—A—
Maryland Album

QUILTMAKING TRADITIONS
1634–1934

A Maryland Album

QUILTMAKING TRADITIONS
1634–1934

Gloria Seaman Allen *and* Nancy Gibson Tuckhorn

Based on the
Maryland Association for Family and Community Education
Quilt Documentation Project

Edited by Deborah Cooney

Rutledge Hill Press
Nashville, Tennessee

Published in Nashville, Tennessee, by Rutledge Hill Press, 211 Seventh Avenue North, Nashville, Tennessee 37219-1823. Distributed in Canada by H. B. Fenn & Company, Ltd., 1090 Lorimar Drive, Mississauga, Ontario L5S 1R7.

Typography by D&T/Bailey Typesetting, Inc., Nashville, Tennessee
Design by Harriette Bateman
Photography, unless otherwise indicated, by Richard and Ann Rohlfing

The authors thank Jennifer B. Greenstein for her production expertise.

Library of Congress Cataloging-in-Publication Data

Allen, Gloria Seaman.
    A Maryland album : quiltmaking traditions, 1634–1934 / Gloria Seaman Allen and Nancy Gibson Tuckhorn ; based on the Maryland Association for Family and Community Education quilt documentation project edited by Deborah Cooney.
        p.   cm.
    Includes bibliographical references and index.
    ISBN 1-55853-341-9 (hardcover)
    1. Quilting—Maryland—History.   2. Quilts—Maryland—History.   3. Maryland—Social life and customs.   I. Tuckhorn, Nancy Gibson, 1955–   II. Title.
TT835.A454   1995
746.46'09752—dc20   95-2387
                                                                                          CIP

Printed in China through Palace Press
1 2 3 4 5 6 7 8 — 99 98 97 96 95

Contents

Author Acknowledgments

MANY PEOPLE ACROSS THE STATE have contributed their time and talents to preserving Maryland's rich quiltmaking heritage. Long before we were asked to write this book, hundreds of volunteers from the Maryland Association for Family and Community Education (MAFCE) and local quilters' guilds participated in documentation days and arranged quilt exhibitions. Without their efforts, and especially the dedication of Elaine Crow, MAFCE's quilt book chairman, Alice Skarda and Belinda Crews, quilt documentation chairmen, and Cindy Edinberg, Annapolis Quilt Guild member and organizer of the Timonium Quilt Show, this book would not be possible.

We are personally indebted to the quiltowners who have welcomed us into their homes and have shared their quilts, photographs, and family stories with us. We are grateful to members of the Maryland-DC museum community for contributing their expertise and allowing us access to their files and photographs. They include Jennifer Goldsborough of the Maryland Historical Society, Anita Jones of the Baltimore Museum of Art, Diane Dunkley, Catharine Tuggle, M. Cricket Bauer, Alden O'Brien, Tamara Humphrey, and Renee Bomgardner of the DAR Museum, Jane Sween and Sally D'Albora of the Montgomery County Historical Society, Jay Graybeal and Joe Getty of the Carroll County Historical Society, John Potts of the Dorchester County Historical Society, Martha Hahn and Roseanne Shuttleworth of the Alleghany County Historical Society, and Judy Proffitt and Angie Brosius of the Frederick County Historical Society.

Quilt historians, all active members of the American Quilt Study Group, have made their personal research available to us and have directed us to other sources. We are especially grateful to Merikay Waldvogel for allowing us access to Mildred Dickerson's collection of quilting ephemera, and also to Cuesta Benberry, Barbara Brackman, Ricky Clark, Joyce Gross, Virginia Gunn, Nancy Hornback, Laurel Horton, Joanne Manwaring, Celia Oliver, Lee Porter, Wendy Reed, and Julie Silber for answering our endless questions.

Other people—not necessarily known for their Maryland quilt expertise, but experts in their own fields—have contributed to our knowledge of material culture. These include Orlando Rideout of the Maryland Historical Trust, John Vlach of the American Studies Department, George Washington University, Rev. Edwin Schell and Betty Ammons, United Methodist Historical Society of Lovely Lane Church, Elizabeth Brown of the Quaker Collection, Haverford College, Anne McCullough Pettit and William G. Bodenstein of Talbot County, and Elizabeth Hughes of St. Mary's County.

Anne Ruta, in addition to assisting us with records and photographs from the DAR Museum, brought order to our chaos at a time when the details seemed overwhelming.

Mary Beth Kurth, a special friend, spent a summer driving with us around the state to examine quilts and interview owners. Her meticulous research on several quilts made our task much easier.

Without the computer expertise of Sue Cheng, half the manuscript would have been lost to a Russian virus. Needless to say, we are grateful for her talent in a field incomprehensible to us. We also appreciate the assistance received from John Scheifer in installing software.

Debby Cooney has spent hundreds of hours reading and editing our drafts. She has tried to bring our diverse writing styles into conformity with the *Chicago Manual of Style* and she has caught our most grievous mistakes. Amy Lyles Wilson, our Rutledge Hill Press editor, has efficiently guided us through the final editing process. Her professional, business-like manner and wry humor have made our job much easier and more enjoyable. The errors that remain are entirely our own.

Finally, without the love, support, and patience of our husbands and children, who have put up with research clutter, late or missed meals, endless phone calls, computer glitches, and car breakdowns over a two-year period, this book would not have reached completion.

We sincerely thank them all.

Gloria Seaman Allen
Nancy Gibson Tuckhorn

Pieced and appliquéd Irish Chain quilt made around
1840 by Ann Amanda Floyd Dunbar (1819–1903), in
St. Mary's County, 108.5 x 105.75 inches, cottons.
Owned by Lucie Dunbar Abell. The Irish Chain is one
of Maryland's most popular quilt patterns. More than
seventy examples made between 1830 and 1930 were
documented by the Maryland Association for Family and
Community Education.

Maryland Association for Family and Community Education
A BRIEF HISTORY

*I*N 1988, THE MARYLAND ASSOCIATION for Family and Community Education (MAFCE) initiated a project to document quilts made in Maryland between its founding in 1634 and its tercentenary in 1934. These quilts are irreplaceable records of the social, economic, and artistic history of Maryland. They play a vital role in helping us understand the state's colorful past. Thanks to the single-minded dedication of numerous volunteers, an exhaustive search was conducted to locate quilts made in Maryland.

A statewide survey is a time consuming and costly undertaking that requires a large, cohesive group of workers. MAFCE was such a group with 10,000 members located throughout the state at the start of the project. To comprehend MAFCE's involvement in this project, one needs to understand the organization.

Having concern for the health and well being of their families, women have always searched for proper methods of food preparation and preservation, fabric care and clothing construction, and economic ways to furnish their homes. Until the passage of the Smith-Lever Act and the establishment of the Cooperative Extension Service (CES) in 1914, trial and error was often their best source of information. Through the CES, education could be "extended" from land-grant colleges into communities to meet the needs of families.

Extension agents trained in home economics began visiting homes and encouraging neighbors to gather together to learn approved and improved homemaking skills. The new knowledge and opportunity to socialize with neighbors were popular. Soon clubs, which met on a regular basis, were formed and the idea for "each one to teach one" was developed.

As more clubs were started, they became known as canning, tomato, or home improvement clubs. Their popularity spread from the rural community to urban areas. Members represented many nationalities, religions, and walks of life. They shared a common thread: the value of strong families and communities. Educational materials were, and still are, related to current needs. In 1930, homemakers were learning to can and cook on an electric stove; in 1960, they were learning techniques of freezing foods; and in 1980, they were learning to cook in a microwave oven. Throughout the same years they learned the proper way to care for wool, cotton, rayon, nylon, polyester, and fabrics of mixed fiber content.

By 1936, there were many clubs in communities all over the United States. In June of that year representatives from twelve states gathered in Washington, DC. They resolved to reach out to others in their communities with information on health and farm and home management by organizing the National Home Demonstration Council. Over the years, the organization has undergone several name changes from the National Home Demonstration Council to the National Extension Homemakers Council to its present name, the National Association for Family and Community Education, Inc. (NAFCE). The name changes embrace the continued commitment of the organization to the changing community. The organization's mission and strengths have always been to improve the quality of life for the individual, the family, and the community through education and leadership development. Through the years it has remained a non-profit organization totally designed and governed by its volunteer membership.

From its inception, NAFCE has influenced the development of pertinent community service programs throughout the country. The nationwide school lunch program was envisioned as members prepared and delivered hot lunches daily to students in their community schools. "Bookmobiles" were introduced as members hauled carloads of library books out to schools lacking access to libraries. Educational programs have become varied to include not only health, nutrition, parenting,

Maryland Association for Family and Community Education's (MAFCE) fiftieth-anniversary quilt, 1938–1988. To acknowledge the value of strong families and communities, each Maryland county, and Baltimore City, contributed a square depicting a local place of worship. These were incorporated into this thirty-square quilt, which will be presented to the state for permanent display in a government building or museum.

been carrying water as much as seven miles daily, use of vitamins to prevent childhood blindness, and simple formulas to prevent dehydration in children, to name a few.

NAFCE is a non-profit educational organization that reaches into the community through its national, state, county, and club components. Throughout its history it has had a unique partnership with the U.S. Department of Agriculture (USDA) and the CES in the state land-grant universities and county governments. CES has acted principally as advisors and programming specialists, training local volunteers to bring up-to-date information to local associations. All programs are offered to the entire population.

A popular program for rural women started by the Maryland CES was the Rural Women's Short Course. Once a year during the summer, women from all over the state met at the University of Maryland to spend a week as "college students," attending a planned series of educational classes. They lived in dormitories, ate in the cafeteria, and received a diploma during graduation at the end of the week. This often served as a vacation and a highlight of the year for the "students." As years passed, the Short Course became College Days and is still held annually.

The Maryland organization—Maryland Home Demonstration Clubs—began February 23, 1938, and has had more than fifty years of successful program development. A project worth noting was designed to increase the use of safety belts by Maryland drivers and passengers. MAFCE wrapped a huge safety belt around the Maryland capitol in Annapolis to "buckle up" on a windy 22-degree day in January 1985. The secondary safety belt law was passed the following year and much of the credit was given to MAFCE members, who also served non-alcoholic punch throughout the state at public functions to say, "Don't drink and drive."

To celebrate MAFCE's fiftieth anniversary, each member association created a twelve-inch square featuring a local church that was then stitched into a quilt to be presented for public viewing in a state government building or museum. The interest generated by this anniversary quilt and classes held across the state on quilt conservation led to the documentation project. MAFCE members recognized the value of studying the social and cultural traditions represented in their heirloom quilts.

financial management, and safety but also today's concerns on environment, children and TV, literacy, and neighborhood crime issues. Family and Community Leadership (FCL) curriculum is taught to encourage leadership skills and self-esteem. Many NAFCE members donate community service hours to Head Start, Meals on Wheels, literacy tutoring, providing books for youngsters, and knitting items for children, the homeless, and the elderly. The list of community service projects goes on and on.

In addition to community and national projects, NAFCE reaches worldwide with projects that help those in the global community. NAFCE is a member of the Associated Country Women of the World, an international organization with representation at the United Nations. Global projects have included providing wells or supplying other means of water to communities where women have

To raise funds for this project a quilt in the Postage Stamp pattern was produced by members of MAFCE as a raffle fundraiser, and it traveled throughout the state. The quilt was shown at fairs, luncheons, and other public gathering places where raffle tickets could be sold.

Having seed money on hand from the raffle, MAFCE applied for grants. The grant proposals called for statewide quilt documentation and stressed the importance of preserving this part of Maryland's rich cultural history.

Documentation sites were publicized for each county and Baltimore City, a standard method of documentation was established, and documentation was done by volunteers whose training covered terminology, style, construction, fabrics, dating, recording procedures, and photographing of quilts.

Fifteen quilts were shown for two weeks in July 1990 at the Threads of History exhibit at the 4-H Center on the University of Maryland campus in College Park. One hundred twenty-seven quilts were viewed in the September 1990 exhibition at the Maryland State Fair and Agricultural Society, Inc., in Timonium. A quilt pin was designed and sold at the September quilt show and at other events. Demonstrations, lectures, and documentations were held at both exhibitions. To date, more than 2,400 quilts have been documented and many member associations have exhibited quilts and held quilt shows.

The governor of Maryland recognized MAFCE members for preserving an important part of the state's history. MAFCE continues to promote Maryland's history by displaying documented quilts annually at the Maryland State House in Annapolis. MAFCE quilts also were exhibited at the United Way convention held in Baltimore. A "quilt-in" featuring quilters and antique quilts was held at the state office building in Baltimore and received nationwide TV coverage.

It was the desire to share the stories about the quilts and the quilters with a wider audience that led to the appoint-

In December 1990, the governor of Maryland honored MAFCE for its quilt documentation project. Left to right, Belinda Crews, Governor William Donald Schaefer, Elaine Crow, Alice Skarda. (Photo by Richard Tomlinson, Governor's Press Office)

ment of a MAFCE publications chairman in 1990. Volunteer efforts and fundraising continue to support the project. Some of the stories are lost to time; others are in the hearts and minds of the quilt owners. Through the efforts of thousands of volunteer hours, many of these stories have been recorded for future generations in MAFCE files. This book is based on selected quilts and stories discovered during the project and expanded on by the writers.

The information contained herein, revealed through the eyes, ears, and talents of a dedicated group of volunteers, is a part of Maryland history, perhaps never before told.

Maryland Association for Family and Community Education

Mathematical Star quilt, c. 1840, quilted in 1953. Made by Elizabeth Dahle (b. 1812) and quilted by Lydia Kautsch (1906–86), Baltimore County. Cottons, 104 x 101 inches. Owned by Mr. and Mrs. Warren Schlenker.

Maryland Quilts and Quiltmakers: A Patchwork of Cultural Traditions

MARYLAND IS A SMALL STATE, YET its 360-year history is rich with people and events that represent a variety of often conflicting lifestyles and viewpoints. Historian Robert Brugger put it best in his book, *Maryland: A Middle Temperament, 1634–1980*, when he wrote, "Here the tensions and ironies of the American experience have taken concrete form and become vividly, at times painfully, a part of everyday life. Marylanders both championed liberty and relied on slavery. They welcomed opportunity yet clung to tradition."[1] Maryland quilts were made by women from all walks of life and of all manner of means. Elizabeth Wintkle (p. 43), the wife of a Baltimore house and sign painter, and Sophia Pearce (p. 53), a member of the landed gentry, are just two examples of the heterogeneous mix of quiltmakers working in Maryland during the early nineteenth century. By the end of the century quilts were still being made by such wealthy, educated Baltimore women as Florence Sands (p. 165), and such rural farm women as Nancy Miller (p. 173), an Amish woman living in a small community in Garrett County. The twentieth century ushered in many changes in the country and in the state. Maryland quilts reflect those changes. Quiltmakers in the state retained the status quo in terms of social and economic factors, yet the designs of their quilts show fewer regional influences. They began to adopt the national design vocabulary partially inspired by the many quilt patterns published in newspapers and magazines during the period. Even now, during the post-modern quilting revival, Maryland quiltmakers mirror a diversity of social, economic, and cultural factors evident in the state. From Jewish quiltmakers in Baltimore and Montgomery counties to Amish quiltmakers in Garrett, Alleghany, and St. Mary's counties, quiltmaking is prospering in all segments of society and in all parts of the state. The diverse and colorful social and cultural history of the people of Maryland is illustrated here through the quilts made by the women whose life stories appear on the following pages.

The Maryland Association for Family and Community Education (MAFCE) quilt documentation project registered 2,417 quilts.[2] The earliest dated bedcover was made in 1803 (p. 37) and only one (p. 43) has a date range that spans the last decade of the eighteenth century and into the nineteenth century. There is written evidence of quilts existing in Maryland since the state was first settled in 1634 (see "Maryland's Lost Quilts"), but because of the fragile nature of textiles, the majority of these pre-nineteenth-century Maryland quilts have not survived. A very small number are in museum collections and historical houses in and around the state.[3]

Maryland is divided into three geographical regions: the Chesapeake Bay/Tidewater region, the Piedmont region, and the mountainous region in the westernmost part of the state. Quilts made in these areas mirror the history of the people who settled them. In the early years, Maryland was colonized primarily by English and German immigrants. The largest nationality represented by identifiable quiltmakers (415) in this project, the English, established a plantation society based on tobacco and slave labor. They built large plantations along the rivers that flowed into the Chesapeake Bay and were dependent on these rivers to transport their products to ships bound for the Caribbean and England. Support systems, such as shipbuilding and slave trading, grew up around the Bay.

Quilts made by women of English ancestry during the late eighteenth and early nineteenth centuries reflect the English classical design tradition. Characteristics of this style include a medallion format surrounded by numerous borders and finished with a wide outer border. These characteristics are evident on all-white quilts, appliquéd, and pieced quilts. Fabrics used by these quiltmakers were most often elegant chintzes imported from England.

Appliquéd Album quilt, 1844. Possibly made for William T. Pindell and Georgianna Burris, Baltimore City. Cottons, cross-stitched and inked inscriptions. 100 x 101 inches. Owned by Emma Albrecht Hofferberth.

Sophia Myers Pearce (1805–71) of Richmond, Virginia, made her chintz medallion quilt after her marriage and subsequent move to Baltimore County (p. 53). The design of her quilt reflects the English quiltmaking tradition usually found on pre-1840 Virginia quilts, but, in this case, the fabrics she chose are those associated with early Maryland quilts. By the second quarter of the nineteenth century English design characteristics were evident on quilts made by non-English quiltmakers. The assimilation of these designs into a larger segment of society represents the crossover of design traditions between cultural groups. Another example of this crossover is visible on the earliest inscribed album quilt documented in the MAFCE project. Dated 1844, it incorporates glazed chintz appliquéd vases and floral bouquets of the type identified with quiltmakers of English and French ancestry, along with numerous appliquéd cutwork designs visible on quilts made by quiltmakers of German descent. The style of each appliquéd square does not necessarily match the nationality of the signer of that square. This, too, is the case with other inscribed quilts illustrated in this book and is further evidence of the transmission of designs between cultural groups.

The MAFCE quilt documentation project listed 293 identifiable quiltmakers of German ancestry, the majority of whom migrated from Pennsylvania and settled in the Piedmont and mountainous regions of western Maryland. They brought with them a culture and farming tradition learned from previous generations. Their farms, between 150 and 300 acres, were small and centered around the cultivation of such crops as corn and wheat. To meet the needs of this growing population, German artisans and craftsmen, as well as people of other nationalities, settled in the small towns that sprang up along the roads that connected them to their markets. Decorative furnishings, especially quilts, were made and saved by generations of families descended from these early German settlers.

Quiltmakers of German ancestry brought with them customs and traditions from their native country. German folk designs can be identified on nineteenth-century decorative furnishings, including quilts. For instance, the fylfot, or pinwheel, is a design often used by Germans. This motif is visible on a large number of quilts made in western Maryland. Elizabeth Shriver of Carroll County placed a fylfot in the center of her all-white quilt (p. 44) made at the beginning of the nineteenth century. The makers of the Frederick County Hargett family quilt incorporated many fylfots into the quilting designs on a quilt pieced in 1848 (p. 97). Fylfots, tulips, hearts, leaves, vines, and abstract cutwork designs are common German folk designs decorating Maryland quilts.

The lives of past Maryland quiltmakers were strongly influenced by their religion. Denominations of the quiltmakers documented by MAFCE include: Methodist, German Reformed, Lutheran, Catholic, Episcopalian, Baptist, Church of the Brethren, Amish, Mennonite, Quaker, and Mormon. Methodism, the largest denomination in the state by the mid-nineteenth century, had the largest number of identifiable quiltmakers represented in this project during all time periods. At the 1784 conference of sixty Methodist ministers at the Lovely Lane Church in Baltimore, the American Methodist Church formally separated from the Church of England after years of holding unofficial services in homes all over the state. For many years thereafter, Baltimore was the site of the Methodist Episcopal Church's annual meetings. Evangelical Methodism attracted Baltimore's working people and

MUTUAL RIGHTS AND METHODIST PROTESTANT.

NEW SERIES--VOL. 1.]   BALTIMORE...APRIL 22, 1831.   [NO. 16.

EDITED BY GAMALIEL BAILEY, M. D.—PUBLISHED FOR THE METHODIST PROTESTANT CHURCH, BY J. J. HARROD, BOOKSELLER, BALTIMORE.

POETRY.

THE OSTRICH.

BY MARY HOWITT.

Not in the land of a thousand flowers,
Not in the glorious spice-wood bowers,
Not in fair islands, by bright seas embraced,
Lives the wild ostrich, the bird of the waste!

PARAPHRASE OF THE CXXXVII PSALM.

BY ANNE BRADSTREET.

1612.

"From hearts oppress'd with' grief, did they require
A sacred anthem on the sounding lyre:
Come, now, they cry, regalè us with a song—
Music and mirth the fleeting hours prolong.
Shall Babel's daughter hear that blessed sound?

the remainder of our days. Youth is the spring of life; and by this will be determined the glory of summer, the abundance of autumn, the provision of winter. It is the morning of life, and if the Sun of righteousness do not dispel the moral mists and fogs before noon, the whole day generally remains overspread and gloomy. Piety in youth will have a good influence over our bodies: it will preserve them from disease and deformity. Sin variously tends to the injury of health; and often by intemperance the constitution is so impaired, that late religion is

eventually became the largest denomination in that city. It expanded throughout the state by way of circuit riders or itinerant preachers who traveled among local meetings within a "station," or region. In 1828 the Methodist church separated into two factions: Methodist Episcopal and Methodist Protestant. This split was caused by conflicting opinions on the method of governing the church. In 1844 the Methodist Episcopal Church split, this time over the question of slavery. The pro-slavery faction formed the Methodist Episcopal Church South. It wasn't until 1939 that these churches joined to form the Methodist church. In 1968 the Methodist church merged with the Evangelical United Brethren Church to form the United Methodist Church. In Maryland, the act of quiltmaking and the practice of Methodism seem to go hand in hand. Several quilts illustrated in this book have direct associations with Methodist churches and preachers. Despite this connection, the quilts made by women of differing religious backgrounds are indistinguishable from each other for much of the nineteenth and twentieth centuries, with the exception of a small number of Amish and Mennonite quilts made in western Maryland during the last quarter of the nineteenth century.

The second quarter of the nineteenth century is considered the high point of quiltmaking in Maryland, as represented by the chintz and album quilts. It is during this period that the classical medallion style faded from the quiltmakers' repertoire and was replaced by bedcovers constructed in the block format. This explosion of creativity expressed by quilts made during these years

Methodist Protestant, April 22, 1831, published for the Methodist Protestant Church by J. J. Harrod, bookseller, Baltimore, Maryland, 1831, new series, vol. 1, no. 16. (Courtesy of Nancy Gibson Tuckhorn)

can best be explained by putting them in a broader cultural context. During the first half of the nineteenth century decorative arts flourished in Baltimore. Many artisans and craftsmen working then are still familiar names to us today, and their work continues to be held in the highest regard. Benjamin Latrobe, Hugh and John Finlay, William Camp, Francis Guy, Joshua Johnson, Thomas Sully, Samuel Kirk, Andrew Warner, and members of the Peale family are a few names that come to mind. Designs on painted furniture from the Finlay shop and silver worked in the elaborate repoussé style from the Kirk firm are mirrored in the motifs decorating album quilts made in the 1840s and 1850s. Quiltmakers of yesterday, like those today, were influenced by the objects around them. An elaborate design on a piece of Kirk silver or a fancy painted motif on the back of a Finlay chair might have inspired a creative quiltmaker to appliqué or quilt a similar design into her bedcover. The borders and designs on Staffordshire ceramic wares may have had a similar influence. English potters produced these wares strictly for the American market with transfer-printed scenes of Baltimore being popular in Maryland. The design explosion that occurred in Maryland during the first half of the nineteenth century probably inspired a large number of local quiltmakers to reach beyond their usual repertoire to produce some of the most beautiful and charming quilts

Crazy quilt, September 1, 1889. Made by Joanna Gosnell Greenwood (1827–1901), New Windsor, Carroll County. Silks, wools, cottons, silk embroidery and inscriptions. 79.5 x 67 inches. Owned by A. Elaine Wantz, Doris R. Green, and John W. Welty Jr.

of the nineteenth century. Prized today for their technical excellence and beauty, these much sought after quilts document the results of the creative explosion among ordinary middle-class women in Maryland.

The occupations of the quiltmakers' husbands, as indicated by the MAFCE documentation project, give us a clue to their families' economic status. Included are farmers, blacksmiths, sailors, bottlers, cabinetmakers, and storekeepers. The men and women of this tier of society comprised the growing middle class of the nineteenth century.

The MAFCE project documented eleven quilts made during the Civil War. Of these eleven, most were made in rural communities during 1861 and 1863. This small number may reflect the uncertainty and turbulence of the times (see "Maryland Women and the Civil War"). After the war Maryland quiltmakers fell into the mainstream of the American quiltmaking tradition. The fad for album quilts had faded after the middle 1850s, and a

very small number were made between 1855 and 1870. The designs on these quilts have some characteristics in common with earlier album quilts, but fabrics used reflect what was available to quiltmakers in the later years. The latest album quilt recorded in the MAFCE project was made by a twelve-year-old Frederick County girl in 1867—fifteen years after the peak of the craze (p. 163).

The majority of quilts made in Maryland during the second half of the nineteenth century were pieced with cotton or wool fabrics. Appliqué quilts were still being made, but not in great numbers. Like quilts made in many other parts of the country during this time, Maryland quilts reflected national, rather than regional, design trends, such as the crazy quilts popular in the 1880s. Maryland crazy quilts were usually pieced with wools and contained a minimal amount of embroidery. Most crazy quilts recorded in the MAFCE project are in a distressed condition as a result of heavy use, or, in the case of the small numbers of crazy quilts worked in silks, the mineral salts used as a finish have deteriorated the fabric beyond repair. Crazy quilts remained popular in Maryland through the first decade of the twentieth century. One outstanding crazy quilt was made in Carroll County in 1889.

A substantial number of quiltmakers were documented who worked outside the home during the last quarter of the nineteenth century. Of 292 identified quiltmakers from the period, their occupations included: servant, teacher, seamstress, milliner, buttonhole maker, dressmaker, secretary, storekeeper, and plantation owner. This is the first period to document working women, yet in almost every case, except the latter two, their occupation is one traditionally accepted by society as appropriate for a female.

The twentieth century introduced a revival of American quiltmaking and Maryland women played an active role. More than 700 quilts were documented by MAFCE as having been made between 1900 and 1934. This represents the largest number documented during any time period. The cutoff date, 1934, corresponds to the state's tercentenary.

The MAFCE files list only three quilts made during the years of the Great War. With more than 62,000 Maryland men and, for the first time, women, in the military, quiltmakers were busy at jobs vacated by those away at war. Clerical or nursing duties were the jobs of choice for many Maryland women. The Women's Civic

League promoted "Liberty Gardens" and male laborers in the state encouraged women to become farmerettes.[2] Quiltmaking as a pastime would have to wait until after the war.

During the post-WWI colonial revival years, many Maryland newspapers ran regular columns featuring quilt patterns. In the 1930s the *Baltimore Sun* featured the Air Ways pattern. Sarah Timko of Brentwood, Prince George's County, made a quilt in this pattern as a surprise gift for her young son Bernard when he was home in bed with the measles. Such national magazines as *Good Housekeeping* and *Needlecraft* were read by Maryland women, and the patterns for quilts and other needlework arts found in those publications were popular with local quiltmakers. Twentieth-century Maryland quiltmakers found patterns for their quilts in many places: newspapers, magazines, on batting wrappers, from friends, and like those quiltmakers who came before them—on the everyday objects around them.

During the last two years the authors have reexamined more than 250 quilts, with more than 95 being illustrated here. The quilts chosen for this book were arranged in a loose chronological order based on their style and fabrics. This enabled each quilt to be placed in a broad social and cultural context. Art historical styles became evident as the quilts were compared to other decorative furnishings made and used in Maryland during the corresponding years. For instance, quilts made in the neoclassical style, such as the all-white bedcovers, fell into a specific time period and were grouped together. The colonial revival quilts of the early twentieth century, which often imitated earlier quilt designs, brought Maryland quiltmaking full circle. The quilts made by members of the Poffenberger family of Washington County exemplify this influence (pp. 202–05).

The authors interviewed every quilt owner, sometimes many times. Some had moved or passed away since their quilts were originally documented; thus those bedcovers had to be tracked down. Only a handful of quilts remained unlocated. Fortunately, many owners got caught up in the detective-like search for information about their ancestors and their quilts. To these curious people the authors give their heartfelt thanks. Many research hours were saved and often the owners were able to obtain otherwise inaccessible information. After reinterviewing the owners, the authors

Pieced Air Ways quilt, 1930–40, made by Sarah Apperson Timko (1884–1953) for Bernard Timko, Brentwood, Prince George's County. Cottons, 86 x 77 inches. Owned by Myles Timko.

attempted to verify every piece of pertinent information given to them. This was accomplished by using primary records, such as wills, inventories, administrative accounts, diaries, deeds, land surveys, Bible records, church records, census records, tax books, and sundry other original documents. Newspaper accounts were helpful, as were reports from the Montgomery and Carroll counties' agricultural fairs and the fairs at the Maryland Institute in Baltimore. Early maps were an important tool used to research the quilts. An original Frederick County tax assessor's account book, found in a country antiques shop, provided much-needed information regarding the financial status of several Frederick County families.

More often than not, a thread of accuracy was passed down through the generations of a quiltmaker's family and could be verified using primary records. The phrase "according to family history" was frequently used when information provided by the owners could not be verified

Celanese quilt, c. 1930, made by Georgia Weese, Cumberland, Alleghany County. 84 x 72 inches. Owned by the Alleghany County Historical Society. This arresting quilt took first prize at the Alleghany County Fair in 1931 and netted the owner one dollar. It was pieced of acetate fabrics from the local Celanese Corporation textile plant in Amcelle.

but was plausible and added to the narrative. If primary evidence was found that contradicted a family's oral tradition, and if the conflict could not be resolved, those quilts were not included in the book. Some quiltmakers left more evidence of their existence behind than others—a few could have ended up comprising a book in themselves. The authors have tried to include as much information as possible about each quilt and its maker while keeping the narrative readable.

The excitement of finding a Joshua Johnson painting of a quiltmaker was only surpassed by seeing the growing appreciation of the historical importance a family quilt had in the eyes of its owner. The owners were as varied as their quilts, but one characteristic was common to most—a healthy appreciation of their roots. When asked how and why they acquired the quilts, some replied that they were the only members of their generation interested in family history and the objects associated with them. We refer to these owners as "keepers of the family history." The quilts probably were transmitted through previous generations by like-minded people. In effect, these quilts link the present generation to those in the past.

The authors have tried to determine the "keep me" factor for each quilt. Why was a particular quilt kept over successive generations of one family? There are many answers—some obvious, some not. Quilts were often kept because they represented the only object associated with a loved one, or because they were made to commemorate a special occasion or passage of life. In many cases the keep me factor is unknown. Some quilt owners keep their quilts because a previous generation, usually a mother or grandmother, placed it in the highest regard. The current generation may not know why it was cherished by prior generations, but because it represents the personal values of an admired and loved relative, the present owner treasures it too.

The quilts illustrated on the following pages have many stories to tell. Each story is a piece of the puzzle that tells the history of Maryland and its people during the past 300 years. The history written on these pages is limited by the particular quilts documented. Very few quilts made by African-Americans were documented; thus an extremely small number of quilts attributed to this group are illustrated in the book. No quilts made by identifiable Jewish women were documented, and very

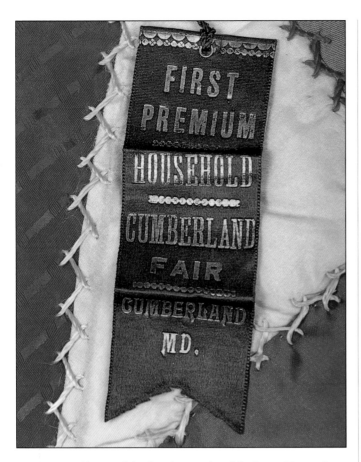

The First Prize ribbon awarded to the Celanese quilt made by Georgia Weese at the 1931 Cumberland Fair. Mrs. Weese received $1 as prize money.

few quilts made by Amish and Mennonite women also were registered. Baltimore was inhabited by a large Jewish population and Jewish girls were among those making samplers in the nineteenth century. Quiltmaking was not a part of their cultural tradition. It was a part of the cultural tradition among the Amish and Mennonite women who settled in communities among the mountains of western Maryland in Garrett and Alleghany counties and later in St. Mary's County. We have tried to include as many quilts as possible that reflect the diverse population of Maryland, and sincerely regret any group we might have inadvertently overlooked. This book is not intended to be the definitive work on Maryland quilts, but the authors hope it inspires other historians to take up where they left off. The research recorded here is meant to be built upon.

The story of quiltmaking in Maryland continues today as women from all over the state participate in the post-modern quiltmaking revival. Perhaps as some of them read this book they will be inspired to sign and date their quilts, thus making the job of future historians easier. And, perhaps they too will reflect on the Maryland quiltmaking traditions recorded here and be inspired to a greater creativity and appreciation of their own work.

This book is dedicated to *past, present, and future Maryland quiltmakers*.

Nancy Gibson Tuckhorn

1. Robert J. Brugger, A Middle Temperament, 1634–1980 (Baltimore: Johns Hopkins University Press, 1988), x.
2. Documentation days were organized by each county association. Each county chose its own level of participation in the quilt documentation project; thus the number of quilts recorded in the individual counties varied. One county registered fewer than five quilts and another more than six hundred.
3. In several cases, local county historical societies (Montgomery and Carroll) or museums (Bannecker-Douglas) cosponsored documentation days. Otherwise Maryland museum and historical society textile collections were not registered.
4. Ibid., 440–42.

Map of Maryland showing the current political division of twenty-three counties and Baltimore City.

A
Maryland
Album

QUILTMAKING TRADITIONS
1634–1934

A Quilting Party, by Enoch Wood Perry (1831–1913), painted in 1876.
(Photograph courtesy of Marguerite Riordan)

Maryland's Lost Quilts

FTER MORE THAN FOUR MONTHS at sea a group of weary and sick passengers disembarked from two storm-battered vessels, the 85-ton *Ark* and the much smaller *Dove*, and set foot on a fertile island in a broad river known by its Indian name, Patawomeck (Potomac). One hundred and twenty-eight survivors of the voyage claimed the land in the name of Cecil Calvert, the second Lord Baltimore. They would call the island St. Clement and the surrounding territory *Terra Maria*, or Mary's land, in honor of King Charles's Portuguese wife, Henrietta Maria. The passengers included Leonard and George Calvert, younger brothers of Cecil, a handful of Catholic gentlemen, two Jesuit priests, and a number of Protestant indentured servants with some experience in farming. After several weeks of exploration they returned to the island, raised a wooden cross, and gave thanks for their safe arrival. The date was March 25, 1634, the Feast of the Annunciation and the first day of the new year.[1]

Master of the *Ark*, Richard Loe (Lowe), disembarked carrying a "flock-quilt" among his personal possessions. Although accompanied by a manservant, Loe could expect to live only a little better than the other settlers. His hastily constructed earth-fast dwelling was furnished with a straw or cattail mattress that he covered with the "old sheete" and "rugg" he had brought from England in addition to his quilt. His other possessions, which he stored in a chest, included several changes of clothing, tools, a sword, and a fowling piece; in addition, his dog and six chickens roamed about. Within four years, Richard Loe was dead; his property was itemized and appraised by a fellow gentleman in the common currency of 2,158 pounds of tobacco.[2] Although the contents of Loe's estate are not exceptional, his probate inventory provides documentation for the use of quilts in Maryland from the beginning of colonization; his flock quilt is the earliest known reference in Maryland literature to a quilt.[3]

The preceding essay and the following album of individual histories describe Maryland quilts that have

survived from the nineteenth and early twentieth centuries. The objective of this essay is to use several types of primary sources to investigate how quilts were made and used during Maryland's early history. By supplementing material evidence with documentary evidence, insights on Maryland's lost seventeenth- and eighteenth-century quilts emerge, in addition to a greater understanding, especially as to process, of Maryland's nineteenth-century quilts. The survivors, illustrated on the following pages, only begin to reveal Maryland's rich quiltmaking traditions. These quilts, and others that were documented by the Maryland Association for Family and Community Education (MAFCE) or are in private and public collections throughout the United States, represent a very small percentage of quilts made by Maryland women and/or used in Maryland homes during the period from 1634 to 1934. These are the "keep me" quilts—quilts that have been carefully preserved by families and institutions for their association with a particular person or event, or for their novelty, rarity, or intrinsic beauty. Utilitarian quilts, fragile quilts, worn-out quilts, and quilts destroyed by war, fire, water, or insects leave no historical record. Unless a woman described her best bed furnishings, which she lovingly bequeathed to her daughter, or a diarist recorded her pleasure in attending a quilting where she completed a silk quilt, or an appraiser of a decedent estate took time to list in detail the contents of an old trunk or chest, there would be no way of comprehending Maryland's true quiltmaking heritage.

Primary sources come in many forms and are readily available to the researcher. Wills and inventories of decedent estates provide evidence of quilt ownership from the beginning of colonization. Newspapers from the eighteenth century to the present day contain advertisements for textiles, ready-made textile furnishings, and textile artisans. Nineteenth-century newspapers describe events, such as fairs and expositions, where quilts were exhibited and awarded premiums. Twentieth-century newspapers often included patterns and directions for the aspiring quiltmaker. Diaries written in the nineteenth century by both men and women relate the process of quiltmaking by women of European background. Slave narratives provide a rare glimpse into the material lives of early African-American quiltmakers.

Probate records include inventories of decedent estates, sales of decedent property, and a final accounting of assets and liabilities. From the itemized lists of the movable property of a decedent, it can be determined whether he or she owned quilts, whether textiles and raw materials were on hand for additional bedcovers, whether appropriate equipment such as a quilting frame was available, and whether there was slave labor to help in the household. The sources present something of the values assigned to quilts but little of their appearance. Analysis of groups of decedent inventories can reveal which economic classes owned quilts, in which geographic locations, and during which time periods. Statistical analysis determines changes in patterns of ownership over time as well as ownership by gender, social, ethnic, and religious groups. Vendues, in which property of the decedent was sold to satisfy creditors and settle the estate, provide information about the sale item, the price, and the purchaser and can often establish a line of descent for a particular household object.

A sampling of Maryland probate inventories recorded in three counties over a period of 150 years reveals diversity in the appearance and ownership of Maryland quilts over time and from one location to another. Inventories taken in Kent County on the upper Eastern Shore between 1710 and 1820 show an increase in quilt usage and some variety in fabrics and construction.[4] The majority of Kent County quilts, where fabrics were specified, were made from calico or cotton, followed in frequency by worsted or woolen. The only indications of construction were for those quilts listed between 1760 and 1800 and noted as patched or stuffed. A 1773 inventory included "1 Pattern of a Work'd Bed Quilt," suggesting that some Kent County women embellished their bedcovers with needlework.[5]

In Frederick County, located in the rolling piedmont of western Maryland, appraisers between 1825 and 1851 described quilts made from such fabrics as calico and cotton, linsey, woolen, worsted, yarn, and flannel. They also were more likely to notice construction; appraisers listed patchwork, pieced, stuffed, hexagon calico, and Marseilles quilts. Several quilts were described as fringed.[6]

Inventories taken in Cecil County on the upper Eastern Shore between 1835 and 1847, approximately the same time period as the Frederick County study, also included quilts made from calico and cotton, worsted, woolen, or moreen. Cecil County appraisers carefully differentiated between types of bedcovers. One household inventory contained "coverlids," "comfortables," "comforts," bedspreads, and counterpanes in addition to quilts.[7]

Very few inventories provide detailed descriptions of appraised objects. The 1762 inventory of Alexander Williamson, late of Kent County, however, is an exception. His bed furniture included the following:

1 figured cotton napt counterpane
2 country made do [ditto]
3 coarse do
4 old calico do
1 stamped cotton counterpane
1 linen do
1 calico quilt
1 suit of china curtains
1 suit of stamped cotton do
1 suit of stuff do
1 suit of stamped linen do
4 Wiltshire rugs
1 worsted do
3 old do
2 old do
1 old bed quilt
3 pr new bed blankets
4 pr old do
3 blankets & 1 rug[8]

This unusually descriptive inventory suggests that by the middle of the eighteenth century quilts and counterpanes had begun to rival the imported woven bed rugs used by most Marylanders as their outer bedcovering. While Williamson still retained bed hangings made from woolen fabrics like china and stuff to go with his woolen bed rugs, he also favored fashionable, lightweight, hygienic cotton and linen hangings with his lighter weight quilts and counterpanes. Perhaps he changed his bed furniture with the change in seasons; woolen pile rugs and heavy curtains would have been

Quilting Party, *painted in 1872 by Henry Bacon (1839–1912). Bacon, a field artist for* Leslie's Weekly *during the Civil War, described the subject of this small oil sketch as a "quilting party about 50 years ago." (Photograph courtesy of the Shelburne Museum, Shelburne, Vermont; photograph by Ken Burris)*

intolerable during hot, humid summers, so common to Maryland's Eastern Shore.

Though not as helpful for understanding what Maryland's early quilts looked like, probate inventories provide a great deal of information about patterns of quilt ownership. In Kent County 32 percent of the decedent population owned quilts between 1710 and 1820; however, in the short period between 1800 and 1820 ownership increased dramatically to 52 percent. In Frederick County 34 percent of the decedent population owned quilts between 1825 and 1851, and in Cecil County 66 percent owned quilts between 1835 and 1847. Among quilt owners, the average number of quilts owned per household varied over time and with location: Kent, 2.7; Frederick, 3.4; and Cecil, 4.8 quilts.

Eight hundred sixty-six Frederick County inventories recorded between 1825 and 1851 yielded 1,031 quilts. The documentation project located approximately four quilts made in Frederick County during the same time period.[10] The figures for Cecil County are equally extreme. Two hundred decedent inventories taken between 1835 and 1847 yielded 649 quilts, whereas the documentation project located approximately three quilts for the same period.[11] In Kent County, in which 360 inventories from the 1710–1820 period were studied, appraisers listed 311 quilts. MAFCE documented no quilts in Kent County from the corresponding time period. These three county studies clearly demonstrate that extant quilts do not begin to indicate the full extent of quilt ownership in Maryland.[12]

Probate inventories are also useful for analyzing quilt ownership by wealth, ethnicity, gender, and religion. In the Kent County study, inventories were assigned to wealth levels; no one with an estate valued at £125 or less owned quilts in 1710, but 50 percent of this group did own quilts by 1820. Among the wealthy, who had estates valued at £500 or more, 50 percent owned quilts in 1710 and 79 percent in 1820. Although distribution of quilts became more democratic in the nineteenth century, quilt ownership was clearly a function of wealth.

In Frederick County, with its large German population, it was important to determine if cultural background of the quiltmaker or owner made a difference in quilt ownership.[13] Of the 347 German decedents in the Frederick County survey, 34 percent owned quilts— exactly the same percentage as ownership by non-Germans during the twenty-five-year period. As early as 1825, 37 percent of the German households owned quilts, and the percentage of ownership remained fairly steady over time. When decedents were divided by gender, a slightly higher number of German women than non-German women owned quilts. Although the evidence suggests that Maryland women of German heritage made and owned quilts in the early decades of the nineteenth century at the same rate as non-Germans, there were differences in the ways appraisers described their quilts.[14] No patchwork, pieced, hexagon calico, or Marseilles quilts were found in German households. However, only Germans had "fancy" and "common" quilts; they also had more woolen and cloth quilts than non-Germans. The early use of quilts in Maryland's Germanic households may reflect more rapid assimilation of the dominant British culture than was true in Pennsylvania's German communities. Quilts made by Pennsylvania-German women generally date from the mid-nineteenth century or later, rather than from the second quarter of the nineteenth century.[15]

A higher percentage of female decedents than male decedents in Frederick County owned quilts. Women made up 17 percent of Frederick's decedent population, and 54 percent of them owned quilts compared with 34 percent of the general population.[16] In Cecil County women comprised 14 percent of the decedent population. Eighty-two percent of them owned quilts compared with 66 percent of the total decedent population. The logical reasons for this gender distinction in quilt ownership are that women frequently bequeathed bed furnishings to daughters and other female family members, and widows, by retaining their dower thirds, often kept their bedstead, bed, and associated textiles.

Ownership of quilts by members of the Society of Friends varied over time and with locality. In predominantly slaveholding regions, like Kent County during the eighteenth century, fewer Quakers than non-Quakers owned quilts. Because there is an apparent correlation between slave ownership and quilt ownership, the lower number of Quaker quilt owners may be attributed to a lack of slaves to assist the white women in the household with plain and fancy needlework or to relieve them of timeconsuming housework.[17] In Cecil County only 12 percent of the decedents, whether Quaker or non-Quaker, owned slaves between 1835 and 1847, so the variable of slave ownership can be discounted. Seventy percent of all Cecil County Quakers owned quilts compared with 66 percent for the total decedent population. In general, Quakers were conspicuous consumers of household textiles and tended to own more bed hangings, blankets, sheets, textile yardage, and textile tools than their non-Quaker neighbors.[18]

Vendues, or sales where the contents of an estate were sold to satisfy debts, indicate the way quilts were dispersed. In Cecil County, the only county analyzed for this purpose, no dominant pattern of quilt dispersal and acquisition existed. When a man died, the widow sometimes removed her quilts and other bedding as part of her "thirds" before or at the time of appraisement. The items were assigned values but were not included with the objects to be sold. James Lynn's widow removed three quilts, valued at $5.37 at the appraisal. Other widows were not as fortunate; they were required to purchase back from the estate their own handiwork. Often quilts listed in male estates were sold, not to widows, but to other male relatives and to sons and daughters of the decedent. When a woman's estate was sold, her quilts generally were purchased by other women, including married daughters. Occasionally an accounting of a sale indicated that a woman had set aside certain legacies. When Mary Hill died in 1842, for example, she left quilts to her three nieces and two calico quilts as "a specific legacy to Rachel Lynch (negro)."

African-Americans also purchased quilts at vendues. Samuel L. Catt, "Col'd," bought one quilt at John Harris's estate sale at $1.25, and "Negro Nero Bacus" purchased two quilts for $1.75 each from the estate of Benedict Craddock. Craddock's widow spent $8 to buy back four new quilts, presumably her own handiwork.

In addition to inventories, other legal documents can be a source of information for bedcovers, especially for the eighteenth century. When Dr. Alexander Fraser, an Annapolis practitioner, made out a deed of gift to his children and sister in 1731, he conveyed his bed furniture along with other property.[19] Dr. Fraser's description provides a glimpse of an early eighteenth-century bed chamber. His high-post bedstead was furnished with calico bed curtains, head cloth, tester, and bases. A matching calico counterpane covered the bed, and white calico curtains hung at the windows. The description does not indicate whether the calico bed hangings and counterpane were also white or stamped with a small-figured motif. If the bed furniture was white, this use predates by many years the early nineteenth-century classical revival fashion for all-white textile furnishings. Perhaps Dr. Fraser's bed furniture was embroidered with silk floss rather than stamped, for his deed of gift also allocated "18 hanks Ingraned working Silk" and "6 hanks More Do [ditto] Silk."[20]

Wills usually contain more detailed information than the itemized lists of objects in probate inventories. Women often bequeathed textile furnishings to their daughters and other female family members. In 1752 Elizabeth Meriott, an Annapolis widow, left her granddaughter Rebecca four new calico quilts along with a "suit of white callicoe curtains bound with red." The 1769 will of Ann Brooke of Prince George's County included bequests of

two Larg new Linin Table Cloaths of princes Linin
one Bed and Bolster on Patchwork quilt
one Bed and Bolster new Stampt Cottens or Callico for a quilt with new Check Linin or Tames[21] to line it
the white Curtins and white quilt
the blew Curtins new stampt Cottens or Callico for a Quilt with new Check Linin or Tames to line it[22]

Mistress Brooke's will states that her bedcoverings consisted of a patchwork or chintz quilt, a white quilt

WM. STEWART & CO.
20 South Charles Street,
Have received by the late arrivals via New York, a handsome assortment of
Seasonable Dry Goods,
Which they offer for sale on reasonable terms, viz.

Super and common printed Calicoes	Schofield's Flannels, assorted bales
Chintz furniture Prints	Printed do
Striped Book and Mull Muslins	8-4 scarlet Cass meres Shawls
Carlisle Ginghams	Black Bombazeens
Chambrays	White plain and Kendal Cottons
Genoa Cords and Velveteens	Worsted and Cotton Hosiery
Cotton Toilinets	English Sewing Silk and Twist
Linen and cotton Bed Ticking	Sail Cloth and Sacking
Super and common Madras Hdkfs.	Brown Linen Hollands
Counterpanes & Quilts	Ravens Duck
Super Cotton Shirtings	Osnaburgs, good quality
West of England Cloths & Cassimeres	Coffee Bagging
Yorkshire Cloths and Cassimeres, a complete assortment	9-8 Hessians
	Wilton Hearth Rugs
Forest Cloths & Flushings	Beaver and Dog Skin Gloves
Rose and Duffil Blank-	Colored Linen Threads
	Cotton Balls, &c.

Advertisement for Wm. Stewart & Co., Baltimore dry-goods merchants, from the August 25, 1820, issue of the Baltimore American and Commercial Daily Advertiser.

with matching bed hangings, and enough new stamped cotton and new check linen for two additional quilts. The references to new fabric for both the quilt top and quilt lining indicate that Ann Brooke did not save fabric scraps for her bedcovers or recycle old bedsheets or table linens for their lining. Her suite of white furnishings provides additional evidence of an early preference for an all-white bed chamber.

Maryland newspapers from the eighteenth and early nineteenth centuries contain advertisements for imported textiles that could be used for quilts and other household furnishings, indicating the types of textiles and sewing accessories available to the quiltmaker. For example, Appleton & Co. of Baltimore advertised in 1806 that they had received from Liverpool "Printed Furnitures . . . Printed Quilting and Calicoes."[23] Possibly the "printed quilting" signified a printed type of marcella, Marseilles, or loom quilting.[24] Wm. Stewart & Co., another Baltimore mercantile firm, advertised in 1820 that they carried a good stock of imported dry goods.[25] Stewart's "Super and common printed Calicoes" and "Chintz furniture Prints" would have appealed to a quiltmaker in addition to their selection of "English Sewing Silk and Twist" and "Colored Linen Threads." Evidently linen thread still found favor with Maryland seamstresses, although it is rarely found in surviving Maryland quilts of the 1820s.[26] Stewart also stocked imported ready-made counterpanes and quilts to supplement domestically made bedcoverings.[27]

Newspapers also ran advertisements placed by artisans who offered their professional services of quilting bedcovers, petticoats, and other clothing articles. The *Maryland Gazette*, an Annapolis newspaper, published notices placed by four professional quilters during a six-year period. In 1745 Sarah Monro boasted that she "performed in

Advertisement placed by Elizabeth Crowder, quilter, in the Maryland Gazette (Annapolis), October 28, 1747.

the best and neatest manner . . . QUILTING of all kinds whether fine or coarse, such as Bed-Quilts, gowns, Petti-coats, & c." In 1749 Anne Griffith advertised that she did "Plain or Figured Corse or Fine quilting in the best and cheapest manner at her house" in Annapolis, and in 1751 Mary Anne March, an Annapolis teacher of "Embroidery, Turkey Work, and all Sorts of rich stitches learnt in Sampler Work. . . . ," also advertised that she took in quilting or needlework. Another advertised quilter came with a somewhat questionable past. Elizabeth Crowder, an English convict, ran away from her contract of indenture with quilter Sarah Monro in 1746. By 1747, Elizabeth had established herself in Annapolis and advertised that she did "all sorts of QUILTING in the best Manner, and at the most reasonable Rates."[28]

The practice of using professionals to quilt a bedcover or otherwise make or embellish quilts continued into the nineteenth century. Mrs. Handlen advertised in the August 7, 1816, issue of the Baltimore Federal Gazette that she ". . . continues to ornament bed quilts, table covers & c . . ." A few years later Matchett's Baltimore Directory included a business listing for Thomas Jordan, "bed quilt manufacture."[29] Thus, many of the quilts used in early Maryland homes were made in part, or totally, outside of the household.[30]

Middle- to late-nineteenth-century Maryland newspapers carried information about state and local fairs and expositions. Their reports confirm materials and patterns that were popular in Maryland during the second half of the nineteenth century. State agricultural society fairs were held from the 1840s on, and the annual expositions held in Baltimore at the Maryland Institute for the Promotion of Mechanic Arts commenced in 1848. Local newspapers listed exhibition classes, exhibitors, and prize winners.[31] In the domestic department, awards were given for quilts and counterpanes of several different types—silk, cotton, calico, and Marseilles[32]—and quilts were described as album, fancy, ornamental, or by a specific pattern name. Mathematical stars, hexagons, octagons, and Job's Troubles appeared frequently in the judges' reports of the Maryland Institute Fair, but no quilts described by these pattern names are in the MAFCE database. Incomplete quilts and scrap quilts also were considered for premiums at the Maryland Institute. In 1848, Mrs. Farrell of Baltimore entered "one save-all quilt," which prompted the newspaper writer to comment that "in the making of [the quilt] every thing but time had been saved."[33]

Newspaper reporters occasionally elaborated on the novelty or artistic merit of an entry, providing the reader with a visual description of delights to come. Mrs. Gibbons, of Pikesville in Baltimore County, entered a knit cotton shell quilt and table cover in 1848. The Baltimore American and Commercial Daily Advertiser described the articles in laudatory terms:

They are formed of shells, each shell being made separate, and the whole then sewn together. The quilt contains 950 of these shells, each of which contains 2636 stitches, making the aggregate of stitches in the quilt amount to two million, five hundred and four thousand, two hundred. An elegant specimen of female taste, ingenuity and perseverance it certainly merits much praise. Supposing this lady to have knit at the rate of one stitch a second, or 3600 stitches an hour, which is probably an overestimate, it would have taken her 695 hours to finish the quilt alone.[34]

Newspapers also informed their readers when interesting or curious objects were placed on display. The September 19, 1845, edition of the Baltimore American and Commercial Daily Advertiser reported that a quilt made for Henry Clay was on exhibition in a local shop.[35] Clay was a favorite with Baltimoreans. Many residents treasured banners, ribbons, and other textile souvenirs of the National Whig Convention, held in Baltimore in May 1844, that nominated Clay for president of the United States.[36] Although the Clay quilt was not described in the newspaper, it could have been pieced from some of the campaign textiles printed and sold by Baltimore businesses. Exhibitors at the Maryland Institute fairs also entered political quilts: the 1848 exhibition included "One Harrison Quilt (silk)" and "One Clay Quilt."[37] In 1851 a young girl entered a "Henry Clay Cradle Quilt."[38]

When out-of-state newspapers mentioned Maryland quilts, their comments sometimes were reprinted in local papers. The *Baltimore Republican & Argus* quoted from a Washington City paper when it described an exceptional quilt made by Mrs. Fowler of Baltimore on display at the Smithsonian Institution: "Four American flags, with tassels ornament the quilt, worked in silk, and two eagles with America's shield, are worked at either side."[39] No Maryland quilts meeting this description were documented, although the 1855 date of Mrs. Fowler's quilt suggests a relationship to the small blocks with appliquéd eagles and flags found on Baltimore album quilts.

Useful information pertaining to quilts occasionally appeared in nineteenth-century Maryland newspapers. During the period of nonimportation brought on by war with Great Britain, readers of the *Maryland Republican* were advised to turn to domestic manufacturers to replace their formerly imported European goods. The following article appeared on January 29, 1812, and provided Annapolitan housewives with a detailed cost analysis for making a reversible calico quilt with a warm woolen filling:

This article of domestic manufacture has been introduced into most of our families, in consequence of the scarcity of blankets, produced by nonintercourse with Britain. As a cheap and comfortable substitute, it merits general attention. The materials can be had without difficulty. It can be made in every family, with one day's work of a seamstress, and will not cost more than $2.75. It is as warm as two blankets, which would cost $2.50—it is remarkably light and pleasant, and the wool, with a small addition of new wool, may be applied to making a new cover, when the calico of the old one shall be worn out. I have had four made in my house, and find the cost of each not to exceed the above estimate, viz.:

2 pieces of India calico at 6s6d 5yds, each	1 74
3¼ lbs. wool, reducing by carding to 3 lbs.	1 30
Carding 12½¢ a lb.	37
Quiltin in squares of 6 inches, 1 day's work	27
Cotton thread	6
	$3 75[40]

The brief document quoted above provides information about quiltmaking that both supplements and contradicts our impression of early nineteenth-century Maryland quilts. Although there were sporadic prohibitions on the importation of European trade goods from 1807 through the War of 1812, Indian cottons evidently could "be had without difficulty" from local merchants. India calico was priced so cheaply—approximately seventeen cents per yard—that it was recommended for the quilt lining as well as for the quilt top. Even during wartime it was not suggested that worn textiles be recycled for this purpose. The proposed filling was a machine-carded wool—a fiber rarely found in surviving Maryland quilts of this period. The writer of the document, who signed himself only as "A Farmer," evidently had little faith in the sewing skills of Maryland women. He allocated twenty-seven cents to compensate a professional seamstress for one day's work to quilt the bedcover in six-inch squares. This widely spaced quilting pattern is unknown in surviving early Maryland quilts that are characterized by fine figurative or closely spaced geometric quilting. Despite the calico covering, which suggests a certain elegance and expense, these simply constructed quilts were warm, utilitarian bedcovers that served in place of imported blankets and when worn out were recycled only in respect to their wool filling.

Maryland diaries are unfortunately not as numerous as those from other areas of the United States. A sample of a few nineteenth-century diaries written by Marylanders is useful, however, in expanding an understanding of the process of quiltmaking.

One of the most detailed accounts was kept by Martha Ogle Forman (1785–1864), a mature Cecil County woman who managed the domestic side of a large plantation and kept a series of diaries with almost daily entries throughout her married life.[41] Her records span the years 1814 to 1845; Martha made quilts during at least five of the years.[42] She records in her diary the quilting process and directly or indirectly the people who helped her quilt. Unfortunately, she does not mention any of the steps she took to make her quilt tops prior to putting them in the frame. There are no references to the cutting, laying out, and sewing of pieces of chintz or to the piecing together of new or scrap fabrics. Although one might wish for more detail, her diaries do provide evidence of the rhythm and context of quiltmaking and the necessity of relying on

Martha Ogle Forman (1785–1864) around 1860. (Photograph courtesy of the Cecil County Historical Society)

others in the plantation community for assistance with quilting. Martha Forman's assistants varied over the years from young unmarried women on neighboring plantations to out-of-town houseguests, hired sewing girls, and "house girls" or female slaves who came under Martha's supervision. Usually Martha quilted with one or two other people; she did not have quilting parties in which a number of people came together to complete a quilt in a day or two. The process of quilting a top was continually interrupted by visitors, visiting, and seasonal and daily plantation chores. As a result some bedcovers remained in the frame for as long as twenty-six days, while others were quilted in as little as four days.

Although Martha's diaries never refer to her patterns or to whether she laid or pieced her tops, they do provide a few clues about her fabrics and their sources. Shortly after the end of the War of 1812, she frugally made her first quilt and covered six chairs out of her old window curtains. For her other quilts she used new material, which was purchased by her husband in Baltimore, or dimity that she paid for herself with the earnings from her poultry, egg, and butter sales. In 1832 she made bedquilts and an easy-chair cover out of chintz. Her homemade quilts were supplemented by Marseilles quilts. Martha's husband purchased the loom-quilted Marseilles fabric in Baltimore and Philadelphia; Martha cut it and made it into bedcovers by adding binding and fringe.

Martha Forman's diaries also provide some evidence for the care of quilts on Chesapeake plantations. Rose Hill, the Forman plantation, was located on the Sassafras River, a swampy estuary of the Chesapeake Bay. Summers were long, hot, and humid; insects were a constant problem. To minimize bug damage and infestation, Martha followed an annual routine that was typical of the Chesapeake region: each May or early June all the bedsteads were taken apart and inspected, bedding was aired, and blankets and quilts were folded and put away. Between late September and early November, the process was reversed, and the house was put back in order. Blankets were aired and shaken; quilts and counter-panes were washed and placed back on the bedsteads for winter use. During some years Martha also had her quilts washed in the springtime when they were taken off the beds. Her all-white Marseilles quilts required frequent washing.

The diary kept by Hannah Mary Trimble (b. 1826), a young Quaker woman living in Baltimore in 1850, contrasts markedly with Martha Forman's description of life on the rural Eastern Shore. The Trimble diary, discovered by the staff of the Maryland Historical Society, revealed the identity of Mary Simon: "The lady who cut and basted those handsome [Baltimore album] quilts."[43] Hannah also described, in detail not usually found in diaries, two elaborate Baltimore album quilts that can be identified today from her description of the designs and fabrics and her naming of the original owners.

The diaries of Margaret Scholl Hood (1833–1919) reflect the life of a young woman in Frederick County between her eighteenth and twenty-eighth years.[44] Margaret kept a daily record of her visitors, people and places she visited, public events, and social customs of her farm community from 1851 to 1861.[45] Frequently her entries are brief and lacking in specific detail. Although she did not marry until much later in life, Margaret Scholl was a fashionable young woman who read *Godey's Ladies' Book* and purchased clothing and accessories in Baltimore and Washington shops. She also made a great deal of her own clothing and borrowed patterns or cut patterns from garments belonging to her friends. Margaret worked collars and quilted skirts; she admired needle and other fancy work at the cattle shows held each October in Frederick County. On occasion Margaret quilted bedcovers. Perhaps if she had accepted the proposal of one of her many suitors, she would have recorded in her diary the preparation of textile furnishings for her future household. Instead, young Margaret

accompanied her mother when she visited other women to assist them with their quilting, or she noted when her mother went out on her own to attend a quilting. During her early twenties Margaret visited with friends her own age and helped them with their quilting: she also made several quilts at home. On June 28, 1855, she proudly noted that she had "Finished stitching [her] quilts. . . ." Margaret does not mention quilting again in the remaining six years of her diary, yet she continued to sew on an almost daily basis. Evidently quiltmaking had no place in her busy life; unlike Martha Forman, Margaret Scholl did not have the responsibility for keeping a large household supplied with bedcoverings.

Carrie Miller (1841–1904), a young Quaker woman living with her family in Alexandria, Virginia, commenced in 1859 a diary,[46] in which she recorded a number of sewing projects she worked on with her mother and sisters. She prepared handkerchiefs for marking, seamed carpeting, knitted stockings, and sewed rags together for rugs; she also worked on her mother's silk quilt and started her own quilt. Along with her sisters, she hosted a rag ball in which twenty-five young men and women socialized over tea and cake, sewed strips of cloth together, and then wound them into balls for rug weaving. In 1867 Carrie Miller married Roger Brooke Farquhar (1837–1924), member

of a prominent Montgomery County Quaker family. Prior to their marriage, Roger had to rely on other women to supply his home with textile furnishings. On April 8, 1859, he hosted a rag sewing party, and on October 10, 1861, he wrote in his diary: "Had a right large company of ladies here to quilt my quilt, & several others to supper had a very pleasant time 33 persons in all here." Carrie Miller was probably among those present; she and Roger had known each other since childhood. The other women would have been relatives and friends, almost all members of the Sandy Spring Meeting. After their marriage, Roger noted in his diary when Carrie gave or attended a rag party or a quilting party. On one occasion, where the diaries cover the same time period, both of them commented on a quilting party. On February 21, 1898, Roger wrote: "Took Carrie to Brooke Grove to a quilting party." In her diary Carrie wrote in greater detail: "I was invited to Brooke Grove to a quilting to day . . . There were a dozen ladies altogether—made nearly three comforts & had a delightful day & delicious dinner." Carrie tells us the size of the gathering, the amount of work completed, and that dinner rather than refreshments was provided. Her reference to comforts suggests that the ladies may have tied the bedcovers rather than quilted them.

Ada Florence Royer (1874–1954), of Frizzelburg in Carroll County, kept a diary during the late 1880s and 1890s.[47] Like young Maryland women before her, Ada spent many hours working on sewing projects. At age fifteen she worked cushions and cut and sewed aprons, dresses, coats, and boys' shirts. She also may have made quilts, for she recorded during that same year (1889) that she washed and put her quilts away in her chest. Ada does not specifically mention quilting on her own or with others, but she does record when her mother and sisters attended local quiltings, which evidently were large social gatherings. On one occasion Ada noted that there were "a good many there," and on another occasion, "there were 10 there."

The Royer diary lacks the detail of the Forman and Miller/Farquhar diaries, but it confirms that little had changed in the social process of quilting over the course of the nineteenth century. Each diary, or series of diaries, documents that quilting was done with other people—relatives, friends, neighbors, professional seamstresses, servants, or slaves. The elaborate laid work and piecing associated with Maryland quilts is almost never recorded by the quiltmaker-diarist. The absence of evidence to the contrary suggests that the preparation of the top for quilting was a solitary and nonsocial activity and not worth noting. The quiltmakers who speak through their diaries may have made quilts from a single type of fabric in which the stitched lines were the only pattern. Examples of quilts of this type, referred to now as whole-cloth quilts, are not common in Maryland. MAFCE documented only forty-five, including a number of all-white quilts. If the diarists and their friends made whole-cloth quilts, they made them for daily use and not for special occasions. The utilitarian bedcovers could be assembled quickly by one person and then quilted at leisure with the assistance of several other people. These simple quilts have not survived to any degree, and no knowledge of their prevalence has emerged other than from clues found in diaries.

Slave narratives—interviews with former slaves taken shortly after the Civil War or in the 1930s and 1940s in connection with the Federal Writers' Project—are an important source for understanding life during slavery. Maryland slave narratives are useful for information they provide about textile production by nineteenth-century African-Americans. They are rich in detail about spinning and weaving by slave women, but unlike narratives recorded in Virginia and other southern states, Maryland narratives rarely mention quiltmaking or quilts. James Deane, who as a child had been a slave on a plantation in Charles County, recalled to his interviewer that his mother had made the quilts that covered the homemade bedstead, but he provided no description of them.[48] Harriet Tubman, a well-known former Dorchester County slave, was a little more informative when she was interviewed in the 1860s about her experiences operating the Underground Railroad. The interviewer wrote down: "By day they lay in the woods; then she pulled out her patchwork, and sewed together little bits, perhaps not more than [an] inch square, which were afterwards made into comforters for the fugitives in Canada."[49]

The most detailed description of slave-made quilts comes from a more recent interview, and therefore must be regarded with some caution. William Diggs, an elderly African-American interviewed in Charles County in the 1970s, remembered seeing slave-made quilts when he was a child.[50] He recalled that the quilts were not the "dainty quilts with fine stitches and small pretty pieces of cloth like you see today. Black women back then didn't have time to fool around with that." Instead their quilts were usually made from large sections of heavy cloth from "old worn-out coats, overcoats, blankets, clothes, or anything they could get their hands on, preferably woolen." He noted that slaves acquired their material secondhand from their owners, swapped worn-out blankets and thick cloth among themselves, or traded with slaves on other plantations. The quilts were thick, durable, and warm. They consisted of large blocks of cloth laid out in rectangular patterns across the backing, and the principal colors were "green, black, brown, and red." Although Maryland quilts of this type are not known to have survived from the antebellum period, Diggs's description does fit several quilts documented by MAFCE that were made by African-American women in the late nineteenth and early twentieth centuries. The preference for quilts with large pieced areas of woolen fabric continued long after the end of slavery.

From a study of primary sources, a different picture of Maryland's quiltmaking tradition emerges. The striking quilts illustrated on the following pages represent a small fraction of the quilts made and used in Maryland during the first 300 years of her existence.

While many of these quilts were saved for their artistic, sentimental, or historical value, many other notable quilts have disappeared. Reports from the Maryland Institute Fair listed numerous album and fancy quilts, far more than are known today. Both the Maryland Institute and the Montgomery County Agricultural Society displayed silk quilts in the 1840s and 1850s; no silk quilts from this early period were documented, and few of these fragile bedcovers are known today. An unusual quilt was described in detail in the "Catalogue of the Third Annual Exhibition" (1850) at the Maryland Institute as "1 silk quilt, representing the coats of arms of several of the States and the late Presidents of the U. S." No quilt fitting this description is known to the authors.

The fair records also suggest that the term "quilt" was used more broadly in the nineteenth century. Knitted and crocheted bedcoverings were called quilts in the Maryland Institute records from the 1850s. In Montgomery County during the 1890s premiums were awarded in the following quilt categories: silk, crazy, worsted, crochet, calico, and knit.

Other documents reveal the extent of quiltmaking and degree of ownership: diaries relate the frequency of the social process of quilting, and probate records indicate the vast numbers of quilts that were made and used in Maryland households. Many of these quilts probably were intended as utilitarian bedcoverings; therefore, they have not survived. Others remain to be discovered.

Many quilts also were made for which no documentation exists: slave-made quilts were not listed in probate inventories, slave women did not enter competitions, and white women's diaries usually fail to mention the participation of African-American women in the quiltmaking process. Martha Forman did note when her "house girls" assisted her with quilting and that they held a quilting party during the Christmas work break. No doubt similar activities took place on other Maryland plantations.

Poor women who made quilts and who rarely had the time or literary skills to record their thoughts and whose meager estates were not subject to probate, left no written record. Their utilitarian quilts have not survived. If it were not for an interview conducted by historian George McDaniel in 1978, their place in

Quilting, *by Mary Lyde Hicks (b. 1866), painted between 1890 and 1910. This colonial revival painting recalls Martha Forman's diary accounts of quilting with her "house girls" at Rose Hill plantation in Cecil County. (Photograph courtesy of the North Carolina Museum of History, Division of Archives and History.)*

Maryland's quiltmaking tradition would be overlooked. Nora Cusic, wife of a white sharecropper living in St. Mary's County before the First World War, told McDaniel that she sewed quilts to keep her family warm. McDaniel observed that they were the most colorful objects in Nora's house, and she was still making quilts at the time of the interview—as many as thirty-five in one year![51]

Historians in recent years have come to appreciate that knowledge gained from studying artifacts can supplement that obtained from documents, and museum professionals also have recognized that primary sources can provide context for their object studies. For a comprehensive investigation of quilts—and especially quilts made and used in a region whose history dates from the seventeenth century—documents are essential. The results of the MAFCE documentation project confirm that quilts were made in Maryland from 1803 on; the documentary evidence proves that quilts were part of Maryland's history from the beginning—1634.

Gloria Seaman Allen

1. This date is now celebrated as "Maryland Day." Before the adoption of the Gregorian calendar, the first day of the new year fell on the Feast of the Annunciation, March 25.

2. William Hand Browne, *Judicial and Testamentary Business of the Provincial Court, 1637–1650, Archives of Maryland*, vol. 4 (Baltimore: Maryland Historical Society, 1887), 74.

3. Ibid., 74–76. Robert Winter (Wintour), who also sailed to Maryland on the *Ark* or the *Dove*, possessed "a quilt" at the time of death. He died approximately five months after Richard Loe, 85. The 1638 inventory of Thomas Cullamore and the 1642 inventory of John Cockshott also include quilts. These gentlemen were not listed among the passengers on the *Ark* and *Dove* and probably came to Maryland on later ships. Cockshott's "very old quilt" was described as "transported from the other side," 96–99.

4. The following comments concerning Kent County have been condensed from my two previous studies, "Textile Furnishings: A Case Study of Kent County, Maryland, 1710–1820," MA Thesis, George Washington University, 1983; and "Kent County Bed Coverings, 1710–1820," in *Uncoverings 1985*, edited by Sally Garoutte (Mill Valley, CA: American Quilt Study Group, 1986), 9–31.

5. Kent County *Inventories*, vol. 3 (1773), 321. Citation courtesy of the Research Files, Museum of Early Southern Decorative Arts, hereafter referred to as MESDA.

6. Gloria Seaman Allen, "Catharine Garnhart: A Quiltmaker in the Context of the Anglo-German Community of Frederick, Maryland," unpublished paper, George Washington University, 1990.

7. Cecil County *Inventories*, vols. 20–25 (1827–47).

8. Kent County *Inventories*, vol. 5 (1759–67).

9. Allen, "Kent County Bed Coverings, 1710–1820," 15–18.

10. The figures from the documentation project are not precise. Documentation teams frequently did not assign dates to quilts. A search for Frederick County quilts brought up ninety-four records, yet only four records had dates that corresponded to the designated time period.

11. The search of the database indicated that thirty-eight quilts were made in Cecil County, with only three having dates within the specified range.

12. Probate inventories, in themselves, may underestimate quilt ownership. The inventoried population was biased toward the older, white male. Young men, women, children, servants, and slaves were either underrepresented or not represented at all.

13. This analysis is based on a subjective determination of whether the decedent's surname was German or non-German in origin. Some Germans were obvious from their clearly Germanic surnames—Derr, Gittinger, Doub, and the like. Other Germans, whose names may have been anglicized, were identified by the presence in their possessions of a German Bible or German books. It is likely that my figures underrepresent the German population of Frederick County.

14. Generally appraisers were of the same socioeconomic class and ethnic background as the decedent.

15. Jeannette Lasansky has observed that "coverlets were the topmost bedcovering of choice in Pennsylvania German families well into the nineteenth century." She found the earliest recorded quilt in an inventory dated 1831. Jeannette Lasansky, *A Good Start: The Aussteier or Dowry* (Lewisburg, PA: Oral Traditions Project, 1985), 7, 43.

16. Women's estates were probated at a lower rate than men's. Usually when a married woman died, her possessions, most of which legally belonged to her husband, were not inventoried. The estates of spinsters and widows were more likely to go through the probate process.

17. See Gloria Seaman Allen, *First Flowerings: Early Virginia Quilts* (Washington, DC: DAR Museum, 1987), 11–13. In my study of York County, Virginia, probate inventories, I have demonstrated that

slaveholders owned quilts at a much higher rate than non-slaveholders.

18. Allen, "Kent County Bed Coverings, 1710–1820," 20.

19. Anne Arundel County *Land Records Book IH1* (1730–33), 239. Document from the Research Files, MESDA.

20. Ibid.

21. Possibly tamis, an open-weave worsted cloth.

22. Maryland Prerogative Court *Wills*, vol. 29 (1754–56), 474 and vol. 38 (1770–72), 178. Document from the Research Files, MESDA.

23. *Baltimore American and Commercial Daily Advertiser*, May 19, 1806.

24. See Florence M. Montgomery, *Textiles in America 1650–1870* (New York: Norton, 1983), 292.

25. *Baltimore American and Commercial Daily Advertiser*, August 25, 1820.

26. Dena Katzenberg quoted an advertisement for linen thread placed by Baltimore merchant Theodore C. Proebsting in 1811. Dena S. Katzenberg, *Baltimore Album Quilts* (Baltimore: Baltimore Museum of Art, 1981), 56–58.

27. There is considerable evidence for the use of imported ready-made quilts. During the eighteenth century, merchants in Philadelphia, Charleston, and other coastal cities imported quilts for sale to their customers. The Philadelphia firm of Francis & Rolfe received eighteen quilts in two different widths from Lisbon, Portugal, in 1761. Invoice from the Henry Francis du Pont Winterthur Museum, Joseph Downs Manuscript Collection.

28. *Maryland Gazette*, July 26, 1745, December 17, 1749, March 27, 1751, April 1, 1746, and October 28, 1747.

29. *Matchett's Baltimore Directory* (Baltimore: R. J. Matchett, 1827), 148.

30. The use of professional quilters and the purchase of ready-made quilts may explain the low number of quilting frames in probate inventories. Many of the Kent County households with quilts did not have frames. Allen, "Kent County Bed Coverings, 1710–1820," 21.

31. The Montgomery County *Sentinel* published the reports just as they were recorded in the minutes of the Montgomery County Agricultural Society. The *Baltimore American and Commercial Daily Advertiser* printed much of the material contained in the judges' reports of the Maryland Institute fairs and sometimes elaborated on specific items.

32. Minutes of the Montgomery County Agricultural Society, 1850–53.

33. *Baltimore American and Commercial Daily Advertiser*, November 21, 1848.

34. Ibid., November 6, 1848.

35. We are very grateful to Jennifer Faulds Goldsborough for sharing with us, in advance of publication, the typescript for *Lavish Legacies*. Her quotation of the Clay quilt notice appears on page 25 in the published version. Jennifer Faulds Goldsborough, *Lavish Legacies: Baltimore Album and Related Quilts in the Collection of the Maryland Historical Society* (Baltimore: Maryland Historical Society, 1994).

36. The May 3, 1844, edition of the *Baltimore Republican & Argus* described the crowds who turned out to watch the Whig procession and to hear the speakers at the Canton Race Track. During the convention, Baltimore merchants sold an array of printed Whig campaign materials with Clay's image, any one of which could have served as inspiration for a quilt design. Jacqueline Atkins illustrates a quilt made from Clay/Frelinghuysen banners, saved from the 1844 Whig campaign. Jacqueline Marx Atkins, *Shared Threads: Quilting Together—Past and Present* (New York: Viking Studio Books, 1994), Figure 114.

37. *Catalogue of the First Annual Exhibition of the Maryland Institute for the Promotion of the Mechanic Arts Held October 31, 1848, at Washington Hall, Baltimore* (Baltimore, 1848), 2, 4.

38. "Catalogue of Articles Deposited at the Fourth Annual Exhibition of the Maryland Institute, Opened in Baltimore, October 20, 1851," *The Book of the Exhibition* (Baltimore, 1852), 18.

39. Quoted by Jennifer Faulds Goldsborough, *Lavish Legacies*, 25.

40. *The Maryland Republican*, Annapolis, Maryland, January 29, 1812. Citation courtesy of the Research Files of MESDA.

41. W. Emerson Wilson, ed., *Plantation Life at Rose Hill: The Diaries of Martha Ogle Forman 1814–1845* (Wilmington: Historical Society of Delaware, 1976).

42. For a detailed analysis of Martha Forman's quiltmaking, see Gloria Seaman Allen, "Quiltmaking on Chesapeake Plantations," in *On the Cutting Edge: Collectors, Collections, and Traditions*, edited by Jeannette Lasansky (Lewisburg, PA: Oral Traditions Project, 1994), 56–69.

43. Goldsborough, *Lavish Legacies*, 16, 17, 21.

44. Rose Barquist, Mary Frear Keeler, and Ann Lebherz, eds., *The Diaries of Margaret Scholl Hood 1851–1861* (Camden, ME: Picton Press, 1992).

45. Another Frederick County diarist, Jacob Engelbrecht, provides considerably more detail about political and social events in Frederick County. William R. Quynn, ed., *The Diary of Jacob Engelbrecht, 1818–1878* (Frederick, MD: Historical Society of Frederick County, 1976).

46. The manuscript diaries of Caroline S. Miller and Roger Brooke Farquhar are in the collection of the Montgomery County Historical Society. Excerpts of Roger Farquhar's diary have been published by the Historical Society in "The Montgomery County Story" between 1958 and 1967.

47. Manuscript in the collection of the Historical Society of Carroll County. The authors thank Tamara Humphrey for transcribing parts of the diary.

48. George P. Rawick, *The American Slave: A Composite Autobiography* (Westport, CT: Greenwood Publishing Company, 1974), vol. 16, 87–88.

49. John W. Blassingame, *Slave Testimony: Two Centuries of Letters, Interviews, and Autobiographies* (Baton Rouge: Louisiana State University Press, 1977), 461.

50. George W. McDaniel, *Hearth & Home: Preserving a People's Culture* (Philadelphia: Temple University Press, 1982), 108.

51. Ibid., 157.

The Eby Quilt

THE EARLIEST DATED QUILT documented in the MAFCE project is pieced and appliquéd in the medallion style, with cross-stitched initials "M. E." and the date "1803" placed directly beneath an openwork calico basket. Long-stemmed, block-printed cotton and linen appliquéd flowers appear to grow from the basket, recreating a design found on seventeenth- and eighteenth-century European textiles. Rows of diamonds and triangles frame the central basket, and the wide outer border is a block-printed cotton, a common design characteristic on Maryland quilts. Flowers, clamshell patterns, and parallel lines make up the quilting scheme.

According to family tradition, Mary Eby of Frederick County made this bedcover in 1803, the year her father died. She was the second daughter and fourth child of Christian and Catherine Wohlfort Eby. Christian was born in Baiertel, a town near Heidelberg in the German state of Baden, and came to America with his parents during the wave of German immigration in the 1740s. Lured by entrepreneurs promoting settlement in the colonies, the new arrivals put down roots only to move on when new opportunities arose. Like most families immigrating from Europe in the early eighteenth century, the Ebys probably came seeking religious freedom, political stability, or economic prosperity. After arriving in Philadelphia, many immigrating families quickly moved to southeast-ern Pennsylvania. As this area became more populated and land more expensive, they moved west to the Pennsylvania frontier or to Maryland. This pattern of settlement some-times took several generations.[1] The "Dutch" (Deutsch), as these settlers were then known, brought native customs and rich craft traditions with them.

The Eby family's journeys followed those of other German families. The Ebys settled in Pennsylvania first, where Christian mar-ried and continued the family business of operating a small farm and grist mill. Shortly before the Revolutionary War he moved to Maryland, settling in the Georgetown dis-trict of Frederick County. Little evidence of Mary Eby's life survives in official records. She is listed in the *Final Account* of her father's estate in 1804, along with her broth-ers and two married sisters. Mary inherited thirteen pounds sterling.[2] Judging from this account, she was unmarried at the time of the settlement.

Mary Eby's quilt, with its appliquéd basket of flowers, numerous pieced borders, and hand-knotted linen fringe, shows that even as a first-generation American living in a largely German community, she absorbed traditions of the larger culture. Overall, her quilt is similar to others made in the mid-Atlantic region in this era. Flower baskets like the one on Mary's quilt embellish bed-covers made by both non-German and German quiltmakers in Montgomery and Charles counties, as well as in Frederick County, in the late eighteenth and early nineteenth centuries.[3]

The appliqué, piecing, and quilting all are worked entirely in a two-ply linen thread.[4] Mary's use of linen thread confirms the belief widely held by twentieth-century textile historians that cotton thread was not generally available to quiltmakers until the early nineteenth century. Fringe such as Mary attached was a fashionable edging among quiltmakers in the late eighteenth and early nineteenth centuries and was also

1. Detail of initials and date on Mary Eby's quilt, the earliest dated quilt found in the Maryland documentation project.

de rigueur as an edging on other such fur-nishings as curtains and drapery for windows and bedsteads.

Inherited by Mary's nephew, Emanuel, the quilt descended in the Eby family along the paternal line. From Emanuel to the father of the present owner, the quilt passed from son to son, along with a blanket chest, a tall-case clock, and a plank rocker. The blanket chest, a prized family heirloom, has held and protected Mary's quilt for more than 190 years.

1. For more historical background on the Germanic immigrant movement into Pennsylvania, see Beatrice B. Garvan and Charles F. Hummel, *The Pennsylvania Germans: A Celebration of Their Arts, 1683–1850* (Philadelphia: Philadelphia Museum of Art, 1982).
2. Maryland State Archives, *Final Account*, G.M., no. 376.
3. For more information about these quilts, see Gloria Seaman Allen, *Old Line Traditions: Maryland Women and Their Quilts* (Washington, DC: DAR Museum, 1985), 10, 12, 15.
4. A microscopic analysis was performed by Nancy Gibson Tuckhorn in 1992.

PIECED AND APPLIQUÉD BASKET QUILT
WITH FRINGE, 1803

Made by Mary Eby (b. 1759)
Frederick County
Linen, cotton, linen fringe, embroidered initials
84 x 78 inches
Owned by Rita Eby Scherping, George and Beulah Eby

Basket Quilt with Classical Lining

THIS CHINTZ APPLIQUÉ QUILT was given to the present owner by her great-grandmother Mathilda Meyers Howard (1864–1961) of Frederick County (4). Great-grandmother Mathilda always referred to the quilt as "Mother's quilt." Her mother, Susan Specht Myers (1827–96), however, could not have made the quilt, as the style and fabrics that compose it predate her birth (3). It probably was made around 1810 by Susan's mother, Catherine Whisner Specht, who died when Susan was six years old. Susan's father, Jacob Specht (1804–95), remarried soon after Catherine's death and fathered six more children. Susan lived with her father and stepmother until her marriage in 1852 to David Myers (1823–1900), a Frederick County shoemaker. The quilt may have been one of Catherine's possessions passed on after her death, thus becoming a treasured object, symbolic of the emotional link between a mother and daughter.[1]

Susan's quilt is similar to Mary Eby's quilt in several ways: both are decorated with chintz openwork baskets that contain sprays of applied flowers; both are framed with a six-to-eight-inch wide border and quilted in grid, clamshell, and simple floral patterns.

Susan's is the earliest documented Maryland quilt displaying an appliquéd sawtooth border—in circular form in this case. The applied sawtooth decoration is one of the design elements that has come to characterize the Maryland style. Susan's quilt is also the earliest documented to include appliquéd birds, one of which is stuffed. These simple, stylized birds were popular folk motifs on textiles and other decorative objects made by members of German communities in western Maryland during the late eighteenth and early nineteenth centuries. Echoing the appliquéd birds in the center of the bedcover are two quilted birds in the top-right and left-hand corners. In a whimsical fashion the quiltmaker embellished the birds with tan cotton embroidered eyes and legs, and she did the same to the blue-resist appliquéd bird under the center basket.

The meandering appliquéd vine surrounding the basket on Susan's quilt is

APPLIQUÉD BASKET QUILT WITH "GOTHIC" PILLAR PRINT LINING, c. 1810

Probably made by Catherine Whisner Specht (1793–1833)
Frederick County
Cottons
101 x 83 inches
Owned by Frances Becker

another design seen often on early Maryland quilts. Grapes, an icon of classical design, are stuffed and quilted and shown growing from the vine. European and English design publications featuring this and other classical motifs were available in limited numbers in the United States at the time. Maryland cabinetmakers, silversmiths, and other craftsmen used the vine and other classical-style elements on everyday objects. Their creations, such as furniture and silver, may have provided some of the design inspirations for Maryland quiltmakers.

The red-ground, block-printed cotton fabric Susan used for the appliquéd designs and border fabric was printed in England between 1800 and 1810 and may have been sent to the Bannister Hall Printworks for production by a designer working for the leading London "linen draper" or upholsterer of the day, Richard Ovey, according to textile historian Florence Montgomery. She discusses the role of the draper in promoting different fabric designs and gives a precise description of the red-ground prints of the first decade of the nineteenth century in her book, *Printed Textiles: English and American Cottons and Linens, 1700–1850*. She describes how "Red backgrounds

3. *Susan Specht Meyers (1827–96), in about 1870. (Photograph courtesy of Frances Becker)*

2. *Detail of pillar print lining fabric. Pillar or columner prints achieved great popularity with London upholsterers between 1800 and 1808. Bannister Hall Printworks in Lancashire turned out large numbers of these designs. Many were imported into the United States for use as curtains and drapery for windows and beds.*

gave a rich effect with a sparkling surface brilliance achieved by means of white outlines surrounding each floral motif. . . ."[2]

The classical block-printed pillar (or columner) print in the "gothic" style, used as lining or backing, also dates from the first decade of the nineteenth century (2).[3] The dark brown columns are set two inches apart by large-scale green (now blue) and yellow (now faded) leaves and acorns. The green dye, produced by layering yellow and blue, was obviously painted or "penciled" on by hand; several small drops and a sizable streak are visible outside the intended design. Fabrics in this color scheme—brown, yellow and green—called "drab," were extremely popular for furnishing fabrics in this period. From 1800 to 1808 the leading English printers produced hundreds of pillar prints. This particular style may be the one commissioned by the Manchester linen drapers Bateman and Todd, who furnished Bannister Hall with a number of pillar print designs during 1806 and 1807.[4]

According to Florence Montgomery, columner prints ". . . may be the precursors to large-scale pillar patterns, long popular

in England. Representations of columns and architectural details have been employed periodically throughout the history of art to create an effect of grandeur and richness."[5] It is possible that the bed furniture in the Whisner household was made of yards and yards of this rich "drab" pillar print, with the remaining yardage used to line the quilt.

1. William Jarboe Grove, *Carrollton Manor: Frederick County Maryland* (Lime Kiln, MD: 1921), 65–66. Also, the Maryland federal census, Frederick County, 1850 and 1860. The authors are grateful to Frances Becker for providing them with family genealogical materials.
2. Florence M. Montgomery, *Printed Textiles: English and American Cottons and Linens, 1700–1850* (New York: Viking, 1970), 149.
3. Obviously the dominant stylistic influence for pillar prints was classical, but the arched detailing on the columns' capitals is in the gothic taste. This style is characteristic of many of the pillar prints surviving from the first decade of the nineteenth century.
4. Peter Floud, "English Printed Textiles: The Pillar Print," *The Magazine Antiques*, 72 (October 1957), 352–55.
5. Montgomery, 129–30.

4. *Mathilda Frances Ellen Meyers Howard (1864–1961), celebrating her eighty-seventh birthday with her seven-year-old great-granddaughter, Frances Becker, on December 5, 1951. (Photograph courtesy of Frances Becker)*

In the Classical Style

At its peak from 1800 to 1840, classicism affected more objects, reached more deeply into American society, and more profoundly shaped national symbols than any previous international style.[1]

AMERICANS HAVE BEEN IMBUED with the spirit of classical Greece and Rome from the beginning.[2] From politics to art, Americans have adopted many tangible and philosophical aspects of ancient Greece and Rome for their own times. Classical ideals of virtue, morality, and patriotism were replayed throughout the eighteenth century. Educated Americans were influenced by such scholars as German-born Johann Joachim Winckelmann, leader of the classical movement in Europe, who wrote, "There is only one way for moderns to become great . . . by imitating the Ancients."[3]

The early phase of classical style was defined by Robert Adam, a noted English architect and designer, who had a profound impact on the revival of classical taste through the publication of his books, *Ruins of the Palace of the Emperor Diocletian at Spalatro in Dalmatia* in 1764, and *Works in Architecture*, two volumes published between 1773 and 1779. Adam coordinated architecture with interior decoration by repeating such motifs as medallions, swags, and bowknots in a variety of media. He influenced artisans and their patrons to build and decorate in the revived classical style. Influential design publications from England and Europe were available to the Maryland gentry in the eighteenth and nineteenth centuries. A 1783 book sale in Baltimore advertised several English furniture design books; the Library Company of Baltimore was the repository for others.[4]

A second phase of this movement emerged in France during the reign of Napoleon I. Known as late classicism, this style was promoted by Napoleon through his architects Charles Percier and Pierre-François-Leonard Fontaine.[5] Classical designs of this period were popularly called Grecian. The works of two tastemakers who promoted the style were available to Americans— *Household Furniture and Interior Decoration* executed from designs by Thomas Hope in 1807 and Rudolph Ackerman's journal, *The Repository of Arts*, published from 1809 to 1828. These publications based their Grecian interiors on examples in design guides of Percier and Fontaine. Decorative motifs of the late classical period, many of which are found on quilts in Maryland, include baskets of flowers and fruit, swags, drapery, oak and acanthus leaves, laurel wreaths, rose garlands, grapevines, and lyres. In addition, such militaristic symbols as helmets, chariots, arrows, trophies, and eagles also grace Maryland furnishings.

Artistic workmanship of the highest quality flourished in Baltimore, the largest city in Maryland, during the peak years of the classical movement. As the principal port on the Cheasapeake Bay, Baltimore daily received ships laden with consumer goods from England and Europe. Some of the merchandise sold locally; much of it headed west and south by the growing turnpike system and the National Road—and by the 1830s the Cheasapeake and Ohio Railroad. Imported textiles with classically inspired designs were plentiful in Baltimore dry-goods stores. Susan Markey Rohrback of Frederick wrote in 1916 of her father's trips to Baltimore in the midnineteenth century to purchase

5. *Painted fancy chair, 1820–30, Baltimore. This chair, which retains its original painted decoration, has a history of ownership in the Key family of Maryland. Its painted motifs include many common classical designs; acanthus and anthemion leaves, helmet, and sheathed sword. From the collection of the DAR Museum, Friends of the Museum Purchase Fund. (Photograph courtesy of the DAR Museum)*

6. *Inked center wreath on a quilt made in 1846 by Mary Rooker Norris for her one-year-old granddaughter, Mary Norris, in Hagerstown, Washington County. From the collection of the DAR Museum, Friends of the Museum Purchase Fund. (Photograph courtesy of the DAR Museum)*

style. Mary Rooker Norris, teacher and sister of the founders, made a medallion-style quilt in 1846 that epitomizes the classical influence in quilt design. A large floral-olive branch wreath surrounds an inked scroll, and the wreath is flanked by four inked floral medallions containing penned family genealogies (6). Six borders of various designs complete the quilt. Two of the last three borders are strips of fabric printed in a Greek key design.[8]

The classical style caught on quickly in Baltimore and then filtered out into rural areas. It remained popular on decorative arts in Maryland through the 1850s, when a distinctly Victorian style took over.[9] Almost every quilt chosen for this book made between 1803 and 1860 includes some appliquéd, quilted, or inked classical motifs; they are the focal designs on some quilts and are secondary to folk motifs on others.

Nancy Gibson Tuckhorn

French fabric for her grandmother to make quilts. "She used to pay one dollar a yard for the French chintz she used, and father always bought it in Baltimore."[7]

Immigrating upholsterers, cabinetmakers, and other artisans brought with them the latest in fashionable taste and technology. "Lately from London . . ." was a common introduction in newspaper advertisements of the period. These newly arrived artisans joined native-born craftsmen working in Baltimore who had knowledge of fashionable European tastes and the skills to turn that taste into products with a distinctly Maryland flavor. Several of the city's many renowned craftsmen working in the classical style between 1800 and 1840 included Robert Mills, architect of the city's Washington Monument; Benjamin Latrobe, designer of the reconstructed U.S. Capitol and Baltimore's Roman Catholic cathedral; John and Hugh Finlay, cabinetmakers and ornamental furniture painters; and the Peale family of portrait painters.

A popular girls' school, the Misses Rooker's Seminary for Young Ladies, operated in Baltimore from 1810 to 1837, offering instruction in reading, history, geography, French, music, drawing, and needlework in the classical

1. Richard L. Bushman, introduction in *Classical Taste in America: 1800–1840*, by Wendy Cooper (New York: Abbeville Press Publishers, 1993), 14. Published in conjunction with a major exhibition at the Baltimore Museum of Art, this catalogue contains many examples of Maryland art and architecture made in the classical style.
2. See Graham Hood, "Early Neoclassicism in America," *The Magazine Antiques*, 140 (December 1990), 978–85, for specific examples of classicism in the colonies prior to the Revolutionary War.
3. Quoted in Cooper, *Classical Taste in America*, 8.
4. Gregory R. Weidman, *Furniture in Maryland: 1740–1940* (Baltimore: Maryland Historical Society, 1984), 77.
5. The design guides of George Smith, *A Collection of Designs*, London, 1808, and Pierre de La Mésangère, *Collection des Meubles et Objets de Goût 1808–1810*, Paris, were owned by the Ridgely family of Hampton near Towson, a town just north of Baltimore. These guides may have been the source for a suite of painted and gilded furniture billed to the Ridgely family in 1832 by the Irish-born Baltimore cabinetmaker and ornamental painter John Finlay. Cited in Cooper, *Classical Taste in America*, 145.
6. Charles Percier and Pierre-François-Leonard Fontaine, *Recueil de Décorations intérieures comprenant toût ce qui a rapport à l'ameublement* (Paris, 1801–12).
7. Letter to Ruth Markey Carter from Susan Markey Rohrback, 1916. The authors thank Catherine Sharoky for sharing this letter. Catherine Garnhart's quilts represent the assimilation of the classical style and a Germanic folk tradition.
8. The nineteenth-century period term for the Greek key design was "Wall of Troy."
9. During the colonial revival period in the early decades of the twentieth century, many Maryland quiltmakers returned to the classical style, taking inspiration from earlier quilts.

White Basket Quilt

IKE SO MANY QUILTS THAT survived the rigors of two centuries, this one came to the present owners with a note written circa 1920 that reads, "made by Elizabeth Wintkle prior to 1799 owned by her great-granddaughter (Mrs. Paul H. Miller) neé Bertha Jenkins" (8).[1] Elizabeth Wintkle was the wife of James Wintkle (c. 1775–1810), a house and sign painter and glazier. They were married on October 22, 1795, and probably attended St. Paul's Episcopal

7. *Mrs. James Wintkle (Elizabeth Jenkins) and her daughter, Elizabeth Adelaide Wintkle, painted by Joshua Johnson in Baltimore, 1802–03, oil on canvas. A companion portrait of James Wintkle and son was also painted by Johnson. (Private collection, photograph courtesy of the Maryland Historical Society)*

Church in Baltimore, where their marriage was dutifully recorded in church records. They raised four children, two of whom were painted (seated with their parents) in portraits by the African-American artist Joshua Johnson (active: 1796–1824) (7). The Wintkle family lived on Holliday Street near Johnson. In 1803, James Wintkle operated the Union Hotel on North Gay Street.[2]

The quilt descended to Elizabeth's daughter, Elizabeth Adelaide. She married Hugh Jenkins (1798–1863), a wealthy coffee importer and nephew of her Irish-born mother. Jenkins came from Waterford, Ireland, to live with the Wintkle family in 1819; a year later he wed Elizabeth Adelaide. They had four children, three of whom survived to adulthood. On the death of Elizabeth Adelaide, Hugh married her sister, Henrietta, and fathered two more children, only one of whom survived.[3] The quilt passed to Elizabeth Adelaide's eldest son, John Stricker Jenkins (1831–79), who took over the family coffee-importing business and became well known as a collector of fine art and paintings. Part of his collection is now in the Baltimore Museum of Art.[4]

The white quilt is designed completely in the classical style. The central openwork basket sprouting large flowers is similar in design to the appliquéd baskets decorating the two quilts made in Frederick County, illustrated on the preceding pages. Wendy Cooper, curator of decorative arts at the Baltimore Museum of Art, discusses the popularity of this type of basket as a design element on American decorative arts in her 1993 exhibition catalogue, *Classical Taste in America: 1800–1840*.[5] The openwork basket filled with flowers and/or fruit is derived from ancient Greek and Roman motifs. Cooper cites the Thomas Hope design guide of 1807 picturing an openwork "flower basket." She found that though the French and English were producing such items in porcelain, silver, and silverplate in the late eighteenth century, the basket did not become a popular design motif in much of America until the 1820s.[6]

Maryland quiltmakers, however, were familiar with the flower basket as a design by the end of the eighteenth century and were eager to use it on their choice quilts. The

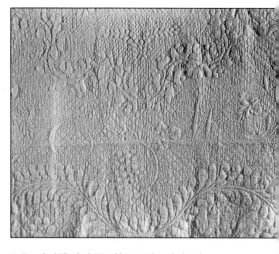

9. *Detail of Elizabeth Wintkle's initials quilted in the center of her bedcover.*

basket motif remained popular with Maryland quiltmakers for many years. In the 1830s and 1840s they used cottons imported from England and France with block- and roller-printed flower baskets similar in design to the one on this white quilt. The noted Frederick County quiltmaker

8. *Clara Jenkins and her daughter, Bertha Jenkins Miller, photographed by Flett in 1915 in Atlantic City. (Photograph courtesy of Mr. and Mrs. Henry Evans Hooper)*

Vandervoort, Bertha's maternal grandmother. Little is known of her, not even her first name, except notations recorded and passed down through generations of her family. Her husband, Robert, died in Baltimore in 1842; she probably died shortly after the birth of her daughter in 1840. By 1860 their young daughter, Eliza, was living with her sister, Clara, and Stricker Jenkins. These quilts have descended to the present owners along with many other family treasures.[10]

1. The spelling of Wintkle (Winckle) varies from source to source. The quilt is pictured with the note attached in William Rush Dunton Jr., *Old Quilts* (Catonsville, MD: n.p., 1946), 258.
2. Carolyn J. Weekly and Stiles Tuttle Colwill, *Joshua Johnson: Freeman and Early American Portrait Painter* (Williamsburg, VA: Abby Aldrich Rockefeller Folk Art Center and Maryland Historical Society, 1987), 111–13. Biographical information from the J. Hall Pleasants File, no. 3291, Maryland Historical Society.
3. In the 1860 federal census for Baltimore City, Hugh Jenkins is listed as a sixty-year-old merchant, owning $80,000 in real estate and $120,000 in personal estate. His wife, Henrietta, was fifty-five years old, and only one child, a son, still lived at home. Four black servants also were listed in the Jenkins household.
4. In the 1860 federal census for Baltimore City, Stricker Jenkins resided across the street from his father, Hugh. He was listed as a thirty-year-old merchant with $15,000 in his personal estate. Clara was twenty-six years old and the mother of two small boys. Two white domestics from Pennsylvania also resided in the house, along with twenty-year-old Eliza Vandervoort, Clara's sister.
5. Wendy Cooper, *Classical Taste in America: 1800–1840* (New York: Abbeville, 1993), 179.
6. Ibid., 179–80. French silk manufacturers also were producing costly furnishing fabrics in this design during the eighteenth century.
7. Nancy Gibson Tuckhorn was curator of an exhibition of nine of these quilts at the DAR Museum in 1991 titled, A Family Legacy: The Quilts of Catherine Garnhart *(1773–1860)*.
8. Dunton, 258.
9. In the photograph of the quilt in Dunton's book, the top ruffle is not visible. It hangs down the back of the quilt in order to reveal the designs at the top.
10. The authors thank Tracy Hooper and Mrs. J. Albert Chatard for making their family genealogies available to them.

Catherine Garnhart made several quilts using this popular chintz basket.[7] The design evolved into the red and green cotton appliquéd baskets seen on Maryland album quilts of the 1840s and 1850s (see p. 118).

Surrounding the flower basket is a classical-style floral wreath. An undulating running feather encircles the central basket and Elizabeth's initials (9). The outer edge is filled in with a series of floral designs, and the ground is quilted in different size grids, which William Rush Dunton Jr., the first to write comprehensively about Maryland quilts, thought helped "in bringing out the designs."[8] The quilt is edged on all four sides with a wide nine-inch ruffle of the same cotton fabric as the ground cloth.[9] Original ruffles are rarely found on a quilt made in the early nineteenth century. Many were removed in mid-century when the fashion for such embellishments had subsided. They

WHITE STUFFED QUILT WITH RUFFLE, 1790–1820

Made by Elizabeth Winkle (c. 1771-1833)
Baltimore City
Cottons, quilted inscriptions
92 x 82 inches
Owned by Mr. and Mrs. Henry Evans Hooper

were resurrected in the late nineteenth and early twentieth centuries during the colonial revival years when quiltmakers sought to imitate the traditions of their ancestors.

A chintz quilt made about 1825 was left to Bertha Jenkins along with this classically inspired white quilt. The all-cotton chintz quilt is decorated with an unusual central arrangement of four palm tree and pheasant appliqués. A note sewn to the bottom attributes the quilt to Mrs. Robert Bruce

The Shriver Quilt

Beloved by her friends, respected and esteemed by her acquaintances, this amiable lady has finished her course, closing her lengthened pilgrimage under the same roof which, for near half a century, afforded shelter to a family circle rendered happy by her cheerful good nature, and to a domestic board which derived new attraction from her hospitable kindness. She leaves a numerous list of relatives and descendants to cherish her memory and emulate her virtues.

—A tribute to Elizabeth Shriver on her death in 1839[1]

*E*LIZABETH SCHULTZ SHRIVER probably quilted and stuffed this all-white bedcover in the first quarter of the nineteenth century. The central figure is a stuffed fylfot surrounded by a stuffed and corded grapevine. The fylfot, a German folk symbol, is combined with the grapevine, a classical motif; together these designs reflect the two major influences on decorative arts in western Maryland from 1800 to 1860 (11). The stuffed work stands out in relief because no ground quilting fills in the open spaces. The quiltmaker obviously was an expert needlewoman capable of quilting many tiny round grapes and yards and yards of running feathers. The three-inch netted and tasseled fringe was applied to four sides with a section left out for the head of the bed.

Elizabeth Shultz married Andrew Shriver (1762–1847) in 1786. Her father, John Schultz, was a respected and wealthy leather merchant in Baltimore. Elizabeth was one of four daughters, three of whom married into wealthy Baltimore families. In the early years of their marriage, Elizabeth and Andrew lived for a brief time in Littlestown, Pennsylvania. Their move to Pennsylvania was not uncommon, as many western Maryland families had relatives in both states and moved back and forth over the border in search of better land and economic opportunities.

The Shriver family was one of the most prominent in western Maryland in the nineteenth century. Their home, Union Mills, is located in Carroll County (Frederick County until 1837), along Big Pipe Creek

WHITE STUFFED QUILT WITH FRINGE, 1800–25

Probably made by Elizabeth Schultz Shriver (1766–1839)
Union Mills, Carroll County
Cottons, cotton fringe
96 x 91 inches
Owned by Union Mills Homestead Foundation, Inc.

10. Union Mills Homestead. (Photograph courtesy of Union Mills Homestead Foundation, photographer, M. E. Warren).

of the Shriver family continued to be active in politics well into the twentieth century; R. Sargent Shriver, great-great-grandson of Andrew, was appointed the first director of the Peace Corps by his brother-in-law, President John F. Kennedy. Shriver later was the Democratic nominee for vice president on the ticket with George McGovern in 1972.

On Andrew Shriver's death in 1847, four quilts, six white "coverlids," one quilting frame, and numerous other sewing utensils were listed in the probate inventory of his estate.[3] The quilt pictured here is among the many objects owned and used by one or more of six generations of the Shriver family and can still be seen at Union Mills Homestead today.[4]

near the Pennsylvania border (10). Andrew Shriver purchased the property in 1797 and soon after built a brick grist mill and log house. Andrew and his brother, David, improved the property, building and operating a tannery and cooper shop as well as running a prosperous farm. For a few years they also operated a wool-carding mill. Families of both brothers lived at Union Mills for many years, until David built a home of his own outside Westminster, the nearby town.

Union Mills became a way station for people traveling between Baltimore and Pittsburgh on the Reistertown turnpike that cut through the Shriver property. In fact, David Shriver was the superintendent of the turnpike for several years. The house was constantly filled with friends, businessmen, and community leaders talking politics with the brothers. Andrew Shriver was a Jeffersonian Republican and active in local politics for most of his life. He was a justice of the peace and well-respected by his neighbors, often settling family disputes. It was once said of Andrew and Union Mills, "his homestead, which he founded and greatly embellished, was, for many years, the seat of hospitality and social enjoyment."[2] Members

1. Samuel S. Shriver, A History of the Shriver Family and Their Connections: 1684–1888 (Union Mills, MD, 1888; revised edition by Robert Campbell Shriver, privately published, 1976), 51.
2. Ibid., 49.
3. Carroll County Inventories, J. B. no. 3 (1847), 51.
4. The authors are grateful to Esther L. Shriver and Helen Shriver Riley for providing information about the Shriver family and quilt.

11. Blanket chest with fylfot decoration, nineteenth century, Pennsylvania. (Photograph courtesy of James and Julie Kappler)

Classical White Basket Quilt

13. The Maples, home of the Jacob Huyett family. (Photograph courtesy of the estate of Helen E. Gladhill)

DESCENDANTS OF THE Huyett family of Washington County inherited this white quilt with little oral tradition to accompany it. The letters "J" and "H," quilted above the basket in the center of this classical design, led the family to believe it was made circa 1820 for the marriage of Jacob Huyett and Elizabeth Ingram (12). The quilted-and-stuffed basket that holds exotic flowers is similar to baskets decorating many pieced and appliquéd quilts of this period. An inverted swag border worked in a feather design surrounds the basket, a classical motif similar to swag designs found in English and French design guides of the late eighteenth century.[1] A field of perfectly round, stuffed circles encompasses the inverted swag. Another feather gracefully drapes around the entire center section, its curving arms coming together in each of the four corners to form a point. Next, a thin delicate grapevine echoes the running feather, and a final element of bold running feather serves as a frame for the quilt.

All the designs are stuffed, and the background quilting, a simple grid, is quilted twenty-two stitches to the inch. The quilt's edging is handmade cotton netting and fringe. Unlike many white quilts, this one is backed with a tightly woven cotton. The maker inserted stuffing from the back by parting individual warp threads and pushing cotton into the empty spaces. For long narrow designs, such as vines and tendrils, twisted cotton

cords were inserted, then pulled through the spaces using a needle.[2] Overall, the design of the quilt is balanced and harmonious; and its maker surely was an expert designer and needlewoman.

Jacob Huyett was the grandson of Franz Carl Huyett, a descendant of Huguenots who had fled to the city of Zweibrucken in

12. Detail of the center of Jacob Huyett's white quilt. The borders symmetrically arranged around a central design—in this case a flower basket—is classical-inspired.

the German Palatinate. Franz emigrated to Pennsylvania in 1738. Louis Huyett (1739–1828), eldest son of Franz and father of Jacob, was born in Berks County, Pennsylvania; he moved with his family to Frederick County, Maryland, around 1774, the year his first land transaction in the county was recorded.[3] In 1799 he purchased 430 acres in the valley at the foot of South Mountain, near the village of Cavetown, becoming one of the largest landowners in the new Washington County. He named his tract of land Huyett's Meadows.

In 1811, at the age of 72, he divided the property between his two sons, Jacob and Daniel. Young Jacob served as a sergeant in the cavalry unit raised in nearby Hagerstown during the War of 1812, fighting at the Battle of North Point in defense of the city of Baltimore. After the war he was appointed captain of the local militia (15). Soon after that, he wed his neighbor Elizabeth Ingram (14). Jacob built a fine stone manor house, which he named the Maples, and settled there with his wife and six children (13).[4]

On October 8, 1840, Jacob and his family attended a political rally

WHITE STUFFED QUILT WITH NETTING
AND FRINGE, c. 1820

*Probably made for the marriage of Jacob Huyett
(1783–1840) and Elizabeth Ingram (1795–1878)
Near Cavetown, Washington County
Cottons, cotton fringe, quilted initials
104.25 x 101.75 inches
Owned by the estate of Helen E. Gladhill*

14. Mrs. Jacob (Elizabeth Ingram) Huyett (1795–1878). (Photograph courtesy of the estate of Helen E. Gladhill)

slightly less than "one and a half dozen chairs" and valued by the appraisers at $2.75. A pair of crimson quilts also was listed at $2.00. Elizabeth may have sewn some of these quilts with the help of her daughter, Cynthia Ann, who remained at home throughout her life.

A lot of calico remnants was listed in the inventory at 75¢. Fifty-four yards of bleached muslin and fifty-six yards of unbleached muslin also were counted. Six coverlids, seven pairs of blankets, two comforts, and one spread made up the remaining bedcovers in the inventory. A lot of old quilts and blankets valued at $2.50 was found in the garrett. The most valuable single item in the household inventory, however, was 280 plus yards of homemade linen at 18¢ per yard, for a total of $50.51. Perhaps a local weaver produced this large amount of linen, as no spinning wheels or looms were recorded.[6] Because seventy-five acres of wheat, rye, and oats were still in the ground when the inven-

15. Jacob Huyett (1783–1840), watercolor on paper. (Photograph courtesy of the estate of Helen E. Gladhill)

in nearby Cavetown during the presidential campaign pitting Martin Van Buren against William Henry Harrison. When the horses harnessed to Jacob's carriage bolted, Jacob was caught under the wheels and killed, a tragic death of one of Cavetown's leading citizens that has become part of the lore of Washington County.

Elizabeth Huyett died in 1878 at the age of eighty-three, leaving an estate worth $3,027.53.[5] An inventory of the estate taken in April that year documents a working farm that included several horses and a large amount of livestock (16).

The list of Elizabeth's household possessions indicates that she was a woman of means: she owned a variety of textiles, including ten quilts of varying descriptions and one "square." The most valuable was described as a leaf quilt, worth $6.00, the same value placed on her "stanley stove and pipe." Another quilt, perhaps the one documented here, was described as a white quilt worth more than a "lot of Queensware" and

Pieced Pinwheel quilt, 1840–50. Made by Cynthia Ann Huyett (1833–1906), the Maples, Washington County. Cottons, inked initials. 87 x 84 inches. Owned by John Gladhill.

tory was taken, the linen may have been saved to make grain sacks.

The Huyett inventory provides somewhat of a visual description of the interior of the house in 1878. Many yards of carpeting were found in several rooms—the dining room, parlor, hall, and stairs. Even a set of stair rods for holding the carpeting in place was listed. The parlor contained two arm chairs and three rocking chairs; and the dining room held a dozen chairs, a table, sideboard, decanter and box, a safe, queensware, glassware, silverware, two waiters, and five fine tablecloths and fifteen old ones. Tangible evidence of the number, value, description, and use of household textiles in Maryland in the late nineteenth century is well represented in this inventory.

1. Gregory R. Weidman, *Furniture in Maryland: 1740–1940* (Baltimore: Maryland Historical Society, 1984), 77. Weidman states that furniture design books were available in Maryland in the late eighteenth and early nineteenth centuries. In 1783 John McClure advertised a sale of several hundred books, several design books being among them. She also writes that Hepplewhite's, *The Cabinet-Maker and Upholsterer's Guide* (1788, 1794) was available at the Library Company of Baltimore, founded in 1795. At least one known Baltimore cabinet-maker of the period—Gerard Hopkins—was a member.

2. Today quilters sometimes refer to this as "trapunto." According to Maryland probate inventories studied by the authors, quiltmakers and appraisers during the classical period referred to quilts such as these as "stuffed."

3. The western part of Frederick County became Washington County in 1776.

4. Daniel Huyett (1786–1869), Jacob's brother, built the Willows less than a mile down the road from the Maples. Both the house and brick slave quarters are still standing and are owned by Huyett descendants. The authors thank John Gladhill for providing extensive genealogical research and background material on the Huyett family.

5. Washington County *Inventories* CR 8547-2 (1878), 391–92. The authors are grateful to Debby Cooney for the hours she spent researching this quilt.

6. It was a common practice in the nineteenth century for rural households to send home-grown wool, flax, or cotton to local spinners to be spun into fibers and then to a weaver to be woven into long strips of cloth. Returned, it was made into objects of domestic use such as clothing, sheets, pillowcases, and towels.

16. *Page from inventory of Elizabeth Huyett's Estate in 1878. (Photograph courtesy of the Maryland State Archives, Washington County* Inventories, Original, *Box 9, p. 10.)*

Clarksburg Chintz Quilt

*I*N 1797, AT THE AGE OF FIF-teen, Sarah Clark married William Willson (c. 1775–1859), son of Jonathan Willson, who was owner of considerable acreage and an activist in colonial politics. Sarah was the oldest daughter of Ann Archer and John G. Clark of Clarksburg, Montgomery County. The village of Clarksburg was situated along the Georgetown to Frederick Road in the northern part of the county; its inns and taverns served numerous travelers passing through by stage on their way west (17).

John Clark was the grandson of Indian trader William Clarke, for whom the village

17. View of Clarksburg and Sugar Loaf Mountain from an 1810 pencil sketch by Benjamin Henry Latrobe. William and Sarah Clark Willson probably owned several of the dwelling lots illustrated by Latrobe along the main road in Clarksburg. The Willson family also owned a large tract of land between the village and Sugar Loaf Mountain. (Photograph courtesy of the Maryland Historical Society)

was named. John Clark built the first house in the village in 1780 and was appointed first postmaster of Clarksburg in 1800. He also owned a general store. After his death in 1802, Sarah and William Willson continued living in a house in Clarksburg given to Sarah by her father; William took over management of Clark's Store, which he operated until his death in 1859. An 1803 inventory of John Clark's store goods and William Willson's 1817 Day Book indicate that the store was well stocked with imported and domestic yard goods (18).[1] The stock included parcels and pieces of kersey, baize, calimanco, oznabrig (mostly unknown fabrics today), plus gingham, muslin, calico, and chintz. In 1803 the selection of calicoes ranged in price from two shillings, four pence to four shillings, nine pence and included striped and India calico. In 1817 chintz sold for sixty to seventy cents a yard and calico for twenty-five to fifty cents a yard. Chintz was costly when compared with the staples of sugar at seventeen cents a pound and coffee at thirty cents a pound, but not nearly as expensive as Imperial tea at $3.25 a pound.

A quiltmaker could find everything she needed at Clark's Store: printed fabrics, imported and domestic linen and cotton for lining, broad and narrow bindings, padding, cording, colored thread and coarse white cotton thread,[2] sewing needles, and large and small thimbles. She could color her cloth from a selection of dyestuffs and mordants, including indigo, madder, and alum.

For those who preferred not to quilt, Clark's also sold Marseilles quilting in 1803 at ten and thirteen shillings a yard.[3]

Sarah Willson probably selected from the store inventory the block-printed fabric, which she used for the borders and some of the appliquéd areas of her quilt. Her glazed blue fabric may have been one of the sixty- or seventy-cent chintzes listed in 1817. The vivid fabric differs from the "lapis" style prints described by Florence Montgomery in *Printed Textiles*,[4] for in Sarah's print, white outlines are left between the red areas and the blue ground.[5]

The appliquéd central bouquet of flowers is composed of several block-printed fabrics. In one print, color was applied to the green leaves and stems by penciling with a brush; another print has leaves textured with dotted pinwork. The white ground fabric still retains stamped marks of an unidentified cotton mill in two places. The appliquéd bouquet is surrounded by a quilted feather wreath and the rest of the bedcover is finely quilted with double crosshatch at twenty-six stitches to the inch. Blue quilting thread was used for the printed fabric areas and white for the rest of the quilt.

Sarah and William Willson had a comfortable lifestyle. The Montgomery County tax lists for 1820 record Willson as the

18. William Willson's 1817 daybook and John Clark's 1803 estate inventory placed on the border fabric of Sarah Willson's quilt. (Courtesy of the Montgomery County Historical Society)

owner of eleven slaves, all or part of four farms, a vineyard, seven lots in Clarksburg, and eighty-two ounces of silver plate. Three slave women, ranging in age from fourteen to thirty-six, may have assisted Sarah with plain and fancy sewing.

Sarah Willson's quilt was probably intended for use on special occasions or on her best high-post bedstead. It has received little wear and does not appear ever to have been washed. It remained in the Willson/Waters family until it was given to the Montgomery County Historical Society by Sarah Clark's great-great-granddaughter.[6]

1. These documents are in the manuscript collection of the Montgomery County Historical Society. We are grateful to librarian Jane Sween for bringing them to our attention.
2. The Triadelphia Cotton Factory, established in 1809 and located in Montgomery County, produced cotton thread in its spinning mill.
3. Montgomery defines imitation Marseilles quilting as "loom-woven patterns of double cloth with an extra heavy cording weft between the layers." She cites a 1784 Philadelphia order for twenty yards of "White Mock Marseilles." Florence M. Montgomery, *Textiles in America 1650–1870* (New York: Norton, c. 1983), 289–92.
4. Florence M. Montgomery, *Printed Textiles: English and American Cottons and Linens 1700–1850* (New York: Viking, 1970), 176. Montgomery states that the lapis style process used a resist mordant to block the indigo dye and "produce red in conjunction with the madder bath. This made it possible to print cloth with areas or even dots of red adjacent to areas of blue without intervening white outlines."
5. An additional blue ground chintz, similar in scale and color scheme but different in design from the chintz used for the borders, has been pieced into the upper-left corner of the quilt.
6. William Willson's 1859 estate inventory included "1 lot Quilts" and "2 Comforts." Montgomery County *Inventories, List of Sales & Accounts*, J.W.S. no. 2 (1858–60).

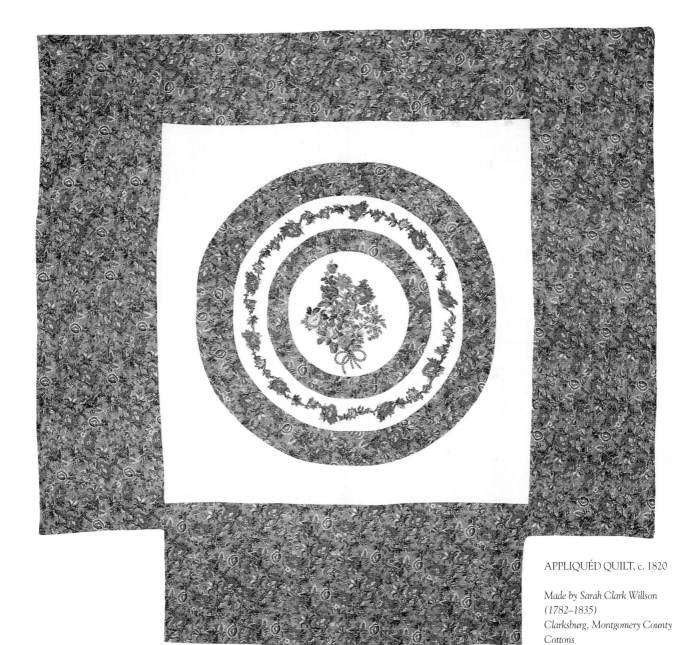

APPLIQUÉD QUILT, c. 1820

Made by Sarah Clark Willson (1782–1835)
Clarksburg, Montgomery County
Cottons
103 x 106 inches
Owned by the Montgomery County Historical Society

Sophia's Fancy Chintz Quilt

WHEN SOPHIA MYERS Pearce set a large chintz diamond on point, she was working in a style more familiar to Virginia quiltmakers than those in Maryland during the late eighteenth and early nineteenth centuries. Although a few Maryland quiltmakers—such as Rebecca Gladstone and her daughter, Rebecca Harker—made quilts in this style, it was more popular in Tidewater Virginia and North Carolina.[1] Sophia may have seen and admired similar quilts when visiting family in Richmond.

Sophia's choice of fabrics to carry out the design was purely Maryland-inspired. She picked some of the most beautiful block-printed, glazed furnishing fabrics available in Baltimore at the time, as did several other Maryland quiltmakers. Eleanora Roche used the same English oval print (p. 55) to encircle a bouquet of flowers in her c. 1840 quilt. Catherine Garnhart and Susan Whitter of Frederick, whose quilts are in museum collections, chose the same block-printed cottons decorated with sprays of lilies, tulips, and roses for their lavish bedcovers. Montell family members of Baltimore selected a rich madder cotton print identical to Sophia's center for several blocks on their quilt.[2] Most of these glazed cottons and the unusual cactus design in the corners of Sophia's quilt are seen on a large group of quilts and unquilted spreads attributed to Achsah Goodwin Wilkins of Baltimore City, a prolific and influential quilt designer.[3] Sophia's fabric choices were dictated by what was available from local merchants and by what attracted her eye; judging from what is documented,

she and other Maryland quiltmakers had similar tastes.

Sophia's quilt also exemplifies the classical style in nineteenth-century Maryland quilted bedcovers: grapes are stuffed and quilted between the appliquéd floral sprays on the outer border, and the remainder of the quilt is stitched in fine parallel lines.

The daughter of Baltimore tobacco wholesaler Jacob Myers (1765–1848), Sophia had a brother (Samuel) who was a tobacco manufacturer in Richmond and operated the notorious Libby Prison in that city. Sophia and John B. Pearce (1800–1874) were married in 1832 and resided with John's widowed father, Thomas (1771–c. 1860), at the family home, Clifford, an estate considered one of the most beautiful in Baltimore County. Thomas Pearce had a notable career as a farmer and soldier: he extended the home farm by several hundred acres over the years, and he fought in the battles of North Point and Bladensburg during the War of 1812. John B. Pearce, although only fourteen at the time, recalled witnessing the bombardment of Fort McHenry as he drove a wagon from Baltimore's harbor. He thought it "a magnificent spectacle, despite the grave apprehensions which filled his mind at the time."[4] Thomas and John Pearce were responsible for building the Clymnleria Methodist Episcopal Church in Baltimore County. During the Civil War "General Pearce," as John was known in his later years, was a staunch Union supporter.[5] In 1862 and again in 1864 he was elected to represent Baltimore County in the Maryland legislature.

John and Sophia had four children, a son and three daughters. Like Maryland quiltmaker Cecilia Jessop, Sophia and John were painted by portrait artist Sarah Miriam Peale (1800–85) in 1835 (19). Sophia, rendered with brown eyes and hair, is dressed in blue velvet with an ermine cape, probably painter's props; John is depicted with black hair and brown eyes.[6] Sophia's quilt descended to the present owner from her mother, who used it occasionally on a family bed.

19. Sophia Myers Pearce (1805–71), painted by Sarah Miriam Peale, c. 1835, Baltimore, oil on canvas. (Photograph courtesy of J. Hall Pleasants File, Maryland Historical Society, #2448)

1. Jennifer Faulds Goldsborough, *Lavish Legacies: Baltimore Album and Related Quilts in the Collection of the Maryland Historical Society* (Baltimore: Maryland Historical Society, 1994), 56. Goldsborough gives a design source for the framed medallion set on point: "This format came directly from ceremonial cloths called rumal from Northern India which presented a central, flower-filled square on point (oriented on the diagonal) surrounded by numerous borders with squares in each corner of the cloth." For examples of other quilts in this style, see Gloria Seaman Allen, *First Flowerings: Early Virginia Quilts* (Washington, DC: DAR Museum, 1987) 16, 17, 26–29, 33; and Ellen Fickling Eanes, Erma Hughes Kirkpatrick, Sue Barker McCarter, Joyce Joines Newman, Ruth Haislip Roberson, Kathlyn Fender Sullivan, *North Carolina Quilts* (Chapel Hill: University of North Carolina Press, 1988), 39–62.
2. The Eleanora Roche quilt is documented as MAFCE #MD-143; Catherine Garnhart and Susan Whitter's quilts are pictured in Gloria Seaman Allen's *Old Line Traditions: Maryland Women and Their Quilts* (Washington, DC: DAR Museum, 1985), 13–15; and the Montell family quilt is published in Allen's, *Old Line Traditions,* 16, and in Jennifer Faulds Goldsborough, *Lavish Legacies: Baltimore Album and Related Quilts in the Collection of the Maryland Historical Society* (Baltimore: Maryland Historical Society, 1994), 58–59.

3. None of these quilts were documented by MAFCE, although they were identified and illustrated by William Rush Dunton Jr. in *Old Quilts*, 184–203. They are presumed to be in the possession of Achsah Wilkins's descendants.
4. J. Thomas Scharf, *The History of Baltimore City and County, Maryland; Part II* (Baltimore:

Regional Publishing, 1971), 907–08.
5. He rose through the ranks of the local militia.
6. J. Hall Pleasants File, Maryland Historical Society, no. 2447, and no. 2448. Sophia's parents, Jacob (1765–1848) and Louisa Spicer Myers (died 1830), also were painted by Sarah M. Peale, no. 2402 and no. 2446, respectively.

FRAMED MEDALLION QUILT, c. 1840

Made by Sophia Myers Pearce (1805–71)
Clifford, Monkton, Baltimore County
Cottons
112 x 112 inches
Owned by Helen Denison Heaton
(Photographer, Mark Gulezian)

Chintz Quilt with Scroll Border

LITTLE IS KNOWN ABOUT the maker of this classical quilt, though the present owner believed it was made by her great-grandmother, Mary Amelia Roche (1837–1917). Because the fabrics in the quilt predate Mary's birth, the quilt was probably made by Mary's mother, Eleanora. Edmund and Eleanora Roche emigrated to the United States from Ireland with Mary around 1837. After settling in this country, they had three more children, two sons and a daughter. Edmund is listed as a bottler in the 1850 federal census for Baltimore. In addition to the children, the Roche household included a seventy-year-old Irish immigrant, William Shehan, possibly Eleanora's father, and two young men Edmund's age who were also bottlers. The Roche family probably attended St. Vincent de Paul Catholic Church, the site of Mary's wedding to David Drohan in 1857. Like many Marylanders in the 1850s, the Roche family went west. By 1851 they were living in Cincinnati, Ohio, but returned to Baltimore in 1857.[1]

The multicolor, block-printed floral nosegay in the center of the quilt was applied by using hidden whipstitches and then surrounded by twelve colorful block-printed medallions, then further encircled by a string of madder-dyed block-printed paterae (20). The oval shapes resemble motifs in an English cotton print produced at the Bannister Hall Printworks around 1826 (21).[2]

Laid-on between the medallions and paterae are several multicolor motifs cut from block-printed cottons in the Indian style. These exotic designs, such as passion flowers and flowering trees, were widely produced on English and French furnishing fabrics in the late eighteenth and early nineteenth centuries. The appeal of these Indian-style cottons coincided with the taste for turbans and paisley shawls worn by fashionable ladies.

The eleven-and-one-half-inch scrollwork border, beautifully block-printed in shades of red and olive green, was a popular English furnishing fabric produced between 1815 and 1824. Classically inspired scrollwork borders were printed vertically along one selvedge edge and used for bordering valances, drapery, and, in this case, bedcovers. The quiltmaker may have sewn window and bed hangings for her home with borders in this graceful print. Scrollwork designs were used on furniture, silver, ceramics, and other decorative art forms in the classical period. Thomas Sheraton pictured scrollwork "borders for pier tables" in his 1794 *Cabinet-Makers and Upholsterer's Drawing-Book*.[3]

The quilting designs on this bedcover also are in the classical taste. The central floral nosegay is encircled by a feather wreath. Several other feather wreaths are intermingled with the appliqué, and the ground is filled in with clamshell, grid, and parallel line patterns. The quilting is twenty-eight stitches to the inch, and the backing is a tightly woven white cotton. The quilt has been passed down through the maternal line, from mother to daughter. The present owner is the great-great-granddaughter of the maker.

1. A sampler made by Mary Amelia Roche while living in Ohio descended to the present quilt owner.
2. See Florence M. Montgomery, *Printed Textiles: English and American Cottons and Linens, 1700–1850* (New York: Viking, 1970), 179. Montgomery states that the Bannister Hall Printworks continued to produce some block-printed textiles after the increase in production of roller-printed textiles in the 1820s. Bannister Hall Printworks led the way among fashionable English furniture printers, but its fabrics were costly and thus widely imitated.
3. Thomas Sheraton, *The Cabinet-Makers and Upholsterer's Drawing-Book* (reprint, New York: Dover, 1969), plate 3.

20. Detail of central floral bouquet in Eleanora Roche's fancy chintz quilt.

21. Detail of block-printed medallion in Eleanora Roche's quilt.

FANCY APPLIQUÉD QUILT WITH SCROLL
BORDER, c. 1840

Probably made by Eleanora Roche (b. 1820)
Baltimore City
Cottons
106 x 106 inches
Owned by Catherine Janet Strauss

William Rush Dunton Jr. (1868–1966)

T HE HISTORY OF QUILTMAKING IN Maryland cannot be accurately written without examining the influence that psychiatrist and pioneer quilt historian Dr. William Rush Dunton Jr. had on the emerging field of quilt history (22). His 278-page book, *Old Quilts*, published in 1946 on the heels of the colonial revival, is still considered one of the most complete investigations of Maryland quilts, particularily those made in the album and medallion styles.[1] The years that Dunton spent actively surveying and documenting quilts in Maryland coincided with the revival of quiltmaking, a time when there was renewed interest in and appreciation for our country's past. The acceptance of his work and its lasting influence is, in itself, evidence of the acceptance of the changing attitudes toward quilts and their importance to U.S. culture in the first half of the twentieth century.[2]

Dunton was born in Chestnut Hill, Pennsylvania, three years after the end of the Civil War. He received B.S. and M.A. degrees from Haverford College and attended medical school at the University of Pennsylvania. A few years later he moved to Maryland, and by 1924 he was medical director of the Sheppard-Pratt sanatorium near Baltimore. In 1947 a *Baltimore Sun* article, entitled "Not-So-Crazy Quilts," chronicled another work, his introduction to quilts, beginning in 1915. "Before the First World War, a Baltimore psychiatrist in search of a pleasant form of occupational therapy for his patients at a mental hospital in Maryland hit upon the idea of quiltmaking." The reporter went on to write, "Believing that the colors involved in making quilts would appeal to his patients, while the cutting and sewing would take their minds off themselves, he started collecting quilt patterns for their use." Dunton was further inspired to organize a quilt show for his patients, "in order to stimulate their interest." Dunton noted that he expected to obtain about a dozen quilts, but surprisingly ended up with fifty.[3]

This event started him on a lifelong quest—studying, documenting, and photographing old quilts. By 1947 he had amassed more than 500 pictures of quilts, the majority from Maryland and the surrounding states, and had begun a close relationship with the Baltimore Museum of Art, where he was curator of at least three quilt shows and where his scrapbooks and correspondence are housed. He stated in the article that he acquired only about fifteen quilts for himself, most of which he later donated to the museum.[4]

Like a true scholar, Dunton relied on evidence rather than an oral history alone to date the quilts he recorded. Realizing that much mythology had developed and misinformation passed along about quiltmaking in the early years, he expanded his study to include early textile printing. He mentioned receiving swatches of old and new cloth from "textile men" in New York, that helped him date more accurately the calicoes and chintzes in the quilts he studied.[5]

An avid letter writer, Dunton corresponded with quilt enthusiasts from all over the country. Because relatively few books had been published on the subject, these quilt lovers had to rely on "round robins," or small groups of people who shared information, kits, and patterns by mail. Correspondence was the only way for some to obtain the specifics they sought about old patterns and methods. In 1939 Dr. Dunton responded to an inquiry from a quilt afficionado in Columbia, Tennessee. He wrote to Mrs. W. Edwin Richardson, providing her with a detailed list of the names and addresses of quilt book authors and/or publishers. He gave his opinion of each source and believed that, "If you can get the photographs or sketches of them [quilts] it is well and also get histories of the makers. You will find this a delightful hobby and I believe will be able to contribute something to local history as I am doing here in Maryland."[6]

Dunton documented Maryland quilts by tapping his extensive contacts within the state. He would set up a date and time for quilt owners to bring their family quilts for him to photograph and sketch and to record the family history or provenance. Almost 200 photographs in the Dunton scrapbooks at the Baltimore Museum of Art have the exact same date recorded on them, suggesting all 200 were recorded and photographed on the same day!

Contemporary quilt historians are presently searching for the whereabouts of the quilts pictured in Dunton's book. Many are housed in museums and historical societies throughout Maryland but also in other states. More than ten quilts are pictured in this book that Dunton studied; some are included in his book. Although he diligently recorded the provenance of each quilt, he did make mistakes, some of which the authors of this book corrected.

The reviews of Dunton's book generally were good, but there were discreet reservations about his scholarship in some circles. The noted New England quilt historian Florence Peto wrote Dunton's friend Mrs. Richardson of Tennessee:

> Our friend Dr. Dunton sent me a copy of the *Baltimore Sun* in which he and his hobbies and book were featured and some nice photos shown; did he send you one? Very nice publicity indeed. Confidentially, we are not alone in our disappointment of his *Old Quilts*. Newark Museum and *Antiques* magazine feel that he was repetitious and tiresome and didn't tell the essential things. The Maryland Historical Society gave him a good review; after all, he DID do quite a job on locally made items.[7]

Nancy Gibson Tuckhorn

22. *William Rush Dunton Jr. (1868–1966) is seen here autographing a copy of his book in a photograph accompanying a 1947 article for the* Baltimore Sun. *(Photograph courtesy of the Enoch Pratt Free Library)*

1. William Rush Dunton Jr., *Old Quilts* (Catonsville, MD: n.p., 1946).
2. Dunton was not the only Marylander to travel the state photographing and cataloguing decorative arts during the colonial revival period. J. Hall Pleasants documented and photographed paintings in Maryland, some of which are pictured in this book. The Pleasants files are housed at the Maryland Historical Society.
3. Carol Forbes, "Not-So-Crazy Quilts," *Baltimore Sun*, Sunday, May 11, 1947.
4. Ibid. Lorena K. Sehgal, assistant to the registrar, Baltimore Museum of Art, kindly provided a list of Dunton's donations. They include four quilts in the following patterns: Baltimore Album, Double Wedding Ring, Le Moyne Star, and Rocky Glenn. He also donated a quilt top described as "a marine life pattern." These bedcovers were given between 1946 and 1949. In 1949 he also donated "two cases of material samples used in American quilts," and an "index of patterns used in quilt M." Two pieces of needlework, a sampler, and a picture were included in this gift along with a linen handkerchief. In 1950 he gave an eighteenth-century needlework counterpane. From 1954 to 1956 he donated quilted petticoat fragments, a pattern block for a bedspread, a patchwork throw, and something listed as "a teabox design in various colored silks." The patchwork throw was his last gift to the museum. Dunton also donated several quilts to the Maryland Historical Society.
5. Forbes, Baltimore *Sun*, 1947.
6. Mrs. W. Edwin Richardson, correspondence, August 21, 1939. The Elizabeth F. Richardson collection. The authors thank June Thomason for permission to quote from this letter, and Bets Ramsey and Merikay Waldvogel for bringing this correspondence to their attention.
7. Florence Peto, correspondence, May 2, 1947. The Elizabeth F. Richardson collection. Peto must have inadvertently recorded the incorrect date on her letter to Mrs. Richardson, as the *Baltimore Sun* article did not appear until Sunday, May 11, 1947. The authors thank June Thomason for permission to quote from this letter.

Pheasant and Plum Tree Quilt

*F*ACTS SOMETIMES BEcome obscure or lost as family histories are repeated and passed down through the generations. The story that emerges about this elaborate chintz quilt paints a poignant picture. Family tradition attributes its making to Arianna Owings of Owings Mills. The initials "A O" are quilted and corded in the center of the quilt (23). Actually, Arianna Owings died in 1807, years before the quilt was made. In William Rush Dunton's 1946 book *Old Quilts*, he attributed the quilt to Arianna Sollers Bouldin (1816–79),[1] the niece of Arianna Owings. Arianna Sollers married Alexander Bouldin in 1834. Although her mother's maiden name was Owings, there is no evidence that Arianna used it as a middle name; thus, Arianna Sollers is unlikely to have inscribed a quilt for herself with those initials only.

A more likely explanation is that Arianna Sollers made the quilt in memory of her niece, Arianna Owings. Ruth Sollers (1802–65), Arianna's eldest sister, married William Owings (1803–70), her first cousin, in 1828. Ruth was the first of six Sollers siblings to marry and start a family. Her first child, Samuel, died at the age of three months in 1830. Her second child, Arianna, lived less than a month in 1831.[2] Arianna Sollers and her infant niece both were named after Arianna Owings, their aunt and grandmother. Arianna Sollers was fifteen years old when her sister's second child was buried. Saddened by the loss of her only niece and nephew within a year, she probably made this quilt as a memorial to the deceased baby.

Girls of this age often had the needlework skills to complete such a task. During the classical era in America, schoolgirl needlework pictures were popular, along with mourning pictures, mourning jewelry, and samplers. Intended to be on display in the home, some included needlework memorials to deceased family members. Arianna's quilt represents a large, quilted version of that type of schoolgirl art. Not only are the initials designed in a script exactly like those seen on needlework pictures, but the laid areas are embroidered with silk thread in a buttonhole stitch.

When Dunton studied this quilt for inclusion in *Old Quilts*, he dated it about 1820 but added a qualifying remark. He wrote, "The fact that the patches are applied with buttonhole stitching would incline me to date this quilt later than given, but the date when this practice began is not yet determined."[3] He was correct in his reservations about the date of the quilt, but his information was incomplete. Although Arianna's quilt is one of the few found in the documentation project appliquéd with a buttonhole stitch, others of this style were made in the Chesapeake region. In a 1985 exhibition of Maryland quilts, the DAR Museum in Washington, DC, displayed a quilt made about 1810 in Port Tobacco, Charles County, in which the central appliqué is worked with cotton thread in a buttonhole stitch.[4] In 1987 the DAR Museum exhibited several appliquéd quilts made in Tidewater Virginia during the late eighteenth and early nineteenth centuries worked in buttonhole stitches with colored silk threads.[5] One quilt was even appliquéd in a reverse buttonhole stitch. Although appliquéd quilts embroidered in buttonhole stitches are not common in Maryland, this technique was used in the region during these years. A coarse, more widely spaced buttonhole stitch is seen on blocks in album quilts made in Maryland during the 1840s and 1850s.

The appliquéd sawtooth border on Arianna's quilt is a typical border design found on many Maryland-made quilts prior to the Civil War. In some cases the triangles are sewn individually to the ground cloth, but usually an entire length of triangles is applied in one piece. Design sources for these sawtooth borders appear on many dec-

23. The initials "A O" quilted and corded in Spencerian schoolgirl script to memorialize Arianna Owings, niece of the maker, Arianna Sollers.

orative objects throughout the centuries, from the Antioch Mosiacs to the patterns on English Staffordshire pottery produced exclusively for the U.S. market in the early nineteenth century. Commemorating American life and events, this pottery was extremely popular, especially with those living in cities depicted in the patterns, such as Baltimore. The tiny borders framing the central scenes on many of these plates, cups, and pitchers are similar to the sawtooth border designs on quilts. The popularity of these border designs on Maryland quilts peaked in the 1840s but did not fade until the last quarter of the nineteenth century.

The chintzes in Arianna's quilt are block-printed cottons with blue penciling. The center appliqué fabric of pheasants and plum trees was printed in England in 1815 and is illustrated in Florence Montgomery's *Printed Textiles*.[6] The ground cloth is a finely woven cotton, corded and stuffed. There is no background or filler quilting. The stitching that outlines the cording and stuffing is worked twenty-three to the inch. The binding is a domestically woven tape in three shades of brown and green.

There is evidence that Arianna Bouldin continued to take pride in her needlework and to pass the tradition along to her daughters, Susannah and Alexina. In 1852 Arianna entered a shell pincushion in the fifth annual Maryland Institute Fair, and a year later Susannah entered a "tidy." That

same year Alexina, future owner of the pheasant and plum tree quilt, entered two jars of peach jelly in the class devoted to "fancy articles."[7]

1. William Rush Dunton Jr., *Old Quilts* (Catonsville, MD: n.p., 1946), 211–12.
2. William and Ruth Owings had eight children, but only one lived to adulthood.
3. Dunton, *Old Quilts*, 212.
4. Gloria Seaman Allen, *Old Line Traditions:* *Maryland Women and Their Quilts* (Washington, DC: DAR Museum, 1985), 10.
5. Gloria Seaman Allen, *First Flowerings: Early Virginia Quilts* (Washington, DC: DAR Museum, 1987), 16–20, 22, 28.
6. Florence M. Montgomery, *Printed Textiles: English and American Cottons and Linens, 1700–1850* (New York: Viking, 1970) 160.
7. "Catalogue of Articles Deposited for Competition and Premiums at the Fifth and Sixth Annual Exhibition of the Maryland Institute Opened in Baltimore," 1852 and 1853, 81, 18, and 80.

APPLIQUÉD CHINTZ QUILT, c. 1831

Probably made by Arianna Sollers (1816–79) in memory of her niece, Arianna Owings (1831–31)
Anne Arundel County
Cottons, corded initials
95.5 x 93 inches
Owned by Roberta Cassard

Pheasant and Palm Tree Quilt

ANN ROE OF QUEEN Anne's County probably made this sunburst quilt shortly before her 1834 marriage to Joseph K. Cook (1803–78). For the appliquéd or laid areas she used a pheasant and palm tree block-printed cotton that dates around 1815 and remained popular for several decades.[1] The print is similar in style to a pheasant and plum tree print found on several other Maryland quilts (p. 59). Textile historians Mary Schoeser and Celia Rufey suggest that these block-printed cottons, with their distinctive "islands" of design, were among those dumped on the American market after the signing of the Treaty of Ghent in December 1814.[2]

Small-figured red and green discharge prints make up the sunburst, the eight-pointed stars, and the pieced sawtooth borders. The block print used for the wide outer border has a dark red or plum ground, which sets off the polychrome floral design and provides a strong frame for the pieced and appliquéd motifs. The border is quilted in the chevron pattern, and the rest of the quilt is stitched in parallel lines.

The second of eight children of Colonel James and Margaret Price Roe, Ann grew up at Sarah's Fancy (also known as Roesville or Roe's Cross Roads), 843 acres granted to Edward Roe by Charles Calvert, fifth Lord

Baltimore, in 1748. Her father and two brothers were active as farmers, merchants, and benefactors in their rural Eastern Shore community. At times they operated a general store at Roe's Cross Roads. Perhaps their store carried English chintz fabrics similar to the ones Ann used in her quilt.

In 1856 brother William Henry Charles Roe inherited Sarah's Fancy; for the next five years he kept a detailed diary of farming activities, political events, weather conditions, and slave holdings. The diary stopped with his death in 1861 but was started again in 1870 by his widow, Mary Wright Roe. Her writings reveal the hardships faced by many, especially widows and children, in Maryland after the Civil War.[3] Although the family home is no longer standing, part of the original land grant remains in the Roe family. Local maps still retain the name Roe's Cross Roads.

Ann's husband, Joseph K. Cook, was active in county affairs. He was a successful farmer with real estate valued at $11,000 in 1860. By the time of his death in 1878, his real estate holdings had grown in value to $27,800 and included 1,100 acres, divided among four farms and a house in Centerville.[4] Like his in-laws, Cook qualified for a seat on the board of the county almshouse. As a slaveholder and Southern sympathizer, Cook served on the committee of the local Methodist church, which rejected the antislavery position set forth by the General Conference of the Methodist Protestant Church of Maryland.

Ann Roe Cook survived her husband by five years. Her estate, which was considerably smaller than her husband's, included her furniture, bed clothing, and Joseph's gold watch.[5] Having no children, her quilt passed to her surviving brother, James B. Roe, and then down the male line to the present owner. In this century Ann's quilt has traveled to Virginia, Rhode Island, California,

24. Detail showing pheasant appliqué, from a print popular with Maryland quiltmakers for several decades.

Pennsylvania, Japan, and back to Queen Anne's County, Maryland. In spite of the many miles traveled in suitcases and packing boxes, this early Maryland quilt has been given loving care and has never required cleaning. The printed fabrics retain their original glazing, and the colors are unfaded.

1. This print is illustrated in Mary Schoeser and Celia Rufey, *English and American Textiles from 1790 to the Present* (London: Thames and Hudson, 1989), 57. The same fabric was used on two quilts, by unidentified makers, documented in Montgomery County. On one quilt, the print was used as the outer border (MO-009); on the other the pheasants, palm trees, and flowers were cut out and appliquéd to the reserves created by an eight-pointed pulsating star (MO-177).
2. Ibid.
3. We are grateful to the Roe family for sharing William Henry Charles Roe's diary with us and to Orlando Rideout for providing us with a typescript of the diary.
4. Queen Anne's County *Inventories*, M.P. no. 1 (1877–80), 147.
5. Queen Anne's County *Inventories*, W.E.T. no. 1 (1880–83), 360.

APPLIQUÉD AND PIECED QUILT, c. 1834

Made by Ann Roe (1807–83)
Sarah's Fancy or Roe's Cross Roads, Queen Anne's
County
Cottons
97.5 x 100.5 inches
Owned by William M. D. and Elizabeth P. Roe

Chintz Wedding Quilt

PIECED CRADLE QUILT, 1840s, Rebecca Gladstone or her daughter Rebecca Harker. This quilt may have been one of those entered in the 1853 Maryland Institute Fair by Rebecca Harker. (Courtesy of Ellen Harker Baer and Mildred Harker Touchton)

FAMILY HISTORY RE-cords that Rebecca Gladstone and her eldest daughter and namesake, Rebecca, made this chintz quilt in 1841 for young Rebecca's marriage to John James Harker (1817–92). The elder Rebecca was the wife of Scottish-born Michael Gladstone (1792–1841), who, according to family tradition, was a cousin of British Prime Minister William Gladstone. Born in Maryland, Rebecca lived her entire life in Baltimore. She and Michael had four children, two boys and two girls. Michael died at the age of forty-nine in 1841, the same year his seventeen-year-old daughter Rebecca married. By 1850, the elder Rebecca's household included her other three children and two seventeen-year-old free black laborers. Sons Andrew, twenty-one, and Charles, sixteen, were both employed as bricklayers. Rebecca's real and personal estate was worth $2,400.[1]

Rebecca and her daughter designed their quilt in a medallion format, popular with Maryland quiltmakers during the classical period but made infrequently after 1840. Appliquéd sawtooth borders outline the circular medallion and diamond-in-a-square configuration. Within this central field they placed birds, butterflies, and flowers cut from glazed, block-printed cottons. The entire central portion probably covered the top of a large bed, with the white quilted and chintz borders hanging over the sides. Polychrome birds, butterflies, and realistic floral patterns found in these furnishing fabrics appear on many quilts made in Maryland during the first half of the nineteenth century. Perhaps the windows and bedstead in the best chamber were hung with curtains and drapery

made of the same glazed chintz as the quilt; perhaps the bed chamber seating furniture was cased in it too.

Like Arianna Bouldin's daughters, Rebecca Harker was an exhibitor at the 1853 Maryland Institute Fair. The quilts pictured here may have been those recorded as "one large and one small quilt, made and deposited by Mrs. R. Harker."[2]

Rebecca Harker bore ten children, but only four survived to adulthood. Between 1848 and 1851 the three eldest died, leaving one-year-old Charles Edgar (1850–1900) as the only child for several years. The Harker

family lived on Harford Avenue, next door to Rebecca's mother.

The quilt descended to Charles Edgar, grandfather of the present owners. Charles was a cabinetmaker in Baltimore; many of his tools, signature dyes, and several pieces of furniture have remained in the family along with the quilt. A cradle quilt, possibly made by Rebecca for the birth of one of her children, also remains.

The owners state that William Rush Dunton Jr. examined the chintz quilt in the years following the 1946 publication of *Old Quilts*. Family history also records that during

Rebecca and John Harker's courtship, Rebecca made a quilt square each time he visited. The resulting quilt was much used and consequently has not survived.

1. 1850 federal census, Baltimore, 8th ward, 460.
2. "Catalogue of Articles Deposited for Competion and Premiums at the Sixth Annual Exhibition of the Maryland Institute Opened in Baltimore," October 3, 1853, 24.

APPLIQUÉD CHINTZ QUILT, c. 1841

Made by Rebecca Gladstone (b. 1795) and her daughter, Rebecca Gladstone Harker (1824–98)
Harford Avenue, Baltimore City
Cottons
96 x 96 inches
Owned by Ellen Harker Baer and Mildred Harker Touchton

Edelen Family Cradle Quilt

A CRADLE QUILT OWNED by the Edelen family of St. Mary's County is thought to have been made by one or more slaves on the family's plantation overlooking Breton Bay. The quilt probably was made during the 1830s or early 1840s for one of the four children of Ellen Leigh (d. 1845) and Dr. William Joseph Edelen (1800–73).[1] The Edelens lived with Dr. Richard Edelen at Society Hill until his death in 1835; William Edelen inherited the home place from his father. After the death of Ellen Leigh, he married Ellen Gough and sired another four children. The Edelen family accumulated a large estate with extensive land and slave holdings. In 1835 Richard Edelen's taxables included 1,231 acres and twenty-three slaves valued at $10,564.[2] By 1850 William Edelen's real estate was valued by federal census takers at $15,000; by 1860 the value of the land had risen to $28,000 and the value of other property, primarily slaves, came to $49,000.

The Civil War brought many changes to Society Hill. William Edelen was forcibly removed from his plantation by Union soldiers, tried, found guilty of aiding the Southern cause, and put in prison.[3] His slaves, who worked the tobacco fields and served in the house, gained their freedom. An inventory from 1860 listed fifty-six slaves, thirty-one females and twenty-five males. An 1867 list of former slaves put Edelen's total at sixty-two, noting which slaves were emancipated by the state of Maryland as of November 1, 1864,[4] which ones enlisted in the Union Army's Thirty-eighth U.S. Colored Troops in May 1864,[5] and which ones left with the military between November 1863 and November 1864.

The Edelen family kept a number of field workers and house servants during the 1830s and early 1840s, the period in which skilled hands—slaves, family members, or both—made the cradle quilt. By the time Richard Edelen died in 1835, his estate included twenty-five slaves, eight of whom were grown women. Several of these slave women must have been textile artisans, for Edelen's inventoried possessions also included three spinning wheels, one quill wheel, three winding blades, and two looms. In addition to the quilt on his bedstead, a large chest in another room contained ten quilts and counterpanes.[6]

The cradle quilt, which has descended in the female line of William Edelen's oldest daughter by his second wife, Ellen Gough,[7] is carefully pieced and appliquéd from a number of block-printed textiles. Fine quilting at twenty-six stitches to the inch outlines the appliquéd floral sprigs and encircles the pieced eight-pointed stars in feather wreaths. Narrowly spaced triple rows of quilting, alternating with plain areas, create a striped background.

An unusual feature of this quilt is the ground piecing. The maker deliberately

26. No photographs are known to exist, but the slave quarters at Society Hill may have resembled those at nearby Sotterly plantation, shown here. (Photograph courtesy of the Historic American Buildings Survey, Library of Congress)

25. The broken lines indicate the pattern created by the piecing of the white ground cloth. The piecing is only visible through close inspection.

pieced the white cotton ground from diamonds, triangles, and sashing to form a grid that connects all the stars while enclosing the appliquéd motifs. The elaborate piecing effort is only visible upon close inspection, yet it adds measurably to the quilt by visually unifying all the design elements (25).

Although this technique is unusual for Maryland quilts, it cannot be ascertained that it reflects an African piecing tradition. Does this quilt represent the conventions of Euro-American quiltmaking or did the maker, thought to have been a slave woman, contribute her own sense of aesthetics? Except for the unusual, elaborate ground cloth piecing, the quilt fits into a chronology of Maryland quilts made by women of British or German heritage. Therefore, it seems likely that the slave woman who made or worked on this quilt sewed under the instruction of her mistress and contributed her considerable skills rather than her creative expression. Probably several of the slave women assigned to the big house were skilled in needlework and sewed quilts for the family with their mistress, Richard's wife, Ann Gough Edelen, or with their young mistress, Ellen Leigh Edelen.

Cecil County plantation mistress Martha Ogle Forman recorded in her diary that she quilted on occasion with her "house girls." Martha also noted that her slaves quilted in their quarters and organized quiltings during the Christmas holidays.[8] The Edelen slaves also may have pieced, appliquéd, and quilted at night in their quarters (26). Out of sight of the master's house they would have had greater autonomy and freedom to express themselves in their needlework.

The cradle quilt, while heavily used, nevertheless was valued and preserved in its fragile state by the Edelen-Gough family long after the names of maker and recipient were forgotten.

1. Margaret K. Fresco, *Doctors of St. Mary's County 1634–1900* (Maryland, 1992), 90–91. Their children included Henry Cornelius, born 1833; Phillip Ford, born about 1837; Alice Leigh, born about 1840; and William Joseph, born about 1842. Although the name of the quilt recipient is unknown, the style and fabrics suggest an 1830 to 1845 date range.
2. Ibid., 89–90. The Edelens and Goughs were among the leading families of St. Mary's County. They frequently intermarried. Anne Edelen, daughter of Richard and Ann Gough Edelen, married Benedict Gough. Her portrait was painted in 1822 by Sarah Miriam Peale. Anne's brother, William, married Ellen Gough.
3. St. Mary's was probably the most pro-South of the Maryland counties. In the 1861 gubernatorial election, fewer than 20 percent voted for the pro-Union candidate, Augustus Bradford. By comparison, Bradford received more than 80 percent of the Baltimore County vote. Suzanne Ellery Greene Chapelle et al., *Maryland: A History of Its People* (Baltimore: Johns Hopkins University Press, 1986), 159.
4. Ibid., 168. The Emancipation Proclamation of January 1, 1863, did not grant freedom to Maryland's slaves. It only freed those held in bondage in the Confederate states "where the people were in rebellion against the United States." The new Maryland state constitution, which went into effect on November 1, 1864, declared that "all persons held to service or labor, as slaves, are hereby declared free."
5. Ibid. In 1863 Congress passed a bill allowing blacks to join the Union army. By 1864, Maryland had six black regiments.
6. St. Mary's County *Inventories* G.C.1.i (1835–40).

7. This daughter, Ellen Leigh, the first child of Dr. Edelen's second wife, Ellen Gough, was named after the first wife, Ellen Leigh.
8. Gloria Seaman Allen, "Quiltmaking on Chesapeake Plantations," in *On the Cutting Edge: Textile Collectors, Collections, and Traditions,* edited by Jeannette Lasansky (Lewisburg, PA: Oral Traditions Project, 1994), 66.

APPLIQUÉD AND PIECED CRADLE QUILT, 1830–45

Possibly made by slave women at Society Hill Near Leonardtown, St. Mary's County
Cottons
49.5 x 36 inches
Owned by the family of Ann Brown Gough

Mathematical
Star Quilt

PIECED AND APPLIQUÉD MATHEMATICAL
STAR QUILT, 1830–45

Possibly made by Sarah Barnett Woolford (1793–1878)
Near Cambridge, Dorchester County
Cottons
100 x 97 inches
Owned by the Dorchester County Historical Society

27. Detail of Sarah Woolford's quilt showing her finely stitched pineapple motif and roller-printed border fabric.

block and roller prints and framed by a narrow border of roller-printed chintz.[2] The middle border is filled with eight-pointed stars appliquéd to the white cotton ground. One star, directly above the central star, has only seven points.[3] The outer border fabric repeats the inner border roller print and is bound with a woven blue and brown tape. Figurative quilting in the form of pineapples and rosettes, worked at twenty stitches per inch, fills in the ground (27).

The star quilt was kept in the Jordan house, a two-and-one-half-story frame house of Georgian design in Cambridge, until it was donated to the historical society. Regrettably the house was demolished in 1967 and replaced by a gas station.

1. The quilt came to the Dorchester County Historical Society with a note, "Made in 1762 by my cousin's grandmother. A duplicate is at Mt. Vernon [New York]." The style of the fabrics and design of the quilt suggest a nineteenth- rather than an eighteenth-century date. The "duplicate" quilt is remembered as a mid- to late-nineteenth-century quilt. It may have been made about the same time as Sophia Reid's quilt. See endnote 3.
2. Blue and brown was a popular color combination in the mid-Atlantic region during the 1840s.
3. Sophia Ruth Peckham Reid of Montgomery County made a similar quilt approximately thirty years later. It, too, has one star with a different number of points, p. 169.

*T*HE HISTORY OF THIS STRIKing star quilt is uncertain. The quilt was given to the Dorchester County Historical Society in Cambridge in 1963 by a relative of Edna Jordan Hirst (1875–1960). The Woolford-Jordan family Bible, also owned by Mrs. Hirst, provides clues to the quilt's possible maker.

Edna Jordan Hirst was the fifth daughter and youngest child of Sarah Jamesina Woolford (1832–1910) and William H. Jordan (1816–85). William had emigrated from Bradford-on-Avon, England, in 1821 and married a Dorchester County native, Sarah Woolford, in 1852. Sarah was the daughter of Sarah Barnett (1793–1878) and James Woolford (1777–1832), a Cambridge innkeeper. The period in which the quilt probably was made, 1830–45, postdates the Woolford's 1826 marriage and suggests that Sarah Barnett Woolford may have been the maker.[1]

The central pulsating star is pieced from numerous small-figured blue and brown

Delectable Mountains Quilt

*L*EWIS SHIPLEY AND ELIZA-beth Mackelfresh, his wife, was married the 10th day of April 1821." This entry is the first of many in the Shipley family Bible detailing important passages in the lives of Elizabeth Shipley and her relatives. The births and deaths of her children, grandchildren, and several family slaves are dutifully recorded, along with her own death in 1865.

Elizabeth was the daughter of John and Margaret Mackelfresh of Reisterstown, Baltimore County. She married Lewis Shipley (1794–1858) and went to house-keeping in 1821. They were members of the Methodist Protestant Church in Reisterstown; three of their six children were baptized by quilt recipient Reverend Eli Henkle (p. 100), who was attached to the Reisterstown circuit for several years in the 1830s.

Like many mid-nineteenth-century parents, the Shipleys lost three of their children in their early years: Adaline in 1834, a year old; Catherine in 1838, six years old; and Miriam one month later, seven months old. These years must have been trying for Elizabeth; for along with three children her mother passed away in 1841. Elizabeth was a beneficiary of her mother's estate in Baltimore County, inheriting cash and personal property. She also was bequeathed sheets, counterpanes, and a large lot of sterling silver, all marked with her mother's initials.[1]

Elizabeth probably pieced this quilt in the early years of her marriage, possibly before her first child was born in 1828. The intricate handwork needed to assemble so many small pieces certainly would have challenged any new mother. Delectable Mountains is the most common name for the pattern of this quilt, made up of 324 five-inch blocks surrounded by a six-inch-wide cotton chintz border. Elizabeth's bed-cover is quilted eighteen to twenty stitches per inch in parallel lines.

The printed patterns of the tiny cotton triangles that comprise the pieced blocks are similar to those found in a book of fabric samples produced at Jonathan Peel's print-works at Church Bank in Lancashire, England, from 1806 to 1817.[2] The block-printed, yellow-ground chintz border fabric probably was produced in England as fur-nishing material during the first two decades of the nineteenth century. All of these tex-tiles reached the United States immediately after the War of 1812, when English textile printers flooded the U.S. market with cheap goods to stifle the growth of a domestic tex-tile industry. According to Mary Schoeser and Celia Rufey's *English and American Textiles from 1790 to the Present*, any time a decline hit the British home trade merchants dumped their unsold merchandise on the American market, a practice that slowed by mid-century.[3]

Elizabeth made at least three other quilts. Sometime in the 1840s she pieced a star quilt with the central figure made of various early cotton prints. Four long-stemmed tulips are appliquéd in each corner. Four pieced sawtooth borders and a seven-inch-

28. A letter to Elizabeth's daughter, Emily, from her cousin, written four days after her mother's death. She wrote, "I am glad she was sensible at her end, and that it was so easy, her head leaning on your breast-Oh how glad dear, I am that you were with her at this time and that she passed away so easily-without pain and suffering."

29. This charming ink and watercolor Reward of Merit was found among the Shipley family papers. It was probably given to one of Elizabeth Shipley's daughters for excellence in orthography, or spelling.

wide red printed border frame the bedcover, which is quilted twenty stitches per inch in a grid pattern. All of these quilts, plus cash and portions of her real and personal estate in Reistertown, were willed to her daughters, Emily and Margaret. The 1857 will includes a codicil, annexed in April 1862, that pro-vides for the manumission of several slaves. She willed that her slave Caroline be freed upon her death and also bequeathed her slave Maria, Caroline's daughter, to her two daughters. Margaret died before her mother in 1861 at the age of thirty-three, with the provision that when Maria reached the age of thirty-one years she would be free and provided with "a good and sufficient deed of manumission."[4]

The quilts descended to Elizabeth's great-grandson, William Grayson Gray (1908–93). Although he and his wife had no heirs, the Grays were keepers of the family history, accumulating many years of treasures and memorabilia (28 and 29). The present owner of the quilts, a twentieth-century

PIECED QUILT, c. 1830

Made by Elizabeth Mackelfresh Shipley (1792–1865)
Reisterstown, Baltimore County
Cottons
106 x 102 inches
Owned by Hildegard A. M. Banes

PIECED STAR WITH APPLIQUÉD TULIPS,
1830–50

Made by Elizabeth Mackelfresh Shipley
Reisterstown, Baltimore County
Cottons
96.5 x 98 inches
Owned by Hildegard A. M. Banes

immigrant from Germany with a young family, met the Grays through their mutual love
of gardening. A fast friendship developed as
the two families traded plants and flowers.
The present owner would sit for hours lis-
tening as the Grays talked about farm life in
the late nineteenth and early twentieth centuries in western Maryland. They showed
her the many original family documents
that gave testimony to the stories they
shared with her. In fact, the present owner
virtually adopted the Grays and their family history as her own, and she also lovingly
watched over the elderly couple in the last
years of their lives. On Christmas Day
1993, the owner and her eleven-year-old
daughter visited the widowed Grayson Gray
in the hospital for the last time, taking presents and singing Christmas carols to him. A
few hours later he passed away. The spirit of
the Grays and their ancestors continues to
live on in the memory of the present owner
and in the minds of those who are touched
by the story of Elizabeth Shipley's quilts.

1. The authors thank Hildegard Banes for
making available copies of Elizabeth Shipley's
Last Will and Codicils, dated 1896.
2. Mary Schoeser and Celia Rufey, *English and
American Textiles from 1790 to the Present* (New
York: Thames and Hudson, 1989), 44.
3. Ibid., 46.
4. Elizabeth Shipley, Last Will and Codicils,
1896.

Ellenborough Quilt

MARTHA ELIZABETH Harris probably made her Ohio Star quilt shortly after she married her first cousin Benjamin Gwinn Harris (1806–95) on October 22, 1833. Martha was the daughter of John Francis and Ruth Tunstill Harris of Mount Tirzah, their home in Charles County. After her marriage she moved to Ellenborough, the Harris family home near Leonardtown in St. Mary's County (30). Their companion portraits were painted a few years later by George Cooke (1793–1849), a native of St. Mary's County who achieved recognition as a painter of southern landscapes and portraits (31).[1]

Benjamin Gwinn Harris gained fame and notoriety for his support of the Confederate cause; he served two terms in the Maryland legislature and was elected to the U.S. House of Representatives in 1863. In 1864 he delivered a speech in Congress proposing compensation for all slaveholders whose slaves were freed, regardless of their loyalty to the Union or lack thereof. He also supported recognition of the Confederacy and an end to war.[2] In April 1865, Harris was arrested at Ellenborough. He was accused of treasonous activities and imprisoned in Washington, DC. Later President Andrew Johnson remitted Harris's sentence and restored his rights. Harris returned to Congress in 1866 and regained his political prestige but not his financial security. His estate, valued before the war at $130,000

including forty-five slaves, was reduced to $43,000. The *St. Mary's Gazette* listed 264 acres of Ellenborough under a "Sheriff's Sale," but Harris managed to retain most of his land.[3] Other residents of St. Mary's County, who strongly supported the Southern cause, were not as fortunate: the local newspaper detailed numerous foreclosures and public sales as many old, established families faced financial ruin.[4]

Martha Harris made her striking quilt during less troubled times in St. Mary's County. The most southern of Maryland's counties, St. Mary's remained a slave-based, tobacco-

31. Portraits of Benjamin Gwinn Harris (1806–95), and Martha Elizabeth Harris Harris (1813–92), painted in 1839 by George Cooke (1783–1849). (Photographs courtesy of the Maryland Historical Society)

growing region long after other counties had switched to a diversified economy and alternative forms of labor. Martha's life centered around Ellenborough. Her daily activities would have included both plain and ornamental needlework. Ellenborough's house girls, or female slaves who were brought up to work in the big house, would have shared in the endless sewing projects required to

30. Recent view of Ellenborough, the Harris family home in St. Mary's County. (Photograph courtesy of Gloria Seaman Allen)

PIECED QUILT, c. 1835

Made by Martha Elizabeth Harris (1813–92)
Ellenborough, near Leonardtown, St. Mary's County
Cottons
100 x 100 inches
Owned by Nelly Key Thompson, George S. Barnes, and
Catherine Waring Barnes

32. *Detail showing block-printed fabrics used for the star and sashing.*

33. *Detail of the lining fabric.*

clothe a large plantation family and furnish a mansion house and quarters.

Martha's Ohio Star quilt is finely worked at twenty-two stitches to the inch in diamond, double-diamond, and chevron patterns. The small-figured block prints cut to form the stars and sashing retain their vivid colors and are typical of fabrics produced at a number of printworks in England during the first decades of the nineteenth century (32).[5] The quilt is bordered in a bold floral roller print and backed by another roller print with an intricate machine ground (33). Martha Harris's quilt passed directly to her granddaughter and namesake, Martha Elizabeth (Mattie) Harris Maddox Key.[6]

1. The portraits are now in the collection of the Maryland Historical Society.
2. Harris probably belonged to an anti-Lincoln faction known as Copperheads. The Copperheads opposed Lincoln's attempts to free the slaves in the South, and they favored compromise with the Confederate states to end the war.
3. Regina Combs Hammett, *History of St. Mary's County, Maryland* (Leonardtown, MD: St. Mary's County Bicentennial Commission, 1977), 125.
4. Ibid.
5. For example, see Mary Schoeser and Gail Rufey, *English and American Textiles from 1790 to the Present* (London: Thames and Hudson, 1989), 44.
6. A related Harris quilt is in the collection of the Maryland Historical Society. Maria Louise Harris Key (c. 1806–79), second wife of Henry

Greenfield Sothoron Key, made a pieced star and appliquéd wreath quilt at Tudor Hall, c. 1840. Maria Louise was the daughter of Susanna Reeder and Joseph Harris. Her younger brother was Benjamin Gwinn Harris, Martha's husband; Martha and Maria Louise therefore were both first cousins and sisters-in-law. Our recent research corrects the genealogical information published in Gloria Seaman Allen, *Old Line Traditions: Maryland Women and Their Quilts* (Washington, DC: DAR Museum, 1985), 31.

Star Quilt

PIECED AND APPLIQUÉD STAR QUILT,
1840–50

Made by Catherine Ann Waring Waring (1787–1867)
Probably Liberty County, Texas, or Prince George's
County, Maryland
Cottons
86.5 x 86.5 inches
Owned by Catherine Waring Barnes and George S.
Barnes

CATHERINE ANN (KITTY) Waring Waring, a native of Prince George's County, may have made her star quilt while living in Texas. She and her husband, Edward, left their 287-acre Germans Clover Farm sometime after 1828 and moved to Liberty, Texas.[1] Declining productivity of tobacco lands prompted many residents of southern Maryland to seek economic opportunity in the western states of Ohio and Kentucky and the Republic of Texas. The Warings, who owned about a dozen slaves, probably took their labor force with them to farm the fertile lands opening up in southeast Texas.

Kitty Waring, as she was usually known, was the daughter of Elizabeth Hilleary and James Waring (34). Her father was a member of a long-established Prince George's County family. On September 8, 1808, she married her cousin Edward Gantt Waring (b. 1788). Their first son, James, was born between 1810 and 1812.[2] In 1831 he received his medical degree; in 1838 he married Anne Maria Thomas, daughter of James Thomas, governor of Maryland. Several years after her husband's death in Texas, Kitty returned to Maryland and took up residence with James at Southhampton, his seventeenth-century farmhouse near Chaptico in St. Mary's County.

During the Civil War, James Waring, by then a prominent doctor, was a staunch supporter of states' rights. He opposed slavery, however, and owned no slaves. Two of his sons, James II and Edward, fought for the Confederacy and were imprisoned nearby at Point Lookout, a Federal prison camp. They escaped under a wagon load of corpses and recuperated while hiding in the woods at Southhampton. Subsequently they rejoined their cavalry unit in Virginia. Edward was killed in battle; James II survived the war.[3]

Kitty Waring died in 1867 at age eighty. In her mature years she had known the rugged and lonely life of a pioneer in Texas, especially after becoming a widow. She also had experienced the anguish and sorrow of civil war, when words and movements were often suspect and loved ones were imprisoned and killed.

Kitty Waring's star quilt pattern is now referred to as Lone Star. Some would assume that Kitty was inspired by the symbol of her adopted homeland of Texas. The solitary star on both the flag and seal of Texas, however, is a five- not an eight-pointed star. Stylistically this quilt dates from the 1840s and coincides with the period when Kitty was most likely to have lived in Texas. Though probably not made in Maryland, this quilt, with its sophisticated imported fabrics, suggests strong ties with the East.

The eight-pointed star pattern was popular with Maryland quiltmakers, and Kitty Waring may have seen similar quilts before departing for Texas or during return visits. An 1849 issue of the *Baltimore Republican & Argus* described a star quilt on exhibition at the Maryland Institute Fair as a "Cincinnati star quilt composed of an infinitesimal number of pieces of calico tastefully and judiciously arranged in the form of a large star."[4]

The fair's judges' reports also listed a number of Mathematical Star quilts exhibited between 1848 and 1853. Kitty's star is pieced from discharge-printed blue and brown calicoes; it is surrounded by four bouquets of flowers cut from a block-printed chintz occasionally seen on quilts made in the Tidewater region. Block-printed fabrics were used for the border and for the lining. The lavish use of printed fabric belies any suggestion of scarcity in furnishing textiles.[5]

Kitty's quilt was passed to her youngest surviving granddaughter, Anne Maria (Nannie) Waring Hayden (b. 1854), who gave it to her great-niece and Kitty's namesake, Catherine Ann (Kitty) Waring Barnes. Kitty Barnes lived at Southhampton from age seven with the Haydens, her parents, and brother (35). Her father was James Waring III. In 1943 Southhampton burned to the ground, but fortunately Kitty Waring's quilt was saved from the fire. Today it remains a tangible reminder of the maker as well as the forgotten connection between southern Maryland and southeastern Texas.[6]

1. It has not been possible to determine exactly when the Warings resided in Texas. Edward Waring was included in the 1828 tax list for Prince George's County, but he was not listed in Maryland census records after 1810. An Elizabeth Waring was listed in Prince George's County in the 1820 census. Elizabeth Waring was probably Kitty Waring; in her obituary she was referred to as "Elizabeth (Kitty) Waring." Kitty Waring was recorded in the 1850 federal census for Liberty County, Texas. At that time she was a widow, living with John Waring (probably her son) and E. A. Lamaine, another Maryland widow.
2. Marriage and death records provide conflicting information.
3. Kitty Waring Barnes has kindly supplied us with a great deal of information regarding the Waring family.
4. Quoted by Jennifer Faulds Goldsborough in *Lavish Legacies: Baltimore Album and Related Quilts in the Collection of the Maryland Historical Society* (Baltimore: Maryland Historical Society, 1994), 25.
5. We have no way of knowing if Kitty took fabrics with her to furnish her Texas home or if she or other family members made frequent trips back to Maryland to obtain the latest in fashionable merchandise.
6. Family members still reside in southern Maryland and Liberty County, Texas.

34. Kitty Waring (1787–1867) in a portrait painted during the 1850s. (Photograph courtesy of George S. Barnes)

35. Kitty Waring Barnes with Nannie and Samuel Hayden in the parlor at Southhampton, about 1938. The arch-framed windows and classical moldings are found in other southern Maryland homes. (Photograph courtesy of Catherine Waring Barnes)

Big Susan's Quilts

APPLIQUÉD FLORAL QUILT, 1840–50

Made by Susan Dawson (1823–80)
Mother's Delight, near Dawsonville, Montgomery
County
Cottons
94 x 94 inches
Owned by Mary E. Conlon

S USAN DAWSON, FIFTH OF nine children of Ann Allnutt (1779–1854) and James Mackall Dawson (1775–1867), lived all her life at Mother's Delight, the family tobacco farm near Dawsonville, Montgomery County (37). Thomas Dawson came to the area from Prince George's County around 1750 and established Dawsonville, a small village with a church, a general store, and several houses. James Allnutt also came from Prince George's County in the 1750s. The Allnutt's original landholding, Thomas' Discovery, was located to the south of the village. Most of the Dawsons and Allnutts were Old School Baptists, and several were prominent Whig politicians. Susan's father was a large landowner and a slaveholder. The Montgomery County tax lists for 1838 and 1841 record that James M. Dawson owned nine-

teen slaves and nearly a thousand acres divided among several farms. By the time his son Americus died in 1891, the Dawson holdings had grown to more than 3,000 acres. Never married, Susan Dawson was referred to in the family as Big Susan, possibly in recognition of her size (36) or to distinguish her from another, slightly younger, Susan Dawson. She is remembered as a formidable lady who could, at times, be very abrupt.[1] She also is remembered for the three quilts she made in the 1840s.[2]

The quilts vary in style and technique and are owned by two different branches of the maker's family. All three have fabrics in common and are stamped "Susan Dawson" on the back in one or more places (38). Two of the quilts have stylized flowers and leaves set in a nine-block format with the reserves finely quilted in a variety of classical and floral motifs. The all-appliquéd quilt features large-scale leafy vines and floral-trail blocks with a flowing vine in the border.

The Peony quilt with its five pieced blocks still retains the pencil lines that marked

tulips, roses, carnations, pineapples, grapevines, and feather wreaths. In addition to design similarities, the two quilts share several of the same small-figured red and green prints. The Peony quilt also has four blocks with appliquéd flowers cut from a roller-printed floral fabric common to other Maryland quilts.[3]

Tiny triangular pieces of this floral fabric can be found on Susan Dawson's third quilt (39). The star quilt is predominantly blue and brown, a color combination fashionable in Montgomery County during the 1840s that rivaled the more familiar red-and-green color scheme in popularity.[4] This quilt is pieced from a large number of printed tex-

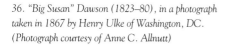

36. *"Big Susan" Dawson (1823–80), in a photograph taken in 1867 by Henry Ulke of Washington, DC. (Photograph courtesy of Anne C. Allnutt)*

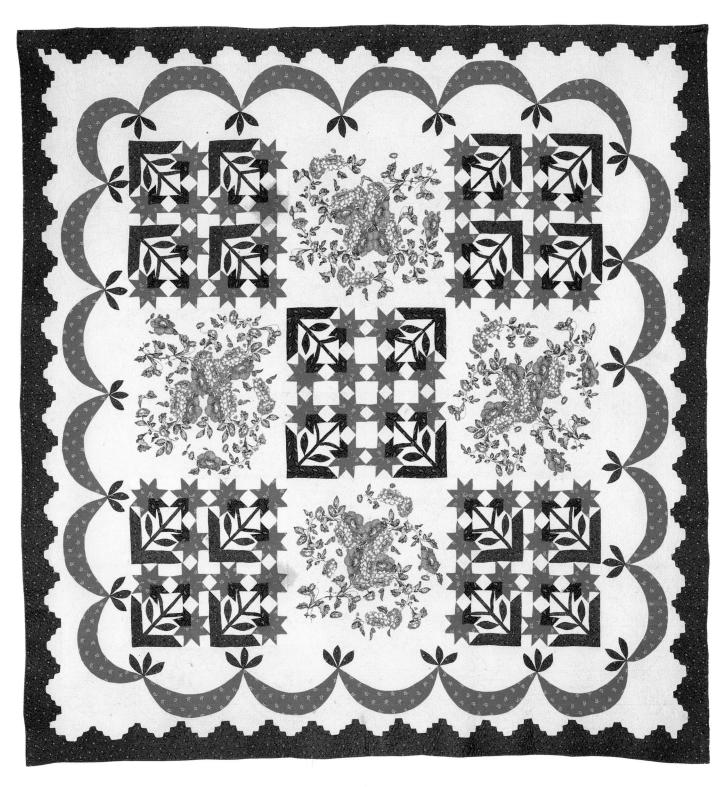

tiles—most likely scraps saved from dress and furnishing fabrics. Some of the individual small triangles that make up the star are pieced from two or three different prints. The bold floral stripe used for the border and the handmade cotton fringe enclose a printed medley that radiates color and movement from center to edge.

Susan Dawson continued to make quilts during her later years. At the time of her death at age fifty-seven, her personal possessions included "11 Colored Quilts," "2 White Counterpains," two additional "Counterpains," and "2 Comforts," along with large stores of linen and cotton sheets, cases, and towels.[5] One of the counterpanes

APPLIQUÉD AND PIECED PEONY QUILT, 1840–50

Made by Susan Dawson (1823–80)
Mother's Delight, near Dawsonville, Montgomery County
Cottons
98.25 x 98.25 inches
Owned by Benoni and Sarah Allnutt

may have earned Susan the premium of a gold pencil in the "Cotton and Linen Goods" competition at the 1850 Maryland Institute Fair. The Report of the Judges listed "A Cotton Counterpane made and deposited by Miss Susan Dawson, Montgomery county, Md." The report went on to state that "This quilt [probably a woven coverlet], manufactured from 3 ply yarn, is highly commended for its intrinsic value."[6]

In 1853, Susan Dawson again submitted articles to the Maryland Institute Fair. Her "2 coverlids and 1 quilt" were "Received too late to go under the regular Classification ["Quilts, Counterpanes; Valances and

PIECED STAR QUILT WITH FRINGE, 1840–50

Made by Susan Dawson (1823–80)
Mother's Delight, near Dawsonville, Montgomery
County
Cottons, cotton fringe
86.5 x 86.5 inches
Owned by Benoni and Sarah Allnutt

37. A recent view of Mother's Delight, no longer owned by the Dawson family. (Photograph courtesy of Gloria Seaman Allen)

Curtains"] but under the 2d Rule, in time for competition." Susan also entered "1 Piece Venetian Carpet" in another class, and her sister, Ellen, entered a counterpane and toweling.[7] Neither of the Dawson sisters took a prize that year. If one of the quilts illustrated here failed to win a premium at the Maryland Institute, the competition must have been formidable.

The Dawson sisters did better at the local Montgomery County Agricultural Society Fair in which they entered competitions and won premiums over a twenty-two-year period. In both 1852 and 1853, Susan Dawson was awarded $2.00 for the best calico quilt. Her counterpanes, carpeting, and knitting took premiums, along with her turkeys and geese, in other years.[8]

Susan Dawson probably resorted to using a sewing machine for some of her later bed furnishings. Appraisers of her estate valued her sewing machine at $25.00, an amount equal to the value assigned to a silver tea set and greater than that given to almost any other possession. Her bedcovers received low values—$1.50 on average for quilts and comforts and $2.50 for counterpanes.[9] The appraised values of 1880 seem especially low when compared with the amounts of the fair premiums awarded in the 1850s. Now, more than one hundred years later, Susan Dawson's quilts are highly valued, not only by her family but by others for their striking beauty and skillful workmanship.

1. Family members relate "a story about Susan Dawson at a funeral: someone stepped on her foot, and she said 'Oh Lord! Get off my foot!' very loudly at whoever stepped on her. This sort of reaction was NOT behavior of that day and time." Written communication from Anne C. Allnutt, June 25, 1994.

2. J. Thomas Scharf mentioned Susan Dawson's name in his 1887 History of Western Maryland (Baltimore: Regional Publishing, 1968), 678. In 1876 Susan Dawson served on the Montgomery County Centennial Committee, which was charged with collecting and exhibiting "centennial relics." The exhibition at the Rockville fairgrounds included a lock of George Washington's hair and a piece of wood from his coffin.

An additional quilt associated with the Dawson family is in the collection of the Maryland Historical Society. An 1849 album quilt contains the names L. A. Dawson, L. E. Dawson, and Mrs. L. Dawson; it is illustrated by Jennifer Faulds Goldsborough in Lavish Legacies: Baltimore Album and Related Quilts in the Collection of the Maryland Historical Society (Baltimore: Maryland Historical Society, 1994), Catalogue 9. L. A. Dawson was probably Lawrence Allnutt Dawson, Susan's oldest brother. Mrs. L. Dawson may have referred to his wife, Mary Elizabeth Kiger Dawson.

3. A red and green Triple Irish Chain quilt with a Maryland history was brought to the DAR Museum for identification several years ago. The quilt had a wide border in the same floral print Susan Dawson used for her appliqué. Fragments of this printed textile are in the collection of Colonial Williamsburg.

4. When the authors conducted research for the Maryland quilt exhibition at the DAR Museum, they discovered a number of blue-and-brown quilts made in Montgomery County in the 1840s. The color scheme was also popular across the Potomac River in Loudoun County, Virginia. Gloria Seaman Allen, Old Line Traditions: Maryland Women and Their Quilts (Washington, DC: DAR Museum, 1985), 32, 39.

5. Montgomery County Inventories, List of Sales & Accounts, R.W.C. no. 12 (1879–81), 380–83.

6. The catalogues from the Maryland Institute fairs suggest that Susan Dawson and her sister Ellen made a variety of textile furnishings. In 1850 they won silver mustard spoons for "Linen Toweling, Table Diaper and Brown Linen." The report noted that they "are alike commended as in a very high degree adapted to their various uses. Firmness of texture and weight are combined in their manufacture." Susan also won a silver butter knife for "1 piece of Carpet and 1 Hearth Rug." "Reports of the Judges," Third Annual Exhibition of the Maryland Institute for the Promotion of the Mechanic Arts, Held October 14,

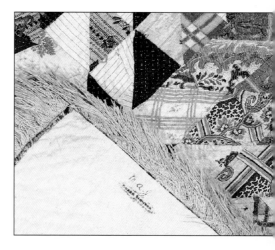

38. Susan Dawson's stamped signature on the lining of her star quilt. "MAJ" are the initials of Mary Ann or Mary Alice Jones, Susan's sister or niece.

39. Detail of pieced star quilt showing printed floral fabric and piecing of triangles.

1850 at Washington Hall, Baltimore (Baltimore: 1850), 11, 12.

7. "Catalogue of Articles Deposited for Competition and Premiums at the Sixth Annual Exhibition of the Maryland Institute Opened in Baltimore, October 3d, 1853," The Book of the Exhibition, Sixth Annual Exhibition of the Maryland Institute for the Promotion of the Mechanic Arts (Baltimore: 1853), 15.

8. Minutes of the Montgomery County Agricultural Society, 1846–68. Manuscripts in the library collection of the Montgomery County Historical Society.

9. Susan Dawson's estate also included a phaeton valued at $175, land holdings valued at more than $5,400, and accounts receivable at more than $6,200. An unusual item in her personal possessions, a photograph album, was valued at $1.50. Unfortunately its whereabouts are unknown.

Counterpanes for the County Fair

O N SEPTEMBER 11, 1851, MORE THAN one thousand people endured the "burning heat and suffocating dust" to attend the opening of the sixth annual fair of the Montgomery County Agricultural Society.[1] In two large tents erected on a two-acre wooded lot in the small town of Rockville, women gathered around the display of household manufactures to admire the craftsmanship and learn the identity of the lucky recipients of premiums.[2] That year the makers of the best silk, ornamental, and calico quilts each received $2.50, a significant prize for handiwork when the average daily wage for a laborer was only $1.[3]

The Montgomery County Agricultural Society Fair, first held in 1846, continued in existence until 1932.[4] It was a popular fall attraction that provided local residents with the opportunity to learn of the latest in agricultural and livestock improvements, to exhibit their farm and home products, and to compete for premiums.[5] It was a time to reconnect with distant friends and relatives, to take pride in one's own accomplishments, and to learn new and better ways of doing things.

Among the earliest and most consistent participants in the fair competitions were the Dawson sisters, Ellen (1809–78) and Susan (1823–80), two of the nine children of Ann Allnutt and James Mackall Dawson. Susan Dawson is remembered today for the beautiful quilts that have descended in her family, but she also excelled in other areas of household manufacture. Her older sister Ellen, whose quilts have not survived, was a woman of many talents. From the minutes of the quarterly meetings of the agricultural society, we learn that the Dawson sisters repeatedly entered the annual competitions and frequently took premiums. The first year the fair was held, the Committee on Household Manufactures awarded the majority of its premiums to Ellen Dawson. She won for "the best pair of blankets . . . the best piece of diaper . . . best piece of striped linsey . . . best piece of carpeting . . . best piece of plain linen . . . best pair of cotton do [stockings] . . . best pair thread do . . . best made suit of gentleman's clothes (coat, vest and pants)." Her sister Susan entered only a hearth rug, but it was judged best in that category. The Dawson sisters no doubt won on the basis of the excellence of their work, but one can not help wondering if their uncle George W. Dawson, a member of the committee, had an undue influence.[6]

Ellen Dawson excelled in knitting and tailoring and in weaving textiles of different weights and construction. Raised in an affluent slaveholding family, she and her sister, nevertheless, acquired skills necessary to produce a range of useful textile products. The fair records do not reveal to what extent Ellen and Susan Dawson were responsible for the textile work they entered. James Dawson owned more than nineteen slaves, and slave women trained as textile artisans may have spun, woven, knitted, and sewed some or many of the items displayed by the Dawson sisters at the fair. Slaves did not enter competitions in their own right, although in some cases they did receive a degree of recognition. In 1856 L. A. Dawson's William earned a $2 premium for doing the best two-horse plowing.[7] At the Maryland Institute Fair, "A Work Box, the ingenuity of a Slave," was entered in 1848, but did not receive an award.[8]

While membership in the agricultural society was for men only, the fair gave their wives and daughters the opportunity to step out of the domestic sphere and into the public sphere where they received wider recognition for their accomplishments. As the minutes from the September 1848 meeting of the society noted, the array of household manufactures "exhibited the skill, industry, and tools of the ladies who encourage our enterprise."

To enter the fair competition, women submitted articles in the advertised classes the day before the fair opened. After judging by an all-male committee was completed, and premiums were awarded, a group of ladies arranged quilts, counterpanes, woven and knitted goods, fruits, vegetables, and flowers for display to the public. They also took responsibility for decorating the exhibition halls and the speakers' stand. In 1847 the fair's organizers appointed a group of women to select appropriate premiums to be awarded for household manufactures; however, when the fair was held that fall, the usual monetary prizes were given out.[10]

At the 1849 Montgomery County Fair, competition in the area of household manufactures reached a new level of excellence. The judges noted favorably "the progress of improvement in this branch of industry," and awarded premiums for a white quilt "of excellence," a patchwork quilt, two patchwork silk quilts, and a "netted cotton quilt."[11] A writer for the *American Farmer* praised the exhibition:

> The ladies made a most beautiful display in the department of household economy. The space allotted for their handiwork was continually crowded, and gave universal satisfaction. A number of the articles were of peculiar merit, and we were promised that they should be on exhibition at the State Fair.[12]

That year, Ellen Dawson again took home many of the premiums—"for Linnen, also for towelling, also for cotton stockings, for thread stockings, also for a counterpane . . . " Susan did not win, but her sister-in-law, Mrs. L. A. Dawson, took a first for her carpeting. Mrs. H. W. Blunt (Harriet Dorsey Blunt), co-maker of the Woodburne quilt (p. 144), won premiums for fulled cloth and blankets. Mrs. Samuel Gaither, kin to several signers of Caroline Magruder's friendship quilt (p. 94), received a premium for "a white quilt of excellence."[13]

The next year, 1850, Ellen Dawson received $1 for the second best calico quilt, and Susan Dawson $2 for the best counterpane. Ellen also received premiums for the best cotton stockings, thread gloves, and table diaper, and for the second best piece of linen, table diaper, and carpeting. Susan took the first premium for her yarn gloves, rug, and green preserves.[14] After their successes at the Montgomery County Fair in September, the Dawson sisters moved up to statewide competition at the Maryland Institute Fair. It appears that they entered many of the same items in Baltimore that they had exhibited a month earlier in Rockville. Ellen's second place calico quilt was probably the "fancy quilt" listed in the Baltimore Fair report; it failed to win a premium. Her thread gloves also did not win, but the table diaper and piece of linen, which she entered jointly with her

sister, earned them a silver mustard spoon. Susan Dawson did even better on her own. Her prize-winning counterpane from the Montgomery County Fair earned its maker a gold pencil, and her hearth rug won a silver butter knife.[15] Altogether, it was a fruitful fall for the Dawson sisters. Not only were their skill and artistry recognized by members of their own community, but their work competed successfully with entries submitted by talented women from across the state.

In 1851, Ellen Dawson again won premiums at the Montgomery County Agricultural Society Fair for woven textiles and a cotton counterpane;[16] in 1852, another of her cotton counterpanes took first prize. Her yarn stockings took second prize with the first premium going to Mrs. Dr. Waters (Mary Waters, maker of the quilt on p. 143), who also won for the best flannel. Susan Dawson entered a quilt for the first time that year and won the $2 premium for the best calico example. In addition, Susan entered "the best lot of ducks" and Ellen "the best hard soap."[17]

Ellen's counterpane and Susan's calico quilt won again the following year.[18] Presumably they entered different articles from the year before. Fair rules stipulated that no article that had received a premium the preceding year would be eligible the following year, although it could be placed on exhibition. The competition was especially strong, and the judges regretted not being able to award more premiums. The minutes of the 1853 fall meeting recorded that "the committee was particularly struck with two quilts, of beautiful and most elaborate workmanship, made and exhibited by Mrs. Emily Beale, and which in our opinion deserves special merit." The Dawson sisters also won premiums for blankets, stockings, and gloves. The sisters decided that year to enter the state competition again in Baltimore. Unfortunately they did not submit their entries in time to be listed in separate classes, but they were still in time for judging. The delay in entering may have hurt their chances. Ellen's prize-winning counterpane and Susan's first place calico quilt failed to take premiums. Their towelling, carpeting, and coverlets also were overlooked by the judges.[20]

In 1854 quiltmaker Harriet Dorsey Blunt took first prize for her woolen cloth, white counterpane, and net work. Ellen Dawson's counterpane came in second. Harriet's husband, Samuel Blunt, had joined the Committee on the Examination of Household

40. *Detail of Susan Dawson's appliquéd quilt showing red and green fabrics and quilting.*

Manufactures in 1847, but he had resigned his committee position by the time his wife entered the competition.[21]

The Dawson sisters continued to enter and win premiums during the 1850s. In 1856 the fair moved to a new location with more land and permanent structures for the display of household manufactures. The society's minutes boasted that "Montgomery County has the most flourishing Agricultural Society and the most beautiful Fair Grounds in the State of Maryland."[22] And the following year, the *American Farmer* observed that the expanded "ladies department contained many testimonials to the good old fashioned home industry of the wives and daughters of Montgomery county."[23]

In 1858, the fair organizers awarded 147 premiums in a variety of categories. Susan Dawson again won with a cotton counterpane. The amount of her $2 premium was in line with those awarded for livestock, tools, produce, baked goods, and preserves, but considerably lower than the $15 award given for the "best conducted farm."[24]

In 1860, the last year before the fair closed down for the war years, Susan Dawson entered in a number of classes and won premiums with her crayon drawing, turkeys, and geese. Tensions were coming to a head as members of the agricultural society fought among themselves over the rights of slaveholders and the stability of the Union.[25]

The war wreaked havoc with the fairgrounds. Union soldiers used the buildings and grounds for a campsite, and the damage was extensive. The $3,000 paid by the federal government only covered part of the estimated $8,300 needed to return the site to its antebellum appearance. When the fair resumed in 1868 the receipts from the three days the fair was opened were not enough to complete the repairs.[26] The Dawson sisters were among those who entered the competitions at the fair and they again took premiums for their counterpanes.[27]

The next year, 1869, the premiums were cut in half as part of an economy move. At ages sixty and forty-six, spinsters Ellen and Susan Dawson, for the first time in twenty-two years since the fair began, were not among the competition entrants. Their world had changed. Their father was dead, no longer were slaves working on the Dawson family farm, and household textile production had become part of the nostalgic antebellum past. A forty-five-minute train ride to Washington, DC, brought the products of New England's mills within easy reach, and the sewing machine facilitated the making of clothing and bedcoverings.

The fair had changed too. The agrarian emphasis gave way to events designed to attract urban visitors. Trotting races and other trials of speed were the biggest draw and carried the largest premiums. A skillful velocipede rider earned greater monetary reward than the farm woman who displayed her household manufactures. While handmade textiles could still be entered, there was a class for factory-made textiles. In 1870 premiums were awarded for the best and second best sewing machines for the first time, and in 1876 the "best machine sewing" was recognized.[28]

Gloria Seaman Allen

1. Manuscript minutes of the quarterly meetings of the Montgomery County Agricultural Society, September 1851. Collection of the Montgomery County Historical Society. Jane Sween, librarian, has kindly brought these documents to our attention.

2. Only members of the society, their wives, and daughters were eligible for premiums. Minutes, June 1854.

3. Minutes, September 1851.

4. The Montgomery County Agricultural Society was founded in 1846,

part of a nationwide movement to encourage agricultural improvements. Many farmers in Montgomery County experimented with guano and other ways to enrich soil worn out by years of tobacco cultivation. The stated objective of the society was one of "advancing the moral and intellectual character of our community, by improving their social condition and material interests." Washington *National Intelligencer*, September 12, 1857.

5. As Virginia Gunn has noted in her excellent study of Ohio fairs, "Competition stimulated invention, and prizes helped people recognize superior quality and design which they could later copy." Virginia Gunn, "Quilts at Nineteenth Century State and County Fairs: An Ohio Study," in *Uncoverings* 1988, edited by Laurel Horton (San Francisco: American Quilt Study Group, 1989), 107.

6. Minutes, September 1846.

7. Minutes, September 1856.

8. *Catalogue of the First Annual Exhibition of the Maryland Institute for the Promotion of the Mechanic Arts Held October 31st, 1848, at Washington Hall, Baltimore* (Baltimore, 1848), 8.

9. Minutes, September 1848.

10. This practice differed from the Baltimore Fair where it was customary to award small items of gold or silver.

11. Minutes, September 1849.

12. *American Farmer*, October 1849, 126.

13. Minutes, September 1849.

14. Minutes, September 1850.

15. "Report of the Judges," *Third Annual Exhibition of the Maryland Institute for the Promotion of the Mechanic Arts, Held October 14, 1850 at Washington Hall, Baltimore* (Baltimore, 1850), 11, 12.

16. Minutes, September 1851.

17. Minutes, September 1852.

18. Minutes, September 1853.

19. Minutes, June 1847.

20. "Catalogue of Articles Deposited for Competition and Premiums at the Sixth Annual Exhibition of the Maryland Institute Opened in Baltimore, October 3d, 1853," *The Book of the Exhibition, Sixth Annual Exhibition of the Maryland Institute for the Promotion of the Mechanic Arts* (Baltimore, 1853), 15.

21. Minutes, September 1854.

41. Detail of Susan Dawson's pieced and appliquéd quilt.

22. Minutes, September 1856.

23. *American Farmer*, October 1857, 129.

24. Minutes, September 1858.

25. Minutes, September 1860. Also, see George M. Anderson, "Growth, Civil War, and Change: The Montgomery County Agricultural Society," *Maryland Historical Magazine*, vol. 86, no. 4 (Winter 1991), 396–406.

26. Anderson, 399–400.

27. Minutes, September 1868.

28. Minutes, September 1870, September 1876.

Plantation Quilts

*Sunburst quilt
Made one hundred and
fifty years ago by
Mrs Mary Mac Pherson
Property of
Jane V. Mac Pherson
1st prize 50¢ C.M.C.*[1]

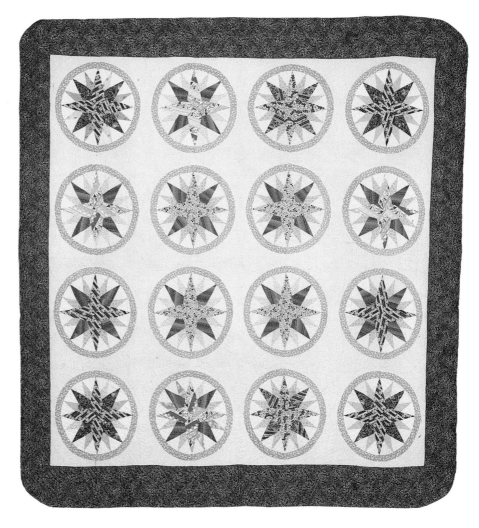

WO FINELY WORKED QUILTS, a handwritten note attached to one, and a solitary tombstone in Charles County are all that remain to recall the life of Mary Ann McPherson (44). According to her tombstone in the graveyard of St. John's Episcopal Church, Mary Ann McPherson was the eldest daughter of Thomas and Jane Benson McPherson.[2] Her parents, who had married in 1808, raised Mary Ann and six other children at Greenway, their tobacco plantation near Pomonkey, Charles County. Slaves labored in the fields and served in the house, and it is likely that slave women took over some of the household chores or tended to the younger children so that Mary Ann had leisure time during the 1840s to do her complex piecing, appliquéing, and fine quilting. She also may have found time to weave and knot the linen fringe sewn to the four edges of her Sunburst quilt.[3]

Mary Ann McPherson's Sunburst quilt is finely quilted, twenty stitches to the inch, in tulips, daisies, leaves, and grapevines (42). Blue, brown, and pink fabrics are pieced together to form four large eight-pointed stars or sunbursts; red and green fabrics are used for the appliquéd flowers, vines, and sawtooth borders. This striking juxtaposition of prints combines two color schemes— red/green and blue/brown/pink—fashionable in Maryland in the 1840s and 1850s.

Handmade fringe, usually associated with earlier quilts, continued to be added by some Maryland quiltmakers through the middle of the nineteenth century (p. 78). In this example Mary Ann left the linen thread in its unbleached state and applied the two-inch fringe to all four sides of the quilt.[4]

The Mariner's Compass quilt is also finely stitched. Areas between the sixteen compass roses are filled with stipple and feather quilting (43). The pieced compass points are cut from blue, brown, and pink block and roller prints. Several of the prints have fancy machine grounds; others are "rainbow browns." A six- to eight-inch border with rounded corners completes the composition.[5]

Mary Ann McPherson never married. In 1850 she and three other maiden sisters were still living at the home place with their twenty-three-year-old brother, William

PIECED MARINER'S COMPASS QUILT, 1840–50

*Made by Mary Ann McPherson (1809–1901)
Greenway, near Pomonkey, Charles County
Cottons
89 x 84 inches
Owned by Mary Lucile Smith Spiller*

Benjamin Benson McPherson, who had taken over ownership of the plantation after the death of their father the preceding year. Thomas McPherson's will left his four daughters equal shares of slaves, livestock, and bedding. Mary Ann, for example, received six slaves, horses, cows, sheep, hogs, two bedsteads with bedding, a carpet, and manure forks.[6]

The 1860 federal census for the Pomonkey district recorded that Benjamin,[7] still a bachelor, continued to provide a home for his four maiden sisters and that he had

PIECED AND APPLIQUÉD SUNBURST QUILT
WITH FRINGE, 1840–50

Made by Mary Ann McPherson (1809–1901)
Greenway, near Pomonkey, Charles County
Cottons, linen fringe
90.5 x 88.5 inches
Owned by Mary Lucile Smith Spiller

42. *Detail showing a corner of the Sunburst quilt with appliquéd flowers, appliquéd sawtooth border, floral quilting, and linen fringe.*

43. *Detail of Mariner's Compass quilt showing feather and stipple quilting.*

amassed a sizable estate, valued at $18,000. Several years later he married Kitty Ann Turner, and the quilts made by his sister, Mary Ann, passed down his family line to his granddaughter, Jane Virginia Mac-Pherson Burton.

In the 1950s Jane Burton, having no children, sold the two quilts illustrated here to Susan Duvall Smith, an antiques dealer and mother of the present owner. Mrs. Burton gave another of Mary Ann's quilts to her husband's doctor, in appreciation of the care given during his last illness. This quilt, remembered as having baskets of fruit with tendrils of the grapes drawn in India ink, was considered to be "the best of the three."[8]

1. This note, written by the last family owner and sewn to the front left side of the quilt, shows clearly in the photograph. Jane MacPherson Burton, a school teacher, was known to be very precise; however, her note presents a problem for the researcher. She credited Mrs. Mary MacPherson with making the quilt; Mary or Mary Ann MacPherson (or McPherson) never married so she was never "Mrs." Her mother, named Suzanna Jane rather than Mary, died in the 1840s so she probably was not the maker. The only Mrs. Mary MacPherson in the family line was Mary Campbell MacPherson, Jane Burton's mother. She was born in the 1870s, too late to have made this quilt. "C.M.C." has not

been identified. The initials may refer to a local Methodist church.
2. Mary Ann is the only McPherson or MacPherson buried in the cemetery of St. John's Church. Her parents and other family members are buried in the cemetery at St. Paul's Episcopal Church in Waldorf. That churchyard is a number of miles from the family plantation, which was near Pomonkey.
3. According to family tradition, the flax for the linen fringe was grown at Greenway. Many Chesapeake plantations continued to raise flax and spin linen thread by hand long after mill-spun cotton thread was readily available.
4. During photography the fringe along the top of the quilt was tucked behind.
5. The black-and-brown print used for the border resembles prints popular in the 1870s and 1880s; however, there is no indication that it was added later.
6. Charles County *Wills*, 1849–52, 263.
7. William Benjamin Benson McPherson was variously referred to in official records as Benjamin or Benson. The family name was spelled both Mc and Mac. Mary Ann McPherson's tombstone has both spellings.
8. The location of this quilt, which was probably an 1840s appliquéd album quilt, is unknown. It was given to a Dr. McDaniel of Washington, DC. Susan Smith saw the quilt at the time she purchased the other two. She later described it to her daughter as "exquisite, the best of the three." Judging by the quality of the workmanship on the other two quilts, it must have been an extraordinary quilt.

44. *Mary Ann McPherson's tombstone in the graveyard of St. John's Episcopal Church, near Pomonkey. (Photograph courtesy of Gloria Seaman Allen)*

Catharine's Wheel Quilt

PIECED AND APPLIQUÉD MILL WHEEL
QUILT, February 14, 1845

Made by Catharine P. Evans (1816–97)
Near Rising Sun, Cecil County
Cotton, ink inscription
102.5 x 102.5 inches
Owned by Alice B. Geiger

CATHARINE P. EVANS was the daughter of James and Mary Patterson Evans of Cecil County. James Evans had settled on a large tract of family land near Rising Sun, along Maryland's border with Pennsylvania. Evans, his brother, and two sons farmed considerable acreage. Unlike many of their neighbors, who were members of the Society of Friends, or Quakers, the Evanses were slaveholders.

On May 30, 1848, Catharine Evans married William Washington Black (1814–87) and moved to Charlestown, in central Cecil County, where her husband owned a store. Later the Blacks lived outside Charlestown at Good Hope, the family home where they raised two sons. Washington Black, as he was usually known, was also from a well-to-do Cecil County family. As a child, his portrait was painted by fashionable African-American artist Joshua Johnson. In later life Black was a prominent Democrat; he received a commission from President Abraham Lincoln in 1864 to serve as major general in the Union army.[1]

Catharine Evans Black made at least two quilts that she signed and dated prior to her marriage. The earlier, dated February 20, 1844, is in a pieced star pattern. The later quilt, Mill Wheel, is dated almost exactly one year later, February 14, 1845 (45). The 1844 star quilt remained in the Evans family until 1985, when it was given to the Maryland Historical Society. The 1845 quilt, illustrated here, came to its present owner without history from an antiques dealer. The connection between the two quilts was only discovered after the DAR Museum in Washington, DC, exhibited the star quilt, and the signatures on the two were compared.[2]

Catharine's Mill Wheel quilt is pieced from a small-figured, blue-and-tan discharge-printed calico and white cotton, sim-ilar but not identical to a print she used in her star quilt. Narrow borders of appliquéd sawteeth enclose a wide border quilted in a scrolling vine pattern. The Mill Wheel design was popular throughout Maryland for many decades. In 1842 Mary Ankenny of Frederick County in western Maryland made an almost identical blue and white quilt, which she signed and dated. In the 1930s Martha Jane Cannon of Caroline County on the lower Eastern Shore used the same pattern for her red and white quilt.

When Catharine died in 1897, her estate inventory listed bed clothes but did not specify

45. *Detail showing Catharine Evans's signature and date on the front of her quilt. The discharge-printed calico has transferred blue dye to the white cloth.*

quilts. Her most important possessions included a nine-piece parlor suite, valued at $30, and a carpet at $25. Twenty-five wood bottom chairs at $6.25 for the lot and a floor cloth at $5 were obviously of lesser quality.[3]

Catharine Evans Black's estate is scarcely memorable, but she lives on for us through her artistic workmanship. Because Catharine carefully signed and dated her quilts, we are able to place them in the context of Maryland's quiltmaking traditions.

1. We are grateful to Alice Geiger for sharing with us her extensive research on the Evans quilt.
2. Gloria Seaman Allen, *Old Line Traditions: Maryland Women and Their Quilts* (Washington, DC: DAR Museum, 1985), 29.
3. Cecil County *Inventories*, R.E.J. no. 39 (1896–1902), 46–48.

Sarah's Sunburst Quilt

ALTHOUGH THIS BRIGHT-ly colored Sunburst quilt was signed by Sarah Griffith, the maker remained unidentified until recently. Sarah Griffith was thought to have lived in upper Montgomery County and to have been an ancestor of Margaret Magruder Clark, the collector from whom the present owner purchased the quilt in the 1970s. A search back through the Magruder family lines revealed several Griffiths, but no Sarah Griffith. A Griffith family genealogy, however, included a number of nineteenth-century Sarah Griffiths,[1] and the 1850 federal census for Montgomery County listed four women between the ages of twenty-four and sixty named Sarah Griffith.[2] Each of these four Sarahs was traced forward until one finally connected with Margaret Magruder Clark.

Sarah Griffith was the great-great-aunt of Margaret Clark's husband, Henry Thomas Clark. Sarah, a sister, and five brothers died unmarried, thus terminating their Griffith line and creating a genealogical impasse. Only sister Ann (Nancy) married, to Charles Holland in 1832. The quilt descended in her Holland/Claggett/Clark line until it was sold out of the family.

Sarah Griffith is now known as a member of a long-established Montgomery County family. She was the second child and oldest daughter of Basil Griffith (1759–1841) and Ruth Gartrell. The Griffiths lived with their eight children at Far View, on land brought to the marriage by Ruth and known before the Revolution as Gartrell's Adventure. Their six-bay dwelling house,

built about 1800 from local rubblestone, commanded an extensive view of rolling countryside to the south and west.[3] The stone barn on the property has the unusual feature of an inscribed date, 1836, cut into one gable end. Basil Griffith and his sons farmed several hundred acres with the help of slave laborers. The 1838 assessment of his taxable property valued his twenty-four slaves at more than $1,600. They probably lived in stone quarters, a building described in 1952 by local historian Roger Farquhar as having its cellar secured by iron bars.[4]

Sarah remained at Far View with her three surviving bachelor brothers after the deaths of their parents, serving as their housekeeper and probably helping to care for brother Davidge, who was described in the 1850 census as "insane." When Sarah died in 1882 at age eighty, she was laid to rest with other family members in the orchard near the house.

Sarah Griffith pieced her intricate Sunburst pattern between 1840 and 1850. She probably worked in the company of her younger sister Nancy, a prolific quiltmaker. Although the whereabouts of Nancy Griffith Holland's quilts are unknown, she left a record of their existence through her estate inventory. When Nancy died in 1876, her personal effects included thirty-one individually listed quilts, eighteen old quilts, three torn quilts, two worsted counterpanes, and a pair of quilting frames—for an impressive total of fifty-four bedcovers.[5] Although the appraisers assigned the num-

bers one through thirty-one to the better quilts, they described only one—a silk quilt, valued at $5. The others ranged in value from 25¢ to $4.[6]

The strong documentation for Nancy Griffith Holland's quiltmaking raises the possibility that she made Sarah Griffith's quilt. A close inspection of Sarah's quilt, however, reveals a certain lack of experience. The piecing alignment is off, causing the sunburst to slope to the left, and the signature is coarsely quilted (46). Perhaps Sarah started her quilt under Nancy's tutelage and finished it on her own. She used a white chain stitch to create the clumsy signature just beneath the central eight-pointed star. The rest of the quilt is stitched with white, green, and brown thread in a double diamond pattern, set one-quarter inch apart.

Sarah's quilt saw little use. The pieced diamonds, cut from a variety of block-printed fabrics, retain their vivid colors. The five-inch-wide border of blue-and-brown roller print, a favorite Montgomery County color combination, is also as bright as when Sarah first selected the fabric.

1. R. R. Griffith, *Genealogy of the Griffith Family* (Baltimore: William K. Boyle & Son, 1892).
2. The 1850 census was selected because it is the earliest one to identify family members by name, age, and occupation. Visually the "Sarah Griffith" quilt dated between 1840 and 1850 and suggested that the maker still would be living in 1850. We assumed that the maker was at least a young adult, so very young Sarah Griffiths were not considered.
3. A plan of the house, drawn as part of the Maryland Historical Trust Historic Sites Survey, shows two rooms up and two rooms down—cramped space for a prosperous ten-member family.
4. Rober B. Farquhar, *Historic Montgomery County Maryland: Old Houses and History* (Baltimore: Monumental Printing, 1952), 155–56. Farquhar's description of the stone building near the dwelling house as a slave quarters must be read with caution. There are numerous inaccuracies in his book. In his discussion on Far View, for example, he mentions Sally (Sarah) Griffith as the daughter of John, her unmarried brother.

46. *Detail showing Sarah Griffith's signature worked in chain stitches. The penciled outline that she followed is still visible.*

5. Montgomery County *Inventories, Lists of Sales and Accounts*, R.W.C. no. 8 (1875–77), 286–93, 348. Because Sarah Griffith died six years after Nancy Holland, the "Sarah Griffith" quilt probably passed to Nancy's heirs at the time of Sarah's death. Sarah Griffith's estate was not inventoried.

6. Ibid. At Nancy Holland's estate sale John O. Clark, father of the last family owner of Sarah Griffith's quilt, purchased the silk quilt, four others in good condition, three torn ones, three old ones, and one of the worsted counterpanes. He paid $13 for the lot.

PIECED SUNBURST QUILT, 1840–50

Made by Sarah Griffith (1802–82)
Far View, near Brookville, Montgomery County
Cottons, chain-stitched inscription
101.5 x 100 inches
Owned by Carolyn Reitman

Calvert County Calico Quilt

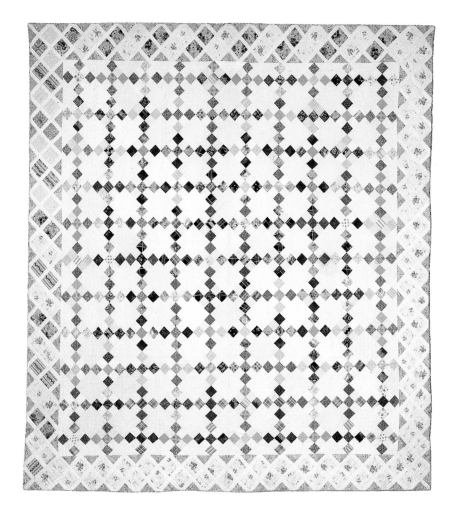

REBECCA MARIAH MAC-
kall Harris, daughter of Mary
Taylor Mackall and
Joseph Harris of Calvert County, quilted her
initials and the date "1847" in the center
blocks of her nine-patch quilt (47). Using
small stitches, eighteen to the inch, she also
quilted sassafras leaves, tulips, hearts, and
other floral and folk motifs in the white
blocks alternating with those quilted in the
grid pattern. Her quilting lines are still visible in some places. For the border Rebecca
cut three-inch squares from block-printed floral sprig fabrics and separated them with white
sashing to create a lattice effect, not usually
found on Maryland quilts. In the top and left
borders she introduced additional printed fabrics to create a darker pattern. The edges are
bound with two different printed fabrics.

An accomplished seamstress, Rebecca also
made a red and green Double Irish Chain
quilt at about the same time. For that bedcover she used twenty stitches to the inch.

Rebecca Harris descended from a long-
established Calvert County family. Her
ancestor William Harris was transported to
Maryland in 1662 as a Scottish prisoner of
war. Although a Quaker and dissenter from
the official religion, he prospered in the tol-
erant colony, acquiring a large tract of land
in the southern Tidewater area, that he
called Duran.[1] By 1800 his descendant
William Harris had expanded the family
land holdings to include Upper Cliffs. Harris
used slave labor, as his neighbors did, to raise
the staple crop of tobacco. At that time
Calvert County and the three other southern counties contained half of all the slaves
in Maryland.[2] Years later, with soil worn out

from one-crop planting, many Calvert
County residents left for fertile lands in the
Southwest. The county's economy was
revived at the end of the nineteenth century by the growth of the oyster industry.

Rebecca Harris grew up witnessing the
change from the old ways of slave-based
agrarian economy to the new maritime economy. Rebecca's quilts descended in the family of her older sister, Mary Harris Laveille
(1806–77) to the present owners. The

47. Detail of Rebecca Harris's signature block. The
initials "RMH" and a tulip motif are worked in quilting
stitches. Nine-patch blocks of small-figured roller prints
and plaids surround the central signature block.

PIECED NINE-PATCH QUILT, 1847

Made by Rebecca Mariah Mackall Harris (1812–96)
Calvert County
Cottons, quilted inscriptions
110 x 100 inches
Owned by Margaret Lomax Lusby

Laveilles were another long-established
Calvert County family. Mary's husband, Uriah
Laveille, descended from French Huguenots who
fled France for Maryland after the revocation of
the Edict of Nantes in 1685. Generations of the
family lived at Laveille House, which still stands
near the head of Battle Creek.[3]

Rebecca Harris continued to sew throughout
her lifetime. At the time of her death in 1896 at
age eighty-four, the inventory of her modest personal effects included "1 old sewing machine,"
along with a bed, bedding, and "3 rocker chairs."[4]

1. Charles Francis Stein, *A History of Calvert
County* (Baltimore: n.p., 1976), 27.
2. Robert J. Brugger, *Maryland: A Middle
Temperament 1634–1980* (Baltimore: Johns
Hopkins University Press, 1988), 46.
3. Stein, 286, 207.
4. Calvert County *Inventories*, C.S.P. no. 1
(1894–1910), 177.

Album Quilts: Souvenirs of the Voyage of Life[1]

ALBUM QUILTS, WHICH REACHED the peak of their popularity in the 1840s, were rooted in Victorian Americans' need to ritualize and sentimentalize the passages or stages of life. Generations of Americans were familiar with the romantic concept of the "Voyage of Life" from the time Samuel Johnson first wrote about it in 1751. The popularity of Thomas Cole's allegorical series by the same name, painted in 1842 and mass marketed through steel engravings, reflected Americans' need to understand and accept the uncertainty and increasing complexity of nineteenth-century life.

More often than not, album quilts were cherished souvenirs representing one of life's many passages, such as birth, marriage, leave-taking, and death; thus, they often were unused and saved by successive generations of a family. In many cases the function of a quilt is lost, but the names inscribed on its surface give us clues to its past. J. Davis Watson, a schoolmaster in Cecil County, presented Mary Ann Alexander with a quilt shortly before her marriage to Joseph England in 1850. Watson was credited with writing all the inscriptions on the quilt, including the square that records his participation (p. 105). The placement of names on the quilt sometimes provides insight into the degree of intimacy between the inscribers and the recipient. Eliza Moore Reynolds probably was deliberate in the placement of names on the quilt she made for her father in 1852. The recipient, David Moore, is in the center, surrounded by immediate family, living and deceased. As the squares move out from the center, the names of cousins and friends fill in the outer edges (p. 107). In some cases, the names on a quilt are the only genealogical record of a family available to researchers today.

Several styles of album quilts were popular in Maryland in the 1840s. Members of the Methodist Protestant church in Westminster made an album quilt in the repeated block style for Rev. Eli Henkle from Turkey red cotton prints, a favorite choice of Maryland quiltmakers at that time. Repeated block album quilts are usually refered to today as friendship quilts, indicating the quilt's function.[2]

Interestingly, the favored pattern for a group of album quilts with Quaker connections was the fleur-de-lis cutwork appliqué design. Again, Turkey red cotton prints were the fabrics of choice for these quiltmakers. Except for one, all the quilts were made in Quaker communities in Cecil County on Maryland's Eastern Shore. The fleur-de-lis quilt not made in Cecil County came from an area of Carroll County settled by Quakers. Although the inscribers of these quilts were not all practicing Quakers by the time the quilts were made, most were descendants of the original Quaker settlers in Cecil and Carroll counties.

Unfortunately, a written or oral tradition disclosing the reasons behind the similarities in design of this group of quilts has not been found and can only be surmised. Travel between western Maryland and the Eastern Shore was aided by a series of roads emanating from Baltimore. Because families from these areas were not isolated and in fact did travel on occasion to different parts of the state, a quilt seen and admired in one community may have possibly inspired a quiltmaker in another.

Two quilts made about fifty miles apart in Montgomery and Frederick counties are pieced in the pattern today known as Turkey Tracks from a virtual sampler of 1840s printed cottons. Both are large quilts measuring between ninety-six inches and one hundred and four inches. The friendship quilt made in Frederick County for a member of the Hargett family (97) is constructed on the diagonal, as is a pre-1860 album quilt from that county (p. 115). The other quilt pieced in the Turkey Tracks pattern was made for Caroline Minerva Bradley Magruder, and the names inscribed on it represent family and friends from neighboring Washington City and Georgetown (p. 94). Most inscriptions are accompanied by drawings, sometimes quite elaborate (48 and 49). The drawings on the Magruder friendship quilt are tangible reminders of the

Victorians' placement of men and women into separate spheres: male signers are represented by such seemingly masculine drawings as a squirrel on a branch or a hunter with a dog, motifs which are in keeping with the appropriate masculine pursuits within the Victorian era man's sphere. Female signers are represented by such designs as classical wreaths, love birds, and floral nosegays. One female signer even drew a house—the ultimate symbol of the woman's sphere!

Album quilts, the quintessential tactile "souvenirs of the voyage of life," are fabric versions of the scrapbooks and autograph albums that were popular with women during the mid-nineteenth century. Like paper albums, album quilts sometimes are decorated with flowers, drawings, poetry, religious verses, and sentimental inscriptions. *Godey's Lady's Book* helped to popularize this fad for immortalizing oneself on the pages of an autograph album. In the mid-1840s, *Godey's* included monthly "Dedicatory Lines for an Album."[3] Women could copy these lines directly from *Godey's* to their autograph books or onto their friendship or album quilts.[4]

At least four of the album quilts pictured in this book were made, according to family histories, to commemorate a wedding. Wedding presents belonged in the female sphere, thus the album quilt was an appropriate gift for a young middle-class bride. Women embodied domesticity in Victorian America and album quilts celebrated it.

The album quilt made to mourn the death of David Firoved is the example included here that represents the final passage of life—death.

Mourning art had been popular since the death of George Washington in 1799, when large numbers of needlework pictures and mourning jewelry were made to immortalize him. Nineteenth-century Americans often dramatized and formalized mourning practices, and by mid-century almost every schoolgirl had worked on mourning art—perhaps a needlework picture, or a brooch containing the hair of a deceased loved one, or an appliquéd album quilt made in memory of a loved one.

The genealogical album quilt made by Mary A. Rhodes in 1856–57, for her son William exemplifies the Victorian spirit of sentimentalizing the passages of life. Mary embroidered her birth and 1850 marriage date, the birth date of her husband, and the age of her son on the bedcover. She also recorded the function of the quilt directly on it, "A Present by Mary A. Rhodes To W L H Rhodes 1856." Her quilt is tangible evidence of the need to romanticize the family as a refuge from the urbanization and industrialization of American society (p. 138).[5]

Quilts as souvenirs of the voyage of life are not restricted to friendship and album quilts. Many other quilts commemorate life's passages and fulfill a need to create something special to honor a person or event. Twentieth-century Maryland quiltmakers continue this timeless tradition. The Needle Chasers of Chevy Chase make quilts for persons with AIDS, while Katherine Brainard of Montgomery County evoked the spirit of the Victorians with a 1990s twist when she made a showstopping quilt—expressing her pain over her divorce![6] As Lou Ellen Slicer wrote when immortalizing herself on the Cronmiller friendship quilt in the 1850s, "*In grief or in glee, till life's dream be over, sweet memories of thee*" (p. 111).

Nancy Gibson Tuckhorn

1. DAR Museum, *Souvenirs From the Voyage of Life*, exhibition checklist, Washington, DC, 1992. The authors thank DAR Museum Director Diane Dunkley and Director of Museum Services Catherine Tuggle for making available their research on the passages of life.
2. Jacqueline Marx Atkins, *Shared Threads: Quilting Together—Past and Present* (New York: Viking Studio Books, 1994), 29, 33, 37, and 38. Atkins pictures several repeated block style friendship quilts with accompanying diary references indicating these quilts were called album quilts by their makers. Also, Atkins illustrates what may be the earliest known reference to a "friendship" quilt from a note written by the maker and attached to the back of the quilt made in 1865 by Mary Field of New York State. Many album quilts were entered in the Maryland Institute Fair records from 1848 through 1853. Because no friendship quilts were recorded, the authors surmise the fair registrar used album quilt as a broad term to encompass those quilts referred to today as friendship or album quilts.
3. Quoted in Linda Otto Lipsett, *Remember Me: Women & Their Friendship Quilts*, (San Francisco, CA: Quilt Digest Press, 1985), 19.
4. Ibid.
5. Gloria Seaman Allen, *Family Record: Genealogical Watercolors and Needlework* (Washington, DC: DAR Museum, 1989).
6. The Divorce Quilt, as it has come to be known, made its debut at G Street Fabrics in Rockville, Maryland. It attracted a great deal of attention and initiated a fad for quilts expressing wrenching life experiences.

Token of Friendship Quilt

Receive thy square, and it, shall be,
A token of friendship from me to thee.[1]

A FRIENDSHIP QUILT MADE for Caroline Minerva Bradley Magruder brings together members of several well-known Montgomery County families. Caroline Bradley, youngest daughter of Hannah Smith (1770–1835) and Abraham Bradley (1767–1838), grew up at the family farm near the District of Columbia line (51).[2] Her father, who came from Philadelphia to Washington in 1800, was the first assistant postmaster general appointed by the federal government.[3] A good many miles north of the White House, his farm served as a temporary residence for several members of President James Madison's cabinet during the British burning of Washington in August 1814.

In 1833 Caroline Bradley married John Willson Magruder (1798–1849), grandson of Col. Zadok Magruder (1729–1811). Colonel Magruder commanded the Home Defense Battalion of Lower Frederick County during the Revolutionary War.[4] His great-grandfather Alexander Magruder came to Maryland from Scotland in 1652. Magruder had joined Scottish Covenanters to fight for the restoration of Charles II to the throne of England after the execution of his father, Charles I, in 1649. Taken prisoner by Oliver Cromwell's army, Magruder was transported as an indentured servant to the English plantations.[5] He survived servitude and eventually amassed a fortune, which included 4,000 acres of land in the colony of Maryland.

In the 1750s Alexander's great-grandson, Zadok, built on Magruder land a two-story brick dwelling. Known as the Ridge, this house was where Caroline Magruder came to join her new husband in 1833 (50) and where they raised seven children and spent the rest of their married lives.

Caroline Minerva Bradley Magruder's friendship quilt contains forty-nine blocks signed by members of the Bradley and Magruder families between 1842 and 1848. Several signatures also appear of Gaither cousins of Oatland, who were members of the founding family of Gaithersburg; two of the Poole sisters of the founding family of Poolesville;[6] and friends from Georgetown and Washington City. In addition to holding a record of prominent families in Montgomery County, the quilt is an encyclopedia of block- and roller-printed fabrics fashionable and available in Maryland in the 1830s and 1840s. Rarely is a fabric repeated from one square to another. The glazed block-printed border fabric, with its small figures on brown ground, dates from the 1830s. The white sashing is quilted at twenty stitches to the inch in the laurel leaf pattern; clamshell and grid quilting fill in the signature blocks.

This friendship quilt may have been among the bedcovers listed in John Willson Magruder's 1849 estate inventory. The appraisers recorded "1 Calico Spread," "7 Quilts," "2 Counterpanes," and "3 unfinished Quilts." A special quilt, such as this one presented to Caroline Magruder, may have been intended for the best bed chamber and included in the listing, "High top bedstead, bed & furniture $12."[7]

Although the stitching of the blocks is fairly consistent, the signatures and drawings suggest that many people contributed to this gift of friendship. The majority of inked names are accompanied by drawings.[8] Some signers placed their names within rococo or neoclassical wreaths. Others drew urns, trophies, lovebirds, flowers, grapevines, and friendship books. One signer, Caroline's niece Annie B. White, drew a house, possibly a portrait of the Ridge (48). The most original drawings are found in the blocks signed by Caroline's husband and six of their children, whose blocks cluster in the lower-right quarter of the quilt. Caroline's own block, with her name encircling a floral bouquet, is in the lower-right corner.

John Willson Magruder's drawing of a hunter with raised gun and hunting dog anticipates a motif found appliquéd on a high-style album quilt from the Baltimore area, and quilted into an 1853 Montgomery County quilt (p. 144).[9] John Willson Magruder may have drawn the design for his son, John, who was not yet two years old in 1843 when his block was signed. The inscription, "My dear mother from her little son/ John Willson Magruder," surrounds a squirrel on a branch (49). Another son, Zadok, who was probably ten when his undated block was signed, drew

48. Detail showing quilt blocks signed by young Zadok Magruder, Caroline's son, and Annie B. White, Caroline's niece.

49. Detail showing quilt blocks signed by John Willson Magruder, Caroline's husband, and young John Willson Magruder, her son.

PIECED FRIENDSHIP QUILT, 1842–48

Made for Caroline Minerva Bradley Magruder
(1812–62)
Montgomery County
Cottons, ink inscriptions
104.75 x 104 inches
Owned by Paul M. Kelley

50. The Ridge, the Magruder family home. (Photograph courtesy of the Montgomery County Historical Society)

death in 1880.[10] His sister Hannah, the only one to inscribe the name of her home on the quilt, and her husband, William E. Muncaster, who was a member of another well-known Montgomery County family, inherited the quilt and the Ridge. The quilt descended to Caroline Minerva Muncaster Kelley, great-granddaughter and namesake of the original owner.

1. Block signed on April 29, 1843, by Elizabeth Young.

2. The original 1747 farmhouse was built on the "Cheivy Chace" plantation, a 560-acre tract granted to Col. Joseph Belt by Lord Baltimore in 1725. Abraham Bradley purchased the old farmhouse and 218 acres in 1814. In 1897 the farmhouse and land were acquired by the Chevy Chase Club to provide space for fox hunting and later a golf course.

3. The Bradley family continued to take an active role in county, state, and national affairs. Caroline's brother Joseph was a prominent criminal lawyer who defended John Surratt, tried for conspiracy to murder President Abraham Lincoln.

4. Lower Frederick County became Montgomery County in 1776.

5. At that time transportation to America and years of forced labor were not particularly preferable to languishing in an English jail.

6. Dunton recorded a quilt with a Gaither and Poole connection from the same time period. A grapevine appliqué quilt is inscribed on the back, "Margaret Anna Poole/ Presented to her/By her Aunt Martha Gaither/ January 1, 1848." William Rush Dunton Jr., *Old Quilts* (Catonsville, MD: n.p., 1946), 242–43. On January 30, 1987, Sotheby's auctioned a Baltimore album quilt that

51. Caroline Minerva Bradley Magruder (1812–62), recipient of the friendship quilt. (Photograph courtesy of Mary Lu Latané)

included the signatures of Sarah and Mary J. Poole.

7. Montgomery County *Inventories, List of Sales & Accounts*, H.H. no. 2 (1847–51), 225. Because husbands generally owned all household possessions, widows frequently were obliged to buy back their own quilts when the contents of the household were sold to satisfy debts.

8. All designs are hand-drawn. No linen marking stamps were used.

9. See Dena S. Katzenberg, *Baltimore Album Quilts* (Baltimore: Baltimore Museum of Art, 1981), 23.

10. Although John Willson joined the Union army, the Magruder family probably sympathized with the Southern cause. They had used slaves to farm tobacco at the Ridge. The senior John Willson Magruder paid taxes on thirteen slaves in 1838.

or had someone else draw a rabbit in a briar patch (48). The names of the four daughters, young girls or infants and probably not the inscribers of their blocks, are drawn with the more feminine symbols of a harp, floral wreaths, and a bouquet of flowers.

The reason for Caroline Magruder's family and friends to piece and sign a friendship quilt between 1842 and 1848 is not known. Perhaps they intended to celebrate her thirtieth birthday in 1842, or perhaps they were offering support and comfort during a period of prolonged illness. Caroline's husband, John, died less than a year after the last block was signed and dated. Caroline Magruder remained with her children at the Ridge until her death in 1862. Her "little son" John Willson grew up to become a prominent surgeon in the Union army and continued to live at the home place until his

Hargett Family Quilt

"TURKEY TRACKS" IS THE popular pattern name for this quilt. The quilt documents a diverse social network centered around the local church and overflowing into a larger community. Although probably made for a member of the Hargett family, the original function of this quilt is lost; however, the people represented by the inscriptions on the quilt allow us to glimpse into a community time has forgotten. Each inscription is neatly written in a different hand with India ink. No stamps or stencils are used and no drawings, such as those on the Magruder friendship quilt made fifty miles away in Montgomery County appear (p. 94). "Mt. Zion Church" is inscribed beneath the names of four signers, all female members of the Smith family. A Lutheran church in Feagaville, Mt. Zion was the house of worship for many other signers, including members of the Hargett family. The inscribed year, 1848, does not coincide with any known important date connected with this family.

John and Barbara Hargett, with other members of their extended family, inscribed the quilt. In 1848 John was a sixty-year-old farmer residing in the Buckeystown district a few miles from Feagaville and the Mt. Zion Church. By 1850 his property was valued at almost $20,000, an impressive sum in those days. Although he farmed in a slave-owning district, he did not own slaves. Members of his extended family lived on adjoining properties but were not farmers.[1] John Hargett may have farmed the land or managed their operations. The most amusing, albeit poignant, reference found in Maryland

records concerning John Hargett and his family is the following description of the burial of John's mother. On October 15, 1831, at 6:00 P.M., the noted Frederick diarist Jacob Engelbrecht recorded the following:

Died- last night. In the 72nd year of her age. Mrs. Mary Hergett Widow Mother of Messrs Peter & John Hergett near the Manor Church, Where She will be buried tomorrow by Mr. Schmaltz,- Mrs. Hergett, was, by far, the largest Woman in this County- both the Hearses in our town are too small to contain her coffin- She was an unweldy woman.[2]

Several members of another Frederick County family, the Buckeys, are represented on the quilt. The name of Peter Buckey (1775–1848) was inscribed just a few months prior to his death at the age of seventy-three. In his will he provided generously for his widow, Mary, and his children. After Peter's debts were paid, Mary was to receive the farm, all household goods, farm implements, stock, slave girl Harriet, plus $2,500. Each child was to receive an equal share ("share and share alike") of his estate upon their mother's death. At that time Harriet was to be freed and given $50.[3]

The name "Erwin Harry" is inscribed in small inked letters on the back of the quilt. She was the daughter of Professor William H. Harry and Mary C. Hargett, and her maternal grandparents were Samuel and Eleanor Hargett. Samuel was the son of John Hargett. At the time the quilt was made, Erwin's mother was six years old and living next door to signer Mary A. Greenwald. The present owner recalls as a young girl seeing Erwin Harry taking tea at the restaurant in the Frederick City Hotel, Erwin's home in her declining years. She does not know when or why her late husband acquired the quilt; possibly it was given to his mother, a cousin of Erwin Harry's.

Thirty-six pieced and twenty-five plain white, nine-inch blocks make up this friendship quilt. The cottons are discharge- and

52. Detail of two inscribed squares in the Hargett family quilt.

roller-printed in floral, stripe, and geometric designs; most retain their glaze (52). The block-printed cotton used for the border probably was an imported furnishing fabric. At eleven inches wide, it created a handsome complement to the squares and fell entirely over the edge of the bed. The 1838 English book *The Workwoman's Guide* describes the use of chintzes "for better purposes" rather than the inexpensive cotton and linen checks and ticking available "for common use."[4]

The quilting designs are simple parallel lines and florals that complete the overall design of the quilt. Although there is evidence of many hands at work, the quilt is finely done at twenty stitches per inch.

The quilt, still in pristine condition, was stored carefully and seldom used. Passed down through several generations of this prominent Frederick County family, the reason for its preservation has been forgotten. The quilt is a final remembrance of a family's forgotten past.

PIECED FRIENDSHIP QUILT, 1848

Made for a member of the Hargett family by their friends and neighbors
Jefferson, Feagaville, and Buckeystown, Frederick County
Cottons, ink inscriptions
96 x 99.5 inches
Owned by Mrs. Virginia Everhart

1. Federal census, Frederick County, Buckeystown District, 1850.
2. William R. Quynn, ed., *The Diary of Jacob Engelbrecht: 1818–1878*, vols. 1–3 (Frederick: Historical Society of Frederick, Maryland, 1976), 666.
3. Frederick County *Wills*, 1849, 324–26.

4. By a Lady, *The Workwoman's Guide, Instructions to the Inexperienced in Cutting Out and Completing Those Articles of Wearing Apparel, & c., Which Are Usually Made at Home; Also, Explanations on Upholstery, Straw-Platting, Bonnet-Making, Knitting, &c.* (London: Simpkin, Marshall, and Co., 1838), 192.

Kemp's Feathered Star Quilt

This quilt was pieced in the year 1840 by Mrs. Mary Kemp in her eighty-second year for her great grand daughter Mary Jane Elizabeth Doub when she was eight years old.

—L. L. Coleman

PIECED FEATHERED STAR QUILT, 1840

Made by Mary Laman Kemp (1758–1845) for her great-grandaughter Mary Jane Elizabeth Doub (1832–1908)
Rocky Springs, Frederick County
Cottons, ink inscription
102 x 102 inches
Owned by Mrs. Anne Fisher

THE ABOVE INSCRIPTION IS written in India ink, set between two floral sprigs, and encircled by a feather wreath on the back of Mary Kemp's Feathered Star quilt (54). The quilt's connection to the inscriber, L. L. Coleman, is unknown. Mary chose to work with a single cotton print, piecing it together with a tightly woven, white-cotton ground cloth. The floral-trail pattern, discharge-printed on a Turkey red ground, is in very good condition, without the usual deterioration in the printed areas. Mary also pieced the sawtooth borders, rather than appliquéing them, as was the usual fashion in Maryland.

The relationships and complex interactions of five generations of the prominent Laman (Lehman), Kemp, and Doub families of Frederick County are represented by this quilt. The quiltmaker, Mary Laman Kemp (1758–1845), was the daughter of Adam (1732–1823) and Margaret (1729–1818) Laman. Adam was a farmer and founding member of the United Brethren Church, whose fondness for "his beloved daughter, Mary," was evident when he willed her his entire estate, "for the many favors of services received from her."[1] He also had appointed Mary the executor of his estate prior to his death in 1823 at age ninety-one.

Mary wed Peter Kemp (1749–1811) in 1779, the year after he and 160 other Frederick County men hired substitutes to take their places in the Revolutionary War.[2] Soon after their marriage, Mary and Peter started housekeeping at Rocky Springs, the home of Peter's father, Frederick Kemp (1725–1804) (53).

In the late eighteenth century, German theologian Pastor Philip Otterbein held several conferences to discuss the future of the German Reformed Church in America, the outcome being the founding of the United Brethren Church at Rocky Springs on September 5, 1800. Mary Kemp's father, husband, son-in-law, and grandson all became United Brethren ministers within a few years. Christian Newcomer (1749–1830), traveling minister and bishop of the United Brethren Church, was a frequent visitor at the Kemp home. He sometimes preached there and recorded many of his visits in his journal.[3]

Mary and Peter had ten children in twenty-three years; all but three lived to adult-hood. Reverend Peter Kemp died in 1811 at the age of sixty-two. On April 6 of that year, a notice appeared in the *Frederick Town Herald* announcing a sale of his personal property. It stated, "Sale by order of Orphan's Court of Frederick County, at farm of late Peter Kemp, two miles from Frederick Town, personal property of deceased: 7 horses, 8 milch cows, 20 sheep, 40 hogs, 3 waggons and geers one of which has broad wheels, cart, ploughs, and harrows, furniture, German books, corn, wheat, 2 stills—Mary Kemp and Jacob Cronise, admirs."

Mary and Peter Kemp's fourth child, Esther (1785–1866), married Valentine

53. *Rocky Springs, the home of Mary and Peter Kemp and the birthplace of the United Brethren Church. (Photograph courtesy of Magrabe and Lebherz, photographer, M. Nikirk)*

Mary Kemp made her quilt for Esther and Valentine's granddaughter, Mary Jane Elizabeth Doub, who was born in 1832. Mary Jane was raised by her parents in Frederick where her father was a merchant. Her marriage to Perry B. McCleery on January 26, 1853, an important social event, was recorded in the diaries of two prominent Frederick County citizens, Margaret Scholl Hood and Jacob Englebrecht. Margaret Scholl (1833–1913) noted briefly in her diary, "Very cold. Mr. Perry B. McCleary and Miss Jane Doub were married today."[6] On the other hand, Jacob Engelbrecht (1797–1879) elaborated in his entry: "Married - a while ago - by the Rev. George Diehl, Mr. Perry Beall McCleery to Miss Mary Jane E. Doub, daughter of the late Joshua Doub, all of our town - they just passed on their way to the cars, for Baltimore, Wednesday, January 26, 1853, 3 o'clock."[7]

Mary Jane and Perry McCleery had six children, and their fifth child, George, inherited the quilt. The present owner was given the quilt in 1953 by George McCleery's widow.

54. *Detail of the inked wreath on the back of Mary Kemp's quilt.*

Doub (1777–1844) in 1804. Soon after Esther's father's death, Valentine and Esther moved to Rocky Springs and took over the farming duties. In 1830 the Doubs founded a United Brethren Sunday school in their home; Esther was the first superintendent.[4]

Valentine Doub died in 1843, and an inventory of the Rocky Springs holdings included the home farm of 224 acres valued at $60 per acre, a mountain lot of 30 acres at $35 per acre, the farm owned by his son Ezra of 103 acres at $63 per acre, and the mountain lot attached to Ezra's farm of 30 acres at $28 per acre. The total value of all real estate was $21,819, an extraordinary sum for 1843.[5]

1. Frederick County *Wills*, HS3, 217.
2. *Maryland Historical Magazine*, vol. III (1908), 259. Peter Kemp's substitute was James Champins. He joined the German Regiment under Lt. Jacob Gromet for the duration of the war.
3. C. E. Schildknecht, *Monocacy and Catoctin*, vol. I (Shippensburg, PA: Beidel Printing, 1985), 396–97.
4. Three years after the death of Valentine Doub in 1843, his sons appointed a neighbor, Daniel Getzendanner, husband of Mary A. Getzendanner, signer of the chintz quilt made for Lauretta Eagle, appraiser of their late father's estate (p. 115).
5. Frederick County *Inventories*, 1847, 241.
6. Rose Barquist, Mary Frear Keeler, and Ann Lebherz, eds., *The Diaries of Margaret Scholl Hood 1851–1861* (Camden, ME: Picton Press, 1992), 28.
7. William R. Quynn, ed., *The Diary of Jacob Engelbrecht: 1818–1878*, vols. 1–3 (Frederick: Historical Society of Frederick, Maryland, 1976), 57.

Methodist Feathered Star Quilt

*Presented To The
Rev. E. B. Henkle
By The
Members Of The Methodist
"P" Church
Of The
Westminster Station
February 5, 1844*

THIS RED FEATHERED STAR quilt was presented to Reverend Eli B. Henkle by the members of the Methodist Protestant Church at the end of his tenure at their church in 1844. Reverend Eli Henkle served the Westminster Station in 1840 and again in 1843–44 (55).[1]

He began his career in 1808 as an itinerant preacher on the Alleghany circuit of the Methodist Episcopal Church. He preached on almost every circuit in western Maryland

55. A detail showing the presentation block in Rev. Eli Henkle's quilt.

until 1829, when he joined a group of reformers in the process of creating a new church—the Methodist Protestant Church.[2] His first assignment with the newly formed church was preaching on the Reisterstown Circuit at Deer Creek. He remained in Carroll County from 1838 to 1849, moving to a different circuit every two or three years. Eli Henkle retired from his calling in 1850 after a last assignment at St. Paul's Evangelical Lutheran Church in Manchester, a small town in northeastern Carroll County.[3]

A red discharge-printed cotton, which has deteriorated in some places as a result of the printing process, is pieced together with plain white cotton to make the Feathered Star blocks. The small white cotton square in the center of each star is inscribed in ink with the names of twenty-four individual members of Rev. Eli Henkle's congregation. Under each signature is the place-name, Westminster. The focal point, an inked inscription in the presentation block in the

PIECED FEATHERED STAR QUILT, February 5, 1844

*Made by the members of the Westminster Methodist Protestant Church for Reverend Eli B. Henkle
Westminster, Carroll County
Cottons, ink inscriptions
106 x 104 inches
Owned by the Historical Society of Carroll County, gift of Mrs. Donald B. Carey, 1959*

central star, stands out from the others in that the white center square is larger, the star is set on point, and the inscription is surrounded by an inked wreath.[4]

Most of the signers of Henkle's quilt were members of the Yingling family, who were early members of the Methodist Episcopal Church but joined the Methodist Protestant Church during the reform movement. The family operated a tannery, one of the first businesses in town, next to their home on Main Street in the late eighteenth and early

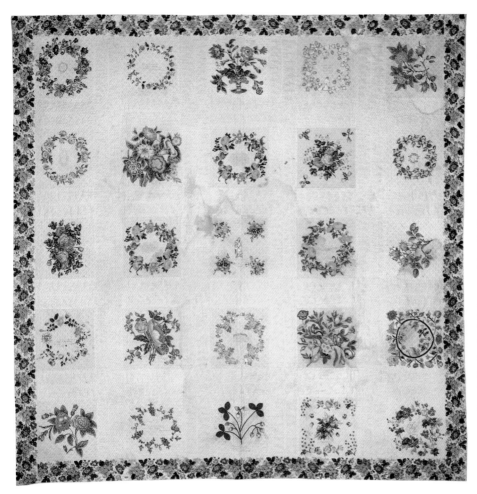

Henrietta Pouder (Powder) (b. 1823) and her sister, Christiana (1826–66), are signers of the Reverend Eli Henkle's quilt, along with their mother, Elizabeth Sundergill. During the 1820s their home was the meeting place for members of the Masonic Order in Carroll County. Henrietta and Christiana's father, Andrew Pouder, died in 1830; their mother, Elizabeth, remarried two years later. The men in the Pouder family were farmers and merchants.[7]

Charles W. Webster, the lone male signer, arranged for his name to appear twice. Nine months after the quilt was presented to Henkle, Charles Webster wed Susanna Waltham of Kent County.

Reverend Eli Henkle's presentation quilt is tangible evidence of a strong social and kinship network. Centered around the church, the communities represented on this quilt overlap and confirm the importance of family and spiritual connections. The role of the quilt in recording these connections serves to open a window into the past.

nineteenth centuries. In 1912, the *American Sentinel* wrote, "At one time no hamlet, village, or town in Maryland tanned more, or better, leather than Westminster. . . . In the early days of Westminster, the tanning industry was its principal industry."[5]

Margaret Yingling, whose name appears on the quilt along with those of her aunt, four sisters, a sister-in-law, and two cousins, married Francis A. Sharrer in 1865. From 1845 to 1917, the Francis A. Sharrer Firm made, repaired, and sold furniture and conducted local funerals. The firm's account books, now owned by the Historical Society of Carroll County, lists in great detail almost every funeral performed in Westminster during those years.

The only name on the quilt inscribed in a different hand is that of Polly O. Shriver (d. 1859). She was related by marriage to

56. APPLIQUÉD CHINTZ FRIENDSHIP QUILT, *1844–46, Carroll County, cottons, ink and cross-stitched inscriptions, 89 x 89 inches, owned by Eleanor F. Mackintosh. This friendship quilt was begun in February 1844 and completed in March 1846 by twenty-two Carroll County women for an unidentified minister. The presentation block in the center of the quilt was made by Mary Whipp, who inked her name under a copper-plate printed robed figure. The figure is framed by four appliquéd floral sprays in each corner of the block. Unlike the makers of Rev. Eli Henkle's quilt, these ladies did not record the name of the recipient on the quilt. The present owner purchased the quilt from a descendent of the original owner in the 1960s, and as time has passed the name of the original owner has faded from her memory.*

Joshua Yingling, brother of several signers. The name of her daughter, Louisa Troxel, also appears on the quilt. After Polly died in 1859, her estate inventory recorded a quilting frame but no quilts.[6]

1. *A Bicentennial History of the Westminster United Methodist Church* (Westminster, MD: Historical Society of Carroll County, 1976), 1–3.
2. In 1828 the Methodist Episcopal Church split into factions over governance of church issues. The reformers who founded the Methodist Protestant Church were opposed to vesting all church powers in the hands of the bishops or the privileged class. They thought the church should be democratic with the power residing in the hands of all.
3. Edna Agatha Kanely, *Directory of Ministers and the Maryland Churches They Served, 1634–1990*, vol. I (Westminster, MD: Family Line Publications, 1991), 313.
4. William Rush Dunton Jr., *Old Quilts* (Catonsville, MD: n.p., 1946), 160–61.
5. Westminster Historical Sites Survey, Public Works Department (Westminster, MD: Historical Society of Carroll County, 1976).
6. Carroll County *Inventories*, 1859, 461.
7. Nellie Whedon, *Jacob Pouder* (Westminster, MD: Historical Society of Carroll County, 1944), 10–21.

Joseph's Quilt

ACCORDING TO FAMILY history, a group of young ladies gathered at an inn in Uniontown, Carroll County, in 1845 to make a quilt as a thank-you gift for a valued friend. Earlier in the year local farmer and bachelor Joseph Rinehart offered to supply the ladies with a room where they could meet weekly to visit and sew. The gift they presented to him for his generosity was this outstanding quilt. Family lore notes that many of the ladies were unmarried and had one eye on the needle and one eye on the altar.[1] Joseph Rinehart was a prosperous farmer and a good catch indeed!

The appliquéd fleur-de-lis pattern of Joseph's quilt is remarkably similar to those on a group of Quaker friendship quilts made in Cecil County (pp. 105 and 107). Joseph's quilt was made in Uniontown, not far from the Quaker settlement of Union Bridge, but none of the makers regularly attended the local Quaker church, Pipe Creek Meeting House.[2]

Twenty-five blocks, each twelve and three-quarter inches square, are sewn together with a sashing and border to make up Joseph's quilt. One pattern probably was cut and then used as a template. As a result the appliquéd decoration in each block is exactly the same size. The laid-on designs are cut from several different red discharge-printed cottons, which appear often on Maryland quilts in the 1840s and 1850s. Technically, the appliqué work is superior; every point is sharp and perfectly turned under with the finest of whip-stitches. Variations in the work of many different hands are virtually invisible.

Each block of the quilt is signed in ink with a linen marking stamp or a drawing (57). Seven signers used a marking stamp of closely inked floral designs; ten used a marking stamp with a simple design of wavy lines; and the rest inscribed their names by hand, with a few signatures embellished by a drawing (58). Linen marking stamps are devices used in the 1840s and 1850s to mark household textiles with the owner's name. A movable type with the name was set into an opening in the marker. The ladies who worked on Joseph's quilt used two linen marking stamps and changed the type for each name.[3]

The sashing is made of a red printed cotton fabric with a stripe-shaded green ground. Such shaded fabrics often are called "rainbow" stripes, a printing technique that usually involved the application of different colors blended together at the edges with a brush. On this fabric only the color green is used, shading from dark to light. This type of print was produced in England and France after many years of experimentation and first imported to the United States in the late 1820s.[4] Printed on cotton and silk, rainbow stripes reached the height of popularity in the 1840s; many a mid-nineteenth-century lady owned a fine silk gown of a rainbow stripe.

A lavish floral glazed cotton border seven and one-half inches wide frames the appliquéd squares. The same print was used on a quilt now in the Maryland Historical Society collection, and family history relates that it was made for Ella Calvert by the mid-wife attending her birth in 1841 at Riversdale, the family home in Prince George's County.[5]

The cotton tatting attached to three sides of Joseph Rinehart's quilt was made by the ladies in the group who were not inclined to quilt, according to the story. The quilting pattern in the blocks echoes the appliquéd designs, and along the sashing and border is a series of unusual horizontal wavy lines. The entire piece is quilted twenty-two stitches per inch.

The present owner, Mrs. W. E. Dackson, lived with her mother and stepfather from the age of six to sixteen in a large two-family home on the outskirts of Westminster, the county seat of Carroll County. Her step-grandparents, the Reeses, lived in the other half of the sprawling brick house. Mrs. Dackson has a hazy memory of an old lady she called Mrs. Foutz sitting in a rocking chair for days on end in the guest room of her stepgrandparents' half of the house. She surmises that the old woman was possibly Elizabeth Foutz, sister of Joseph Rinehart and one of the makers of this friendship quilt.[6] After her stepfather died, the young girl and her mother moved away and had little further contact with the remaining Reese family. But when she married on May 6, 1944, Mrs. Dackson's mother presented her with this stunning quilt. The date was exactly ninety-nine years from the day the quilt was made!

57. Detail of Joseph Reinhart's friendship quilt showing the inked signature of M. A. Shriner stamped on the square with a linen marker.

58. Inked inscription on Joseph Reinhart's quilt noting the place it was made, Uniontown, and the year 1845.

1. The owner wrote down this story in the late 1940s when the quilt was exhibited in the window of Hamburger's Men's Store in Baltimore for Valentine's Day. The quilt also was featured in an accompanying article in the *Baltimore Sun*.

2. Joseph and many of the makers attended Krider's Evangelical Lutheran Church in Uniontown.

3. David Hewett, "Unusual Use of Marking Devices Produces Rarities," *Maine Antiques Digest* (September, 1993), 18-E.

4. For more information, see Florence Montgomery, *Printed Textiles: English and American Cottons and Linens 1700–1850* (New York: Viking, 1970), 306–07; and the August Zindel Dyebooks at the Winterthur Museum.

5. Jennifer Faulds Goldsborough, *Lavish Legacies: Baltimore Album and Related Quilts in the Collection of the Maryland Historical Society* (Baltimore: Maryland Historical Society, 1994), 54–55.

6. "Catalogue of Articles Deposited for Competition and Premiums at the Sixth Annual Exhibition of the Maryland Institute Opened in Baltimore, October 3, 1853" (Baltimore, 1853), 37–38, list in order: "Mrs. Reinhart, made and deposited a quaker veil"; followed by, "Miss C.V. Reese, twelve years old, made and deposited a table mat."

APPLIQUÉD FRIENDSHIP QUILT, May 6, 1845

Made by the ladies of Carroll County for Joseph Rinehart (d. 1866)
Uniontown, Carroll County
Cottons, ink inscriptions
93 X 93 inches
Owned by Mrs. W. E. Dackson

Mary Ann Alexander's Square and Quilt

Presented by
J. Davis Watson
Locust Grove
to Miss Mary A. Alexander
Blue Ball
1849[1]

Miss Mary Ann Alexander's
Square & quilt
"Blue Ball"
Cecil Co. Md.
1849[2]

SHORTLY BEFORE HER 1850 marriage to Joseph Townsend England (1821–1900), Mary Ann Alexander received from J. Davis Watson a friendship quilt in the fleur-de-lis pattern containing the names of forty relatives and friends living in Cecil County, Maryland, and Chester County, Pennsylvania (59). Mary Ann, daughter of widower Joseph Alexander, lived with William and Mercy Biles, a prominent family with a large farm near the crossroads of Blue Ball in Cecil County.[3] According to family history J. Davis Watson was a local schoolmaster; he is credited with writing all the inscriptions on the quilt.[4]

After her marriage to Joseph, Mary Ann left her familiar surroundings to take up residence next to the England family homestead. The quilt accompanied Mary Ann as a tangible reminder of her social network as a single woman. Joseph worked as a carpenter and assisted his father, Isaac, with farming. Eventually Mary Ann and Joseph acquired the England farm, where they produced crops for the Philadelphia market and brought up their three children.

Mary Ann Alexander was a Presbyterian; her husband was a Quaker. Joseph England and a number of other people whose names were inscribed on the quilt were members of the East Nottingham Meeting established in Cecil County by Chester County Quakers around 1700. After the construction of a new meetinghouse in 1724, the meeting became known as Brick Meeting House to distinguish it from the West Nottingham Meeting or Little Brick Meeting. The Brick Meeting House is inscribed on this quilt as the place name of two of the signers (60).

According to family tradition, Mary Ann Alexander made the quilt presented to her by J. Davis Watson. She was known for making numerous quilts; examples of her skillful work remain with her descendants and include a pieced and appliquéd album quilt and a pieced quilt in the Ohio Star pattern. Both quilts date from the mid-nineteenth century.

Mary Ann probably did the appliqué, assembly, and quilting of the friendship quilt pictured here while Davis took responsibility for contacting family, friends, and church members and then writing their names in the individual appliquéd squares. The fleur-de-lis design, common to early Maryland friendship quilts (pp. 103, 107, and 157), was cut from thirty-seven different Turkey red printed cottons.[5] Perhaps Davis also solicited donations of fabric scraps from women of the Cecil-Chester County community.

William Rush Dunton Jr. published Mary Ann Alexander's quilt in his 1946 book on Maryland quilts.[6] At that time the friendship quilt was owned by her granddaughter, Iva Mearns McKinney.

1. Center block in the bottom row of the quilt.
2. Center block of the quilt.
3. Family history relates that the Biles ran the historic Blue Ball Tavern located on the main thoroughfare between Lancaster, Pennsylvania, and New Castle, Delaware. Mary Ann was thought to have lived at the tavern with the Biles. The 1850 federal census, however, lists William Biles as a farmer with property valued at $12,000. There is no indication of tavern employees. By the time the census was recorded, Mary Ann had already married and was living with Joseph.
4. The 1850 federal census for Cecil County records two John D. Watsons, one a seventeen-year-old boarder living with the Washington Alexander family and the other a middle-aged merchant whose household included the boarder Levi R. Mearns. Levi Mearns's name is also on the quilt. His son would later marry Mary Ann Alexander England's daughter.
5. Jacqueline Atkins observed that the fleur-de-lis pattern was well-suited for repetitive block friendship and presentation quilts. Quakers, who had a particular affinity for signature quilts, favored the single-pattern style. Jacqueline Marx Atkins, *Shared Threads: Quilting Together—Past and Present* (New York: Viking Studio Books, 1994), 48.
6. William Rush Dunton Jr., *Old Quilts* (Catonsville, MD: n.p., 1946), 162–65. Mary Ann Alexander is incorrectly listed as "Sarah Ann" in Dunton's caption.

59. *Detail showing recipient block—Miss Mary Ann Alexander's/ Square & quilt/ "Blue Ball"/ Cecil Co. Md./ 1849.*

60. *Detail showing meeting house block—Charles H. Haines/ Brick Meeting House/ 1848.*

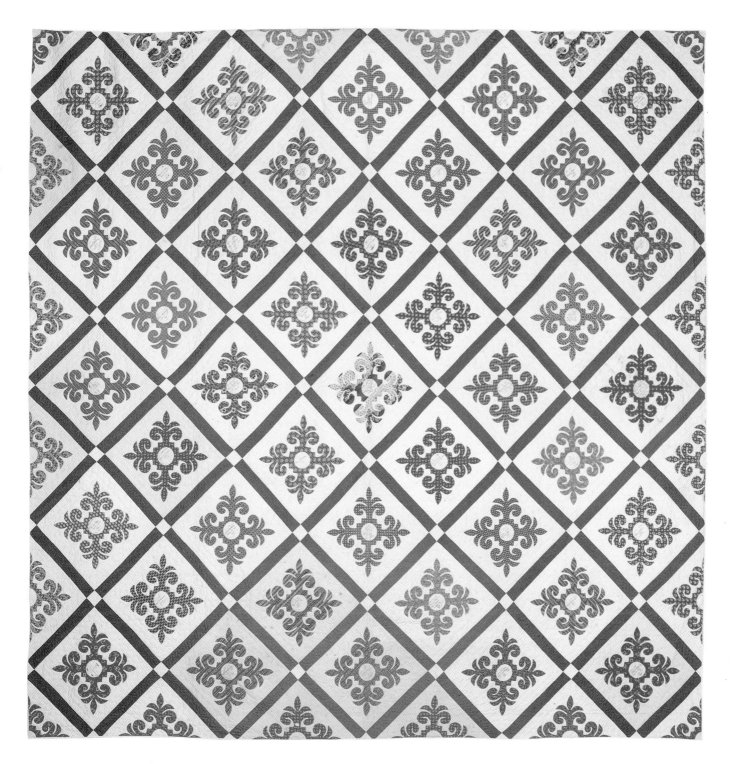

APPLIQUÉD FRIENDSHIP QUILT, 1847–49

Made by Mary Ann Alexander (1824–1909)
Cecil County
Cottons, ink inscriptions
102 x 101 inches
Owned by Frances Hubis

Quaker Community Quilt

*T*HIS QUAKER FRIENDSHIP quilt that documents several social networks in rural Maryland probably was made by Eliza P. Moore Reynolds in honor of her seventy-seven-year-old father, David Moore.[1] Eliza placed her father's name in the central block and surrounded it with names of family members and friends living in northern Cecil County, Maryland, and southern Chester County, Pennsylvania. Many of the signers were also Quakers; thus, David Moore's quilt brings together overlapping communities of family, church, and friends.[2] Quakers, especially, placed strong emphasis on community, both in their faith and in everyday life. The recipient of the quilt was but one part of the many social relationships that made up the whole.[3]

The quilt includes the names of Eliza, her husband, and their two children in the lower left of center; her sister Phebe, her husband, and one of their ten children in the upper left of center;[4] and her two unmarried sisters above and below center. The names of her mother, Sarah, and another sister, both deceased when the quilt was made, are also included immediately above David Moore's name (61). Moving out from the center, cousins, other kin, and friends fill in the remaining blocks. Eliza was deliberate in her placement of names and selective in her inclusion of kin and acquaintances. She omitted the name of her stepmother, Leah, yet included the name of the hired hand living on her brother-in-law's farm. His block is along the outer edge of the quilt.

The Turkey red fleur-de-lis pattern, which appears on this friendship quilt and on a slightly earlier Cecil County quilt made for Mary Ann Alexander (p. 105),[5] was popular with Eastern Shore quiltmakers. The later example shows much greater variation in motifs. They range from delicate to crude and express the dexterity or whim of the individuals who cut them out; some resemble pineapples whereas others are closer in design to a tulip-and-leaf motif usually seen on later quilts.[6] The signatures also show the work of several different hands. Family tradition attributes this quilt to Eliza Moore; she may have been responsible for the planning, assembly, and quilting rather than for all the individual blocks. The quilt is stitched in the grid and clamshell patterns and bordered with appliquéd sawteeth cut from Turkey red and green and black printed cottons.

Eliza Moore and her older sister Phebe married brothers, Henry and Haines Reynolds. The 1850 federal census recorded Henry as a machinist and Haines as a miller; both also maintained farms near Rising Sun in northern Cecil County. The Reynolds family business included a machine shop, a foundry, and saw and grist mills on Stone Run.

The Moore and Reynolds families, in addition to a number of other people named on the quilt, attended the West Nottingham Meeting, established by Quakers from Chester County, Pennsylvania, in 1710.[7] Although Eliza was buried at West Nottingham, her children followed the growing movement away from the Society of Friends and joined the Presbyterian Church.

Eliza's son George, who was six at the time his name was written on his grandfather's quilt, inherited his mother's stitched record of the Rising Sun community and passed it to his son, Curtis, father of the present owner.

61. Detail of Sarah Moore's block. Sarah, who died in 1842, was the mother of Eliza Moore Reynolds and wife of David Moore.

blocks placed several rows away. The expansive Reynolds family reused many of the same Christian names, so it is frequently difficult to sort out family members.
5. An all-white quilt in the fleur-de-lis pattern was made by Rachel Ross Knight or her sister Martha Ross in Cecil County, c. 1845. The quilting lines, rather than appliquéd fabric, form the pattern. The unquilted fleur-de-lis shape is set off by the stipple quilted ground. The motifs are arranged in blocks, set on point. The Rosses were originally Quakers.
A Cecil County friendship quilt made by Milcah Churchman Lesslie Pyle in 1848 contains several blocks with fleur-de-lis motifs. The Pyles were members of the Nottingham Monthly Meeting at one point. This quilt, the Moore quilt, and the Alexander quilt (p. 105), however, have no names in common even though all three were made in northern Cecil County within a five-year period and are associated with Quakers. The Pyle quilt is illustrated in Patricia T. Herr's "Quaker Quilts and Their Makers" in *Pieced by Mother*, edited by Jeannette Lasansky (Lewisburg, PA: Oral Traditions Project, 1988), 15–17.
6. Two later Cecil County presentation quilts have the tulip and leaf appliquéd design. One was made in 1897 by Sarah Elizabeth Tyson for her son Carroll in honor of his twenty-first birthday; the other was made in 1930 for Adella Huston McKee, wife of the departing minister of the West Nottingham Presbyterian Church in Colora. In these two quilts one printed fabric was used throughout for the appliqué, whereas in the quilts of the 1840s and 1850s the appliquéd motifs were cut from numerous Turkey red prints.
7. The Reynolds brothers descended from Henry Reynolds, who received one of the original Nottingham Lots granted by William Penn in 1702.

1. David Moore died two years later. Perhaps his failing health prompted the creation of a quilt that would commemorate his connections to family, church, and community.
2. For a thoughtful discussion of quilts "whose primary function is to reify community," see Ricky Clark, "Mid-19th-Century Album and Friendship Quilts 1860–1920," in *Pieced by Mother*, edited by Jeannette Lasansky (Lewisburg, PA: Oral Traditions Project, 1988), 77–86.
3. Jacqueline Marx Atkins, *Shared Threads: Quilting Together—Past and Present* (New York: Viking Studio Books, 1994), 27.
4. Two additional children of Phebe Moore Reynolds, or possibly cousins, are inscribed in

APPLIQUÉD FRIENDSHIP QUILT, 1852

*Probably made by Eliza Moore Reynolds (1815–85) for
her father, David Moore (1775–1854)
Near Rising Sun, Cecil County
Cottons, ink inscriptions
105 x 105 inches
Owned by Mildred R. Gifford and family*

Family Record Quilt

MARY ROOKER NORRIS made this outstanding bedcover while residing in Hagerstown with her daughter, Sarah (1822–78), and son-in-law Thomas, a Methodist itinerant preacher.[1] The recipient of the quilt was one-year-old Mary Norris, daughter of her eldest son, John (1813–82), and his wife, Henrietta Tyson Norris (1809–71) of Harford County.

Mary Rooker Norris was one of twenty-one children born to Mary Berry Rooker (1762–1814) and Reverend James Rooker (1756–1828), who immigrated with their family from Walsall, near Birmingham, England, in 1807. Shortly after arriving in Baltimore, Mary's sisters, Harriet and Rebecca, opened the English Seminary for Young Ladies on Pratt Street near the downtown area.[2] In 1811 Mary wed John Norris (1774–1829) of Harford County and Baltimore City. The couple lived in Baltimore during the early years of their marriage when John was a partner in a flour milling business. Illness forced John to quit the business and take a long sea voyage to Spain and Portugal in hopes of regaining his health. On returning, John resettled in Harford County, the place of his birth, with his family and built a stately home, Olney, where he was surrounded by relatives and boyhood friends. John and Mary lived at Olney until his early death in 1829. Mary returned to Baltimore shortly thereafter and joined the faculty at her sisters' seminary. In 1830 the *Baltimore American and Commercial Daily Advertiser* contained this notice: "THE MISSES ROOKERS' SEMINARY FOR YOUNG LADIES . . . they now beg leave to add that

their sister Mrs. NORRIS, whose talents as a Teacher will be remembered by many, has returned to the city, and will resume her station in the Institution."[3]

Mary was given a life's interest in her husband's estate. Her son, John Saurin Norris, inherited the farm and dwelling house. His daughter, Mary Norris, recipient of the quilt, was born at Olney in 1845. She spent the first ten years of her life in Harford County until her grandmother and parents sold Olney to her cousin Lloyd Norris in 1855 for $400.[4]

In 1868 young Mary Norris married George Perry (1842–72) of Virginia. The marriage was short-lived: George died at age thirty in 1872 just a few months after their daughter, Henrietta Tyson Perry, was born. Mary Norris Perry was still alive in 1916 when a history of the Norris family was published; she provided the author with much of the family history.[5]

Mary Rooker Norris's bedcover is one of two known Maryland finished genealogical quilts made in the nineteenth century. Mary Rhodes of Dorchester County made a genealogical quilt for her son William in 1857 (p. 138).

Mary Norris was a skilled artist with a pen. The classically inspired ink scroll and wreath in the center of the quilt records the birth, marriage, and death dates of several generations of her family (62). This is surrounded by several appliquéd borders. Her appliqué work is crudely executed and the corners do not evenly match up, giving the quilt an unplanned appearance. Mary used the same glazed and printed cottons for some of the laid areas as did many other Maryland quiltmakers in the 1830s and 1840s. The iris, tulip, and lily motifs show up frequently in quilts made around Baltimore and Frederick Counties. Classical designs, such as the Greek key, or wall of Troy border print were also popular choices for Maryland quiltmakers in the period.[6] She pieced different white cottons for the ground cloth, which have discolored unevenly over the surface of the quilt. The quilt is lined with white cotton; its bleachyard stamp is still visible. In 1986 the DAR Museum purchased the quilt from an antiques dealer.[7]

62. *Birth, marriage, and death dates of successive generations of the Norris family are inscribed in an elaborate inked scroll and four medallions decorating the center of Mary Norris's quilt.*

1. This quilt was published by the authors in Gloria Seaman Allen, *Family Record: Genealogical Watercolors and Needlework* (Washington, DC: DAR Museum, 1989), 93.
2. *Federal Gazette & Baltimore Daily Advertiser*, Baltimore, MD, October 5, 1808, 3. Instruction was given in "Reading, Orthography, English Grammer, Composition, History, Geography, Writing, and Arithmetic, French, Music, Drawing, Stenography, Plain Work, Marking, Netting, Cotton Work, Embroidery, Chimney Ornaments, Bell-Ropes, Table Mats, Baskets, Decanter-Stands, Card Racks, Watch Cases, Hand-Fire Screens, Urn and Tea Pot Rugs."
3. *Baltimore American and Commercial Daily Advertiser*, January 2, 1830.
4. Harford County *Indentures*, 1855. The authors thank the DAR Museum and Mrs. Mabel E. Andrews, corresponding secretary of the Historical Society of Harford County, for providing them with a copy of the indenture of mortgage.
5. Thomas M. Myers, *The Norris Family of Maryland* (New York: William M. Clemens, 1916), 33–57.
6. The DAR Museum owns a quilt bordered in an almost identical fabric as this one. It was made in Baltimore during the 1840s by Mary Tayloe Lloyd Key, the widow of Francis Scott Key.
7. The museum also owns a needlework picture (c. 1810) of a "View Near Exeter," worked by Rebecca Rooker (1793–1862), Mary's sister.

PIECED AND APPLIQUÉD GENEALOGICAL
QUILT, 1846

*Made by Mary Rooker Norris (1785–1868) for Mary
Norris (b. 1845)*
Hagerstown, Washington County
Cottons, ink inscriptions and drawings
102.5 x 104 inches
*Owned by the Daughters of the American Revolution
Museum, Friends of the Museum Purchase*
*(Photograph courtesty of DAR Museum, photographer,
Mark Gulezian)*

Hexagon Quilt

MORE THAN 123 HEXAgons make up this red and white friendship quilt. In the center of each hexagon is a name inscribed in ink. In one center the name "Augusta" is worked with hair in very fine cross-stitches. Several names are accompanied by poems or drawings. Many different Turkey red discharge-printed cottons are combined with plain white cotton to make up the hexagons. The border is an appliquéd stepped-pyramid design of classical inspiration. Although the quilt is in mint condition and the hexagons pieced in an exemplary manner, the borders were unevenly sewn to the field, giving the quilt an unbalanced appearance like a picture placed askew in a frame.[1] The bedcover was lined and quilted well into the twentieth century. Quilting designs include feather wreaths and a running feather along the borders, with stitching at eighteen stitches per inch.

63. Detail of Cronmiller friendship quilt showing inked inscription, "Frank Pierce/Pres U.S." It was in the 1852 presidential election between Franklin Pierce and Winfield Scott that the Democratic party carried Maryland for the first time.

Family tradition records that the Cronmiller sisters of Baltimore County owned the quilt (64). All of their names appear on it except that of the youngest sister, Hester. Nine children were born to Dr. John Cronmiller and his wife, Mary Ann. Eliza Jane (1819–66), Susan Roberts (1822–1912), and Catherine (Kate) Cronmiller (1829–c. 1912) never married. Hester Welling Cronmiller (1835–1922) married Alfred Cole in 1887 at the age of fifty-two. The Cronmiller girls were represented at the Maryland Institute Fair in 1850 by Kate, who entered Fox grape jellies "of excellent flavor"; she was the proud winner of a silver mustard spoon. The oldest sister, Eliza Jane, entered a "crochet-work" hat but failed to pick up a prize.[2]

The inscriptions on the quilt record many members of several Baltimore County families prominent in the local Methodist church. The children of Reverend Henry Slicer (b. 1801) are listed (65).[3] His wife, Elizabeth, was the sister of fellow Methodist preacher Dr. George C. M. Roberts. Several generations of the Roberts family also are listed on the quilt. Susan Roberts Cronmiller was probably named after a member of the Roberts family. Dr. Roberts married several members of the family in the 1840s. Other families affiliated with the Methodist church in Baltimore from 1848 to 1852, are represented on this quilt, giving testimony to the social network alive in Methodist church circles during the middle of the nineteenth century.

The inscription "Franklin Pierce, Pres. US" is neatly written in the center of one hexagon (63). It probably represents the political affiliations of the makers and owners during the time the quilt was being made.[4] In the 1852 election between Democrat, Franklin Pierce (1804–69) and Whig, Winfield Scott, the Democrats carried the state for the first time in a presidential election.[5] This was the last election in which the Whig party mounted a national campaign. Whig's Defeat became the name of a quilt pattern that was popular all across the country.

1. One hexagon quilt and an octagon quilt were entered in the fair at the Maryland Institute in 1848. *Maryland Institute for the Promotion of the*

64. Members of the Cronmiller family, 1905–07, left to right: Dr. John Cronmiller holding dog, John D. Cronmiller, Hester Cronmiller Coale, Eliza Gardner Cronmiller Halverson, Susan Cronmiller, Catherine Cronmiller, and William Welling Cronmiller. (Photograph courtesy of Ruan Robertson)

Mechanic Arts For the Exhibition of October 31, 1848 (Baltimore, 1849), 6.
2. Ibid., 34.
3. It is interesting to note that as a young man Reverend Henry Slicer apprenticed for five years to Messrs. John Finlay & Co., the celebrated Baltimore ornamental furniture painters. The elaborate painted classical designs on Finlay furniture, and those made by other cabinetmakers and ornamental painters in the first half of the nineteenth century in Baltimore, are similar to many of the designs decorating album quilts.
4. It is unlikely the inscription was written by the president.
5. Robert J. Brugger, *Maryland: A Middle Temperament, 1634–1980* (Baltimore: Johns Hopkins University Press, 1988), 258.

65. Detail of Cronmiller friendship quilt showing inked wreath surrounding the name, "Susan Hall Slicer."

HEXAGON FRIENDSHIP QUILT, 1851–55

Owned by the Cronmiller sisters
Baltimore County
Cottons, ink and hair-worked inscriptions
108 x 104 inches
Owned by Ruan D. Robertson

Philena's Turkey Red Quilt

Go, little book; go, wander forth
Mid Friendship's rosy bower
And cull from her, as gems of worth
Her fairest, sweetest flowers.

Let no false pen thy page impress
With flattery's sick'ning tone;
But constancy and faithfulness
Adorn thy leaves alone.

Then home return, without delay
To her who sent thee forth;
And to her searching eye, display
Thy gems of rarest worth.[1]

PIECED SAWTOOTH QUILT, 1857

Made by Philena Rebecca Lee Stephens (1832–97)
Willow Dale Farm, near Rising Sun, Cecil County
Cottons, quilted inscription
99 x 96 inches
Owned by Edwin L. Haines Jr.

TWO YEARS AFTER HER MARriage, Philena Rebecca Lee Stephens pieced together Turkey red and white cottons in a sawtooth block variation to make a bedquilt. In alternating white blocks she finely quilted, twenty stitches to the inch, several different floral designs. The quilted motifs, like many of those appliquéd to album quilts, include floral vines, sunflowers, pineapples, crossed laurel leaves, feather wreaths, and hearts. One block contains her maiden name "P R Lee" and the date "1857."

Philena Lee, daughter of Jane and Samuel Lee, was born and raised on her father's farm in West Nottingham Township, Chester County, Pennsylvania. In 1855 she married Joseph Lincoln Stephens (1828–87), who lived just across the state line in Cecil County, Maryland. Shortly before their marriage, one of their friends presented Philena with a memory or friendship book (66). Philena's album is filled with verses penned

between 1854 and 1862 by members of the Lee and Stephens families as well as by friends living nearby.[2] Another friendship album, dedicated in 1857 to Ellen (Nellie) Stephens, a maiden sister of Joseph's, has descended with Philena'a album and quilt to her great-grandson.[3] Nellie's album contains verses and signatures by many of the same friends and family members who signed Philena's book. The two friendship albums, like many quilts from the same time period and locality, attest to close ties of kinship and community along the Maryland/Pennsylvania border. The sentimental verses, often infused with Christian piety, recall absent friends and past pleasures.

After their marriage Joseph and Philena Stephens moved to his father's farm, Willow Dale, outside of Rising Sun, Cecil County, where Joseph took over farm management and Philena kept house for her father-in-law. Willow Dale, with its stone house built in 1774, had been purchased by Joseph's father

in 1815.[4] By 1860 Joseph was running a profitable farming establishment with more than 100 acres in corn and wheat and assets worth $7,000. His chickens produced a surplus of eggs, and his cows supplied enough milk for Philena to produce butter for the Philadelphia market. Another Cecil County farm woman, diarist Martha Forman, frequently recorded that she made butter and gathered eggs for market.[5] During the 1820s and 1830s Martha produced thousands of pounds of butter for her neighbors' tables and for Baltimore shops.[6] In one week alone, she churned fifty-two pounds.[7] Cecil County was part of the "butter belt" that supplied the nearby cities of Baltimore, Philadelphia, and Wilmington with fresh produce.[8] Farm women in the area gained a degree of economic independence through the sale of butter and eggs. Their production for market "kept the farm household a functional, fundamental, and essential part of the new economy" of the nineteenth century.[9] Their own source of income allowed these women to exercise greater control over purchases. Martha Forman used her butter and egg money, for example, to purchase dimity for quilts and chair cases; she also used her earnings for special gifts for house servants.[10]

In 1862, after his father's death, Joseph inherited Willow Dale, and Philena continued to provide a home there for Joseph's unmarried sister and brother and to raise their six children (67). In addition to her farm responsibilities, Philena taught Sunday school at the local Methodist church, built on Stephens property.

66. Philena Stephens' and Nellie Stephens' friendship albums and a photograph of Philena and Joseph Stephens, taken shortly after their 1855 marriage, are placed on a section of Philena's bedcover quilted in a sunflower motif. (Photograph and albums courtesy of Edwin L. Haines Jr.)

1. Dedication page in friendship album owned by Philena Lee Stephens, Cecil County, Maryland, 1855.

2. The relationship of the signers to Philena can be determined from names in the 1850 and 1860 federal censuses for Chester County, Pennsylvania, and Cecil County, Maryland.

3. We are grateful to the Haines family for sharing their albums, photographs, and family history with us.

4. Interview and correspondence with Edwin L. Haines Jr.

5. W. Emerson Wilson, ed., *Plantation Life at Rose Hill: The Diaries of Martha Ogle Forman 1814–1845* (Wilmington, DE: Historical Society of Delaware, 1976).

6. Unlike Philena, Martha Forman was assisted by one or more slave women who were experienced dairymaids. Joan M. Jensen, *Loosening the Bonds: Mid-Atlantic Farm Women, 1750–1850* (New Haven: Yale University Press, 1986), 84.

7. Ibid.

8. Ibid., 79–91.

9. Ibid., xv.

10. Gloria Seaman Allen, "Quiltmaking on Chesapeake Plantations," in *On the Cutting Edge: Textile Collectors, Collections, and Traditions,* edited by Jeannette Lasansky (Lewisburg, PA: Oral Traditions Project, 1994), 63.

67. Philena and Joseph Stephens in later years. (Photographs courtesy of Edwin L. Haines Jr.)

Friendship Album Quilt

When friendship once is rooted fast
It is a plant no storm can sever
From fixed and needless of the blast
It blooms and flourishes forever

Mary G. Kemp
Oakland Mills
1847

THE FAMILY AND FRIENDS OF Margaret Lauretta Eagle presented her with this quilt before she married Thomas Jarboe (1828–94) in 1850.[1] Lauretta was born and raised on Carrollton Manor in Frederick County. The Manor, as it was called in the nineteenth century, was the original land grant established in southern Frederick County by Charles Carroll, signer of the Declaration of Independence.

The makers of Lauretta's quilt were family members, neighbors, and relatives of neighbors living on or near Carrollton Manor. Margaret Scholl Hood, a neighbor of Lauretta and her twin sister, Frances, kept a diary from 1851 to 1861,[2] recording her day-to-day activities along with those of her family and friends, many of whom signed Lauretta's quilt. Her diaries show a complicated social network of family and friends, and life on the Manor at mid-century.

Evident by the varying degrees of workmanship on Lauretta's quilt, each participant probably designed, sewed, and inscribed her own block. The quilt is composed of thirteen blocks: three floral sprays and ten classically inspired chintz and plain cotton wreaths. The blocks are set on point and separated by plain red cotton bands. Floral branches and chintz half-wreaths are laid onto triangles that fill in the edges of the quilt. Without

enough triangles to complete the composition, the assembler divided several blocks in half. One block, inscribed in ink by Mary R. Grove, was cut down the middle through the date "1847," and then the halves were sewn to opposite sides of the quilt.

The names on the squares represent families of French, English, and German ancestry, each with its own needlework and design traditions. In the past, textile historians have attempted to link chintz appliqué with those of French and English ancestry and red and green appliqué work with those of German ancestry. In fact, no correlation exists between the ancestry of the quiltmakers and the two distinct styles seen on this quilt.

Lauretta was seventeen years old when she was presented with the quilt. Her mother, Margaret Fout Eagle, died at the age of twenty-seven, when Lauretta and her twin sister were two years old. Although their father owned a large farm in the Buckeystown district, the girls grew up several miles away at Locust Hill, the home of their maternal grandmother, Magdalene Fout (1788–1860), and aunt Barbara Fout, both signers of Lauretta's quilt.[3] The girls attended the Frederick Visitation Academy and later St. Joseph's Academy in Emmitsburg, where they learned reading, history, and drawing, along with sewing skills.[4]

Barbara Fout is mentioned many times in the Hood diary. In 1851, Barbara Fout "plaits" [pleats] a dress for young Margaret Scholl. Over the next year Margaret visits Locust Hill for fittings and other meetings related to sewing projects that Barbara undertakes for her. Although Margaret paid Barbara for her services, the visits were often purely social.

Other names inscribed on the quilt include that of Louisa Moffet of Snickersville, Loudoun County, Virginia, one of two signers from the Virginia county located directly across the Potomac River from southern Frederick County (68). Families moved back and forth across the Potomac River, the state line—which was in some cases only a political boundary. Evidence such as Lauretta's quilt suggests that community and social networks were

flexible.[6] Living on farms adjoining Locust Hill were Virginia-born Benjamin Moffet, Louisa's uncle, and his son. In 1850 they owned ten slaves between them, more than the average number for a Frederick County slaveowner.[7]

Nineteen-year-old signer Mary R. Grove of Jefferson and her twenty-one-year-old sister Manzilla, another signer, were the daughters of Jacob Grove, a farmer and slaveowner.[8] Mary G. Kemp of Oakland Mills in Buckeystown, a sixty-year-old widow and one of the few female slaveowners in the county, was the oldest signer. Loretta C. Fout, the wife of Grafton Fout, Lauretta Eagle's cousin, inscribed the quilt a few months before the deaths of two of her children. A neighbor of Margaret Scholl, Loretta Fout is mentioned many times in Margaret's diary.[9]

Of all the signers of Lauretta's quilt, only Vallie Adams (b. 1829) is mentioned more often than the Fouts in Margaret Scholl's diary. Vallie was Margaret's cousin and lived one mile south of Manchester Farm, the Scholl home. Vallie was a frequent visitor to the Scholl home and participated in many social activities with Margaret and her friends. In 1851 Margaret records going to a neighbor's house with Vallie Adams and Frances Eagle to be weighed![10]

Lauretta married Thomas Jarboe in 1850 and settled at Gayfield, a large brick house on 338 acres of land on Carrollton Manor and considered by some to be the most successful farming operation on the Manor. Thomas Jarboe was a prominent politician, one of the few Democrats in a Republican county elected to the county commission—twice.

William Jarboe Grove, a nephew of Thomas Jarboe, wrote in his 1928 book, *The History of Carrollton Manor*, about a celebratory picnic held at Gayfield after Thomas's election as county commissioner. He and his wife hosted a picnic dinner of about a thousand guests and participated in a mile-long torchlight parade, which was made up of delegations from neighboring towns and communities. The event was remembered for its fine food and plentiful drink; the cider and wine were made on the home farm.[11]

Grove repeats another story about a night during the Civil War just before the Battle of

FRIENDSHIP ALBUM QUILT, 1846–50

Made for Margaret Lauretta Eagle (1833–1900) by her
family and friends
Locust Hill, Carrollton Manor, Frederick County
Cottons; silk, cotton, and wool embroidery thread; ink
inscriptions
105 x 102 inches
Owned by Jeanne Golibart O'Brien

Monocacy, which was fought a few miles away. Although Jarboe was a Southern sympathizer, he did not want his horses taken by Confederate soldiers. He willingly sold his best horse, named Andrew Jackson, to a Confederate soldier. The horse returned riderless as the soldier was killed in the fighting.[12]

Lauretta and her family survived the war, and Gayfield was spared its ravages. Lauretta's only child, Margaret, inherited the farm and lived there the rest of her life with her husband, Charles Rohrback, and their five children. She continued the family tradition of naming the children after previous generations: Loretta Jarboe, Ellen Brunner, Thomas Jarboe, Margaret Jarboe, and Francis Eagle all survived to adulthood and were beneficiaries in their grandmother's large estate. The quilt descended to Lauretta's daughter, Margaret Jarboe Golibart, who in turn gave it to her own daughter, the present owner, in 1975.

68. Detail of Louisa Moffett's square on Lauretta Eagle's album quilt. Louisa's square represents a social network that defies political or physical boundaries. The inscription reads, "Cold and cheerless were the earth, and the heart a colder hearth, did not friendship, time and [unreadable], Grace its holy fireside. Louisa Moffett, Snickersville, Loudoun Cty, Virginia, Jan. 1st 1848."

1. MAFCE documented in Kent County another red and white friendship quilt in the Feathered Star pattern inscribed with Frederick County and Baltimore City names and the date 1845. The squares also include the names of members of the Fout family, who also are named on this quilt.

2. Rose Barquist, Mary Frear Keeler, and Ann Lebherz, eds., *The Diaries of Margaret Scholl Hood: 1851–1861* (Camden, ME: Picton Press, 1992). The original diaries are in the collection of the Historical Society of Frederick County.

3. The 1850 federal census for Frederick County lists: Magdalene Fout, seventy-two; Barbara Fout, thirty-four; Frances E. Eagle, seventeen; Margaret L. Eagle, seventeen; and a fourteen-year-old female mulatto slave. Magdalene's son Lewis Fout lived on the adjoining property with his wife and nine children. Next to Lewis was his brother, Grafton Fout, thirty-six, his wife Loretta, twenty-five, and one-year-old Isadore.

4. Betty Ring, *Girlhood Embroidery: American Samplers and Pictorial Needlework, 1650–1850* (New York: Knopf, 1993), vol. 2, 516–21.

5. Hood diaries, 20–41.

6. The 1850 federal census for the Petersville District, Frederick County, recorded a high concentration of Virginia-born residents, including Lauretta's father, William Eagle.

7. Father and son owned one slave family each. The average number of slaves per owner in Frederick County in 1850 was 3.6. Mary Fitzhugh Hitselberger and John Philip Dern, *Bridge in Time* (Redwood, CA: Monocacy, 1978), 455.

8. Grove's slaveholdings consisted of one eight-member family.

9. Hood, 268, 361.

10. Hood, 19.

11. William Jarboe Grove, *The History of Carrollton Manor* (Frederick, MD: Marken & Bielfeld, 1928), 80–81.

12. Ibid.

Baltimore Album Quilt

*Mrs. H.F. Firoved and her niece made
this quilt in the year A.D. 1845.
Yes, we were made to win below
The moon hereafter given
To calmly smile at earthly woe
To find our home in heaven*

THIS INSCRIPTION (PLACED within the appliquéd wreath, top row second from left) probably was written to mourn the death of Hannah Firoved's husband, David, in 1845. The dye from colored silk embroidery thread that outlined his name (bottom of the central appliquéd basket) is all that remains to link this quilt to him. His embroidered name probably was pulled out at a later time when the intent to memorialize a loved one was forgotten.

Margaretta Firoved, Hannah's niece, probably was living in the Firoved home, helping her aunt during her Uncle David's last illness and awaiting her marriage to Oliver Switzer (1822–71). She was the youngest of five children born

70. Margaretta F. Switzer (left) and her daughters standing on the steps of her home on West Lombard Street, Baltimore. A letter written to Margaretta by her brother John, on hearing of the death of Oliver Switzer in 1871. Four generations of Switzer women. From left to right: Margaretta F. Switzer, Lydia Margaretta Culver (mother of owner), Nettie Krout Culver, Martha Margaretta Switzer Krout. (Photograph courtesy of Mr. and Mrs. Z. Vance Hooper)

to Nancy Firoved (d. 1826) and her husband, George (d. 1831), of Carlisle, Pennsylvania. Margaretta, orphaned at the age ten, spent the following fourteen years living with various relatives in Pennsylvania and Baltimore. At school in Carlisle, Margaretta worked an alphabet sampler, stitching in lines from a poem, "The time is short-the moment near/ When we shall dwell above/ And be forever happy there/ With Jesus whom we love" (69). As an orphan, Margaretta was all too aware of the meaning of the message she stitched into her schoolgirl needlework.

Margaretta was living in Baltimore when she met and fell in love with twenty-three-year-old Oliver Switzer. He was the son of Conrad and Mary Rogers Switzer, immigrants from Switzerland. He and all his siblings settled in Baltimore except one brother, Thomas Switzer, who moved to Pennsylvania where he became a Methodist minister. The entire Switzer family, in fact, were devout Methodists. Margaretta and Oliver may have met through their church connections.

Oliver and Margaretta were married on October 25, 1845, by the Reverend Henry Slicer.[1] The Slicer name is prominent on another album quilt made in Baltimore in 1844–45, now in the collection of the Minneapolis Institute of Arts. Although visually different, both quilts are inscribed with religious poetry.[2] The names of Henry Slicer and members of his family also are pre-

69. Sampler, Margaretta Feyroved, 1835, Carlisle, Pennsylvania. (Courtesy of Mr. and Mrs. Z. Vance Hooper)

sent on a red friendship quilt made by or for the Cronmiller sisters of Baltimore (p. 111).

For the first seven years of Oliver and Margaretta's marriage, Oliver's mother, Mary Switzer, lived with the young couple in their home (built by Oliver) at the corner of Fayette and Eden streets. Mrs. Switzer was undoubtedly a help to Margaretta when her first child, Emma, was born in 1849. In 1852, just a few months prior to the birth of Margaretta's second baby, Mary Switzer died.

Oliver operated a family grocery store at Fayette and Central streets until his death in 1871. According to surviving family papers, during the hard times brought on by the Civil War, Oliver allowed his customers too much credit, which strained his own finances. Just before his death he had to close the store. In later years Emma Switzer remembered several

117

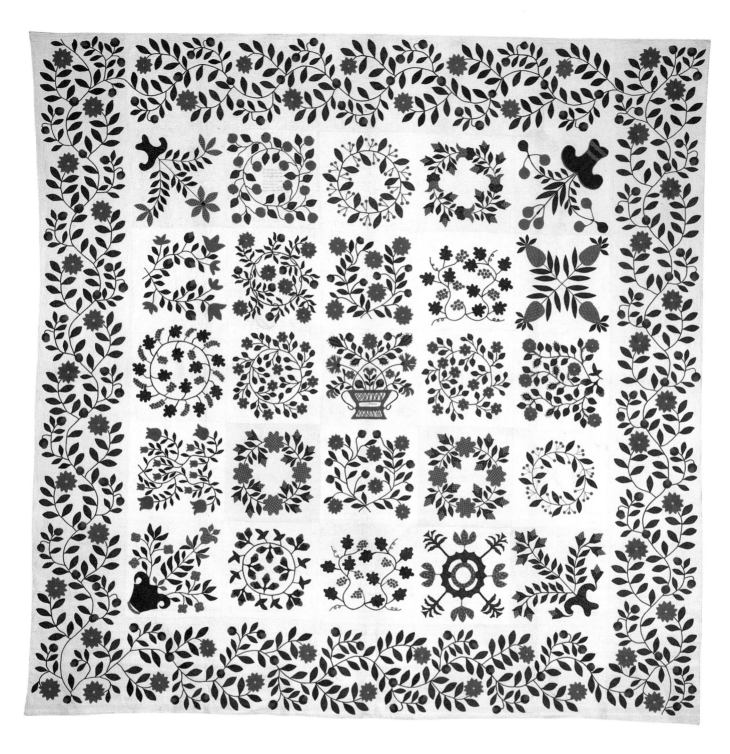

BALTIMORE ALBUM QUILT, 1845

*Made by Hannah F. Firoved (d. 1864) and her niece
Margaretta Firoved (1821–1916) in memory of David
Firoved (d. 1845)
Baltimore City
Cottons, wool, ink inscription
118 x 118 inches
Owned by Mr. and Mrs. Z. Vance Hooper*

PIECED QUILT, c. 1820, of cottons, probably made by a member of the Firoved family in Pennsylvania or Maryland. (Courtesy of Mr. and Mrs. Z. Vance Hooper)

sures 118 inches square. Each appliquéd block is a little more than sixteen inches square, and the border is a broad sixteen inches wide—the largest of any quilt seen. The light, airy effect in the design results from the use of a satin embroidery stitch for the stems and vines. Many hours of work went into making this quilt a tour de force.

Margaretta Switzer died at the age of ninety-five in February 1916. The quilt, in mint condition, has been lovingly handed down through the generations from mother to daughter (71).

1. In 1827, Henry Slicer married Elizabeth A. Roberts, sister of Dr. George C. M. Roberts, Angeline Hoffman's Sunday school teacher (p. 121) and recipient of an album quilt pictured in Dena Katzenberg's *Baltimore Album Quilts* (Baltimore: Baltimore Museum of Art, 1981), 94.
2. Ibid., 72. Katzenberg documents the relationship between Methodism and quiltmakers in mid-nineteenth-century Baltimore. This quilt represents another piece of that complicated puzzle.
3. Z. Vance Hooper, family papers.

events from her childhood. She recalled how frightened she was by the soldiers who came into her father's store. Once she and her mother were alone in the store when a soldier came in. He leaned his rifle against the wall and said, "That's my lady luck!"[3] She remembered being scared and impressed at the same time.

A tradition of quilting in the Firoved/Switzer family is evident by the large number of quilts, nine in all, that have survived. All are pieced except the album quilt. The earliest dates before 1820, but a Maryland provenance is not certain; Margaretta may have brought this quilt with her from Pennsylvania. Three other quilts date from the 1840s, including the album quilt. The remaining five were utilitarian quilts, made in the latter half of the

nineteenth century. A striking characteristic of all these quilts is the prominence of red fabric. Red was a popular color in the Firoved/Switzer household, as it appears in every quilt.

This album quilt, one of the largest documented in the Maryland Quilt Project, mea-

71. Left to right: Nellie Krout Culver, Margaretta F. Switzer, Margaretta Culver, and Martha Margaretta Switzer Krout. (Photograph courtesy of Mr. and Mrs. C. Vance Hooper)

119

Angie's Wedding Quilt

I'll remember my Angie
Whatever betide
I'll think of her often
though waters divide

March 20th/46

THE FRIENDS AND RELATIVES of twenty-four-year-old Angeline Hoffman made this quilt as a gift for her marriage to Lawrence M. Strong (1816–71) of Kent County. She must have announced their engagement sometime before March 18, the earliest dates inscribed on the quilt. The wedding ceremony took place December 21, 1846.

The makers of Angeline's quilt included Virginia Auld, a dressmaker; Emily Brunner, the young daughter of a bookseller and perhaps a relative; Ann Coats, a hair picker; and several other young women from the local Methodist church.[1] Some of the makers were from families living in working-class neighborhoods of Baltimore in 1846.

Angeline's quilt is made of twenty-five squares, sixteen to seventeen inches each in varying levels of needlework skills and techniques. Most of the designs are simple with a few exceptions. The lack of sashing or borders and the simple diamond quilting designs confirm the quilt's purpose as a ceremonial gift of friendship rather than a showpiece of a group of accomplished needleworkers. The center square, however, is an elaborate layered creation, one of those marked among the best quilt styles by later admirers (72). A classical-style wreath of green leaves and red berries surrounds a

brown bird carrying a floral branch in its beak, a square that was probably purchased by the quiltmakers from the Bavarian-born quilt designer Mary Simon. Mary Heidenroder Simon (b. 1810) was the wife of Philip Simon, a Bavarian-born carpet weaver. Mary arrived in Baltimore in 1844 and lived on Chestnut Street with her family, where she "cut and basted" quilt squares and sold them.[2] She was one of thousands of immigrants that arrived from strife-torn Europe in the first half of the nineteenth century. They followed an earlier wave of their countrymen emigrating in the 1730s and 1740s.

Mary Simon's elaborate and sophisticated designs are similar to the complex floral motifs seen on woven carpets popular with the middle class in mid-century Baltimore and elsewhere. The reds and greens, colors found most often on Simon's squares, were used frequently in carpets of the period. Philip Simon's woven designs, made in his shop-residence, undoubtedly influenced his wife's appliqué patterns. Another possible influence on Mary Simon's work was the colorful beaded bags made in Germany during this period and imported to the United States (73). These small bags are decorated with multicolor glass and metal beads in designs similar to the floral squares on album quilts.

Some of the other designs on Angeline's quilt reflect the Germanic folk tradition—the wreath of rings, the heart, and the abstract floral cutwork appliqué. The over-

73. BEADED BAG, 1820–50, possibly Germany, silk, glass beads. The designs on beaded bags echo the elaborate floral designs on many album squares. (Photograph courtesy of the DAR Museum, photographers, O'Brien and Bauer)

riding design influence, however, is classical: the urn, lyre, cornucopia, wreath with bird and bowknot, grapevine wreath, and floral sprays are all common classical motifs (74). Both design and literary influence of the early civilizations influenced western European countries, including the German provinces; thus, classical elements are evident in the Germanic design traditions brought to this country by immigrants such as the Simons.

Lawrence and Angeline were married by Methodist minister the Reverend Dr. Roberts and their marriage was announced four days later in the *Baltimore Sun*. The Reverend Dr. Roberts was George C. M. Roberts (1806–70), leader of Angeline's Sunday school class. The class, some of whose members signed Angeline's quilt, met at the home of R. G. Armstrong on Paca Street at 3 P.M. every Wednesday afternoon.[3]

The relationship between members of the Methodist church in Baltimore and Baltimore album quilts was thoroughly documented by Dena Katzenberg, the Baltimore Museum of Art consulting curator of textiles, in a 1981 exhibition and accompanying catalogue, *Baltimore Album Quilts*.[4] Katzenberg was one of the first to examine the relationship between the names on Baltimore album quilts and members of

72. Detail of square probably "cut and basted" by quilt designer Mary Simons of Baltimore.

BALTIMORE ALBUM QUILT, 1846–47

Made by the friends of Angeline Hoffman (1822–1907)
Baltimore City
Cottons, cotton and wool embroidery, cross-stitch, and
ink inscriptions
83.5 x 83.5 inches
Owned by Amelie W. Porter
(Photographer, Mark Gulezian)

74. Detail of appliquéd lyre on Angeline Hoffman's quilt. During the early nineteenth century it was desirable for cultured women to excel at a musical instrument. Rosalie Stier Calvert of Maryland wrote in 1806, "Music is an indispensible talent for a young lady." Two popular instruments, the pianoforte and the harp, were played by women in the nineteenth century during musical evenings in the home. These evenings were important aspects of the social life of these proper American women. The lyre shape is found on many furnishings during this period, and the classical lyre on Angeline's quilt may represent the importance of music in her life.

Methodist congregations in Baltimore.[5] Katzenberg's catalogue presents several quilts with squares almost certainly designed by Mary Simon and shows a quilt containing blocks similar to those in Angeline's quilt. The quilt pictured there was made for the Reverend Dr. C. M. Roberts in 1847 and 1848 by the members of his Sunday school classes. Katzenberg writes, "Reverend Dr. Roberts received his medical degree in 1826 and entered medical practice in 1829, eventually becoming professor of obstetrics at Washington Medical College. Concurrently,

he served as a trustee of the Methodist Church as well as a traveling minister and was closely associated with the Light Street Church . . . " She goes on to say, "He preached frequently at the Light Street, Eutaw Street, Wesley Chapel, Exeter Street, Monument Street, Columbia Street, High Street, Harford Avenue, and Charles Street churches." The *Baltimore American*, describing Dr. Roberts's funeral in 1870, noted that 2,000 people crowded into Charles Street Church for the service with another 2,000 outside.[6]

By the time Dr. Roberts's quilt was made, Angeline had married and moved to Kent County across the Chesapeake Bay ("the waters divide" from the quilt's inscription) to start housekeeping on Strong family land. Lawrence is listed in the 1850 federal census as a farmer owning real estate valued at $2,000. By then, he and Angeline had two sons, one and two years old. Two years later, the oldest boy died. When the census taker came again in 1860, Lawerence and Angeline had four more children, three boys and five-month-old Florence. From 1846 to 1862, Lawrence and Angeline had a total of ten children, half of whom survived to adulthood.

Lawrence died in July 1871, leaving Angeline with four children at home—an estate valued at $5,134.28. The sale of his personal property included: two bedsteads, five mattresses, six feather beds, six pairs of muslin sheets, pillowcases and bolsters. Two bed quilts were also listed plus three comforts and one Marsails [sic] bedcover.[7]

Angeline survived Lawrence by thirty-six years, dying at the age of eighty-five in 1907. Both Lawrence and Angeline are buried in the Strong family cemetery in Kent County.

The present owner purchased the quilt from a dealer in 1988, who had purchased it at auction in Washington, DC, in 1986. A Kent County antiques dealer had consigned it to auction, having purchased it from the estate of Lawrence and Angeline Hoffman Strong's granddaughter.

1. Ann Coats was one of the many women who worked in the hair industry in Baltimore in the nineteenth century. The industry was established in 1836 and by 1850 there were eleven bristle, ten brush, and five hair mattress manufacturers located in or around the city.
2. For more information on Mary Simon, see Jennifer Goldsborough, *Lavish Legacies: Baltimore Album and Related Quilts in the Collection of the Maryland Historical Society* (Baltimore, MD: Maryland Historical Society, 1994), 16–23.
3. Rev. John Miley, A.M., *Treatise on Class Meetings* (Cincinnati: Methodist Book Concern, 1851), 52. Miley writes about the purpose of class meetings, "Strict inquiry is also made into the religious habits of each member; into the manner of life which each pursues; whether he avoids that which is evil and practices that which is good."
4. Dena S. Katzenberg, *Baltimore Album Quilts* (Baltimore, MD: Baltimore Museum of Art, 1981).
5. William Rush Dunton Jr. published photographs and family histories of many Baltimore and Maryland album quilts in his book, *Old Quilts*. Among those with church connections were several relating to Methodist churches in Baltimore.
6. Katzenberg, *Baltimore Album Quilts*, 94–95. Dr. Roberts's quilt is in the collection of the United Methodist Historical Society, Lovely Lane Museum, Baltimore.
7. *Kent County Sales of Personal Properties, 1872.* All genealogical research was provided by the owner.

Exotic Album Quilt

THIS FORMIDABLE ALBUM quilt has some remarkable features not found on other album quilts recorded by the MAFCE project. It is one of only two album quilts (56) documented that is decorated with a human figure—a silk-clad woman riding a white horse sidesaddle—and only one of two with appliquéd animals[1] (75). The sophisticated design and fine workmanship reveal the skill of an experienced designer and/or needlewoman.

The designs in each of the eighteen-inch squares are perfectly balanced in terms of color and composition, with the laid areas covering most of each square. The squares appear "heavy" compared to those in many other album quilts of the period. The designer may have tried to offset the weight of the squares by separating them with three wide, dark green and white strips of cotton. Unexpectedly, the quilt is delicately bound with a tiny red cotton tape. Although the name of the maker of this album quilt is lost, some of its provenance was preserved. The quilt descended in a Baltimore family until recently, when the present owner acquired it.

Recent research has led to a group of similar bedcovers.[2] A

75. The nineteenth-century woman sits sidesaddle on a white cotton horse with a silk embroidered mane and tail. Her bodice and bonnet are made of brown silk and her skirt of dark-blue silk damask.

quilt in a private collection resembles this one in several aspects: the sashing is red rather than green but the figures are almost exactly the same. The source for these two exotic-looking motifs may be found in a book published in 1848 by John Frost, titled *A Pictorial History of Mexico and the Mexican War*.[3] Maryland soldiers were involved in some of the heaviest fighting in the Mexican War and local newspapers covered the conflict well. Another possible inspiration for these designs may have come from an unlikely source—jousting. It was popular in Maryland during the 1840s and eventually became the official sport of the state in 1962. Maryland historian Robert Brugger found that, "the sport of jousting—galloping on horseback in medieval costume and spearing rings—gained popularity in this romantic period [in Maryland] and often included a ceremony crowning a queen at the post-tournament ball."[4] The horse as the central focus of this quilt is in keeping with the importance of the horse to the sport of jousting. The woman atop the horse may represent the tournament queen.

William Rush Dunton Jr. illustrates three similar quilts in his book, *Old Quilts*, one of which is now in the collection of the Maryland Historical Society.[5] It was made by Rachel Meyer (1818–67) around 1850. The

designs are fundamentally the same as the quilt shown here and they are worked in the same techniques.[6] The figures on the Meyer quilt are similar to those illustrated in *A Pictorial History of Mexico and the Mexican War* by John Frost, published in 1848.[7]

The other two quilts pictured in Dunton's book were made as a pair. They were purchased by the late Mrs. Frederic Leiter, a prominent Maryland collector who scoured country auctions for more than half a century searching for the unusual and the best in American decorative arts. Like most collectors then and today, the history of an object was not her primary interest; thus, most of her quilts have no attributions.[8]

Two other quilts have been linked to this group. An album quilt made about 1850 by Mrs. Joshua Goodman, now in the collection of the Maryland Historical Society, is stylistically the most outstanding of the entire group of exotic album quilts.[9] Appliquéd with wools and tweeds and boldly embroidered in wool yarn, the designs are whimsical birds, bugs, dogs, horses, flying insects, peacocks, and an elephant. A quilt similar to the Goodman quilt is pictured in an article by textile curator Julie Silber in the 1983 inaugural volume of *The Quilt Digest*.[10] Silber attributes this quilt, decorated with whimsical figures similar to those on the Goodman quilt, to two Jewish women: Katie Friedman Reiter and her mother, Liebe Friedman of McKeesport, Pennsylvania. All of these exotic quilts are evidence of talented quilt designers at work in Maryland and environs during the middle years of the nineteenth century.

1. Other figurative quilts documented by MAFCE are the Garden of Eden (p. 171), a Crazy quilt (p. 16), and an Irish Chain quilt where the silhouette of a Victorian bride is worked into the quilting. The Woodbourne Quilt and Mary Waters's quilt (pp. 143–44) also incorporate human and animal figures into the quilting

ALBUM QUILT, c. 1850

Maker unknown
Probably Baltimore
Cotton, silk, wool
84 x 83 inches
Owned by Dr. and Mrs. Richard Palmer

designs. The other album quilt decorated with animals and birds is Mary Brown's quilt (p. 131).

2. Jennifer Faulds Goldsborough, *Lavish Legacies: Baltimore Album and Related Quilts in the Collection of the Maryland Historical Society* (Baltimore: Maryland Historical Society, 1994), 82–87. Goldsborough has identified about ten similar quilts and attributes them to a specific although unknown designer: "designer #III." The authors thank her for sharing her research on this group of extraordinary quilts.

3. John Frost, *A Pictorial History of Mexico and the Mexican War* (Philadelphia: n.p., 1848). The authors are grateful to Jennifer Goldsborough for bringing this book to their attention.

4. Robert J. Brugger, *Maryland: A Middle Temperament, 1634–1980* (Baltimore: Johns Hopkins University Press, 1988), 249.

5. William Rush Dunton Jr., *Old Quilts* (Catonsville, MD: n.p., 1946), plates 33, 63, and 64.

6. Goldsborough, *Lavish Legacies*, 82.

7. Frost, *A Pictorial History of Mexico and the Mexican War*, 1848.

8. Further research is underway on Mrs. Frederic Leiter by Nancy Gibson Tuckhorn for future publication.

9. Goldsborough, *Lavish Legacies*, 84.

76. *Detail of album quilt decorated with a silk embroidered vase flanked by two reindeer. Reindeer were popular design elements on a group of album quilts made in the exotic style.*

10. Julie Silber, "The Reiter Quilt: A Family Story in Cloth," *The Quilt Digest* (1983), 50–55. Acknowledging the significance of the fact that this quilt was made by two Jewish women, Silber notes, "In a limited sampling, I found no other Jews whose European-born ancestors had made quilts." She goes on to state: "Since quiltmaking is generally regarded as an American form, most European-born women learned the skill here. Yet Jews tend to congregate in large cities, associating almost exclusively with other Jews. For most, quiltmaking was an invisible alien craft." The MAFCE project documented no quilts described as having been made by Jewish women or men. Jewish girls were known to have made samplers in the nineteenth century that were indistinguishable from those made by non-Jewish girls.

Carroll County Album Quilt

THE ORIGINAL PURPOSE OF this appliquéd album quilt is long forgotten, but its beauty is as evident now as the day it was made. The overall design and color scheme show harmony and balance. Except for the delicate chintz appliqué square in the top row and the sophisticated floral nosegay in the second row, the squares all seem to be made by the same person or in the same style.

According to family history the quilt was made by or for Mary McIlhenny Shower in the 1850s. Mary McIlhenny was the daughter of Robert McIlhenny of Adams County, Pennsylvania. Only the Mason-Dixon line separates Adams County from Carroll County; Manchester lies about ten miles

77. George A. Shower, seated, and his sons, George and Robert. This photograph taken sometime in the 1880s is shown on a red and green album quilt made by Mary M. Shower. (Courtesy of Mrs. George Shower)

from the border. As this history shows, many families frequently moved across these political boundaries.

The McIlhenny quilt is similar to another quilt made in Manchester in the collection of the DAR Museum. This album quilt dated about 1858, is attributed to Cornelia Everhart Wissler (1836–1921) and was made for her marriage (78). It contains a square virtually identical to the small cornucopia holding a large spray of flowers in the McIlhenny quilt.[1] Both of these quilts are made of sixteen blocks, each eighteen inches square. Sashing is not used to separate the squares in either quilt. The date of 1858 attributed to the DAR Museum quilt is late for album quilts of this type. The relationship of the two quilts and the family was close; the Shower and Everhart families intermarried in several generations. Cornelia and Mary probably were born the same year, lived most of their lives in Manchester, attended Manchester Academy, and died within three years of each other; therefore,

ALBUM QUILT WITH SWAG AND BOWKNOT BORDER, mid-nineteenth century

Possibly made by or for Mary McIlhenny Shower (1836–1918)
Manchester, Carroll County
Cottons
103 x 102 inches
Owned by Mrs. George Shower

the two quilts may be evidence of their friendship.

The floral nosegay square probably was purchased by the maker or makers from quilt designer Mary Simon of Baltimore.[2] This square is almost identical to several others in quilts made in Baltimore. The nosegay appears in the spectacular quilt given to Elizabeth Sliver in 1849, and in an album quilt made for the Methodist church class leader George Holtzman from 1847 to 1849.[3] Manchester, the quiltmakers' hometown, was located on the Reisterstown turnpike. Women there had direct and easy access to goods available in Baltimore and often trav-

1. Gloria Seaman Allen, *Old Line Traditions: Maryland Women and Their Quilts* (Washington, DC: DAR Museum, 1985), 19.
2. For more information about Mary Simon, see p. 120.
3. Dena S. Katzenberg, *Baltimore Album Quilts* (Baltimore: Baltimore Museum of Art, 1981), plates 13, 18, and 19; and Amelia Peck, *American Quilts and Coverlets in the Metropolitan Museum of Art* (New York: Metropolitan Museum of Art and Dutton Studio Books, 1990), 50.
4. Cecelia M. Shower, *A Sketch of the Early Days of Manchester*, unpublished family papers. The authors thank Mrs. George Shower for sharing these papers with them.
5. O. T. Everhart, *History of the Everhart and Shower Families, From 1744 to 1883* (Hanover, PA: O. T. Everhart, 1883), 120.
6. Ibid., 120–22.
7. Shower, *A Sketch of the Early Days of Manchester*, n.p.

written memoirs of Manchester and Carroll County are rich with the small details not often found in official histories: stories from "old family papers and hearing my father and grandfather talk about the early life in the community."[7] Cecelia died at age 100. Having never married, she left many of her possessions to her nephew, George Shower.

78. ALBUM QUILT, c. 1858, made by Cornelia Everhart Wissler, Manchester, Carroll County, DAR Museum, gift courtesy of Kate Wissler Leatherman. (Photograph courtesy of the DAR Museum, photographer, Mark Gulezian)

eled back and forth themselves. Cecelia Shower, daughter of Mary McIlhenny and George Shower, recalls hearing her father and grandfather talk about the "big conestoga wagons that passed over the turnpike going from Baltimore to Pittsburg."[4] This quilt shows that Mary Simon's quilt reputation and quilt squares were spreading to adjacent counties and towns.

Mary McIlhenny married George Shower in 1863, and their courtship must have been an unusual one, in that George was in prison for most of the year prior to their marriage. George, an ardent Southern sympathizer, was arrested by the Federal government in May 1863 on a charge of disloyalty. After a hearing in Westminster, he was committed to the county jail, then sent to a military prison in Baltimore. Tried by a military court, he was sentenced to be sent "behind the lines."[5] George was sent back to prison but released by December of 1863, the month he married Mary McIlhenny. He obviously did not lose standing in the community, for in 1865 he became postmaster of Manchester. In 1868 he was elected school commissioner of Carroll County, as a Democrat. In 1870 he was elected to the General Assembly of Maryland, and in 1878 he was sergeant-at-arms of the Maryland Senate. He served as a census enumerator in 1880 and deputy sheriff of Carroll County in 1882 (77).[6]

George and Mary Shower had three children. The eldest, Cecelia (1865–1966), who taught school in Carroll County for fifty-eight years, inherited the quilt (79). Her

79. From top to bottom: Cecelia M. Shower, quiltmaker Mary McIlhenny Shower, and friends, photograph taken at the Shower home in Manchester. Photographs are shown on a red and green appliquéd quilt made by Mary. (Courtesy of Mrs. George Shower)

Mary Caroline's Wedding Quilt

FAMILY HISTORY RECORDS that this Baltimore album quilt was made to celebrate the betrothal of Mary Caroline Pattison to Robinson Wesley Cator (1826–1902) in December 1849 (80). Only two inscriptions decorate the quilt, those of an unidentified woman, "Mary C. Haslup Feb 1849," and the initials of Annie Spillman, Mary Pattison's married sister.[1] Like the quilt presented to Angeline Hoffman in 1846, the inscriptions were stitched months prior to the couple's marriage (p. 121). Perhaps the squares were made soon after the engagement was announced, then assembled and quilted in the months leading up to the wedding.

Twenty-five squares, each sixteen inches, with a nine-inch border in a stepped-pyramid design, make up Mary Caroline's quilt. All the squares are classically derived in design but very primitive in execution.[2] Seven squares contain flower baskets and one features a lyre. The most unusual and original block (second from the left on the third row) is an abstract design that resembles a flower pot, a lyre, or two cornucopiae with a flower growing from the point where the lines meet. In the center of this unusual square is the red cross-stitched signature and the date. The appliquéd stepped-pyramid border is a classical motif seen on decorative objects from antiquity to the pre-

sent day. Its popularity with middle-class quiltmakers at mid-century is explained by the acceptance of classical designs by a society eager to be instructed in matters of taste and refinement. Quiltmakers of the period looked well beyond their local communities for inspiration.

Mary Caroline Pattison is not mentioned in Methodist class lists, as other album quiltmakers are, but other members of the Pattison family are recorded. Her fiancé, Robinson Wesley Cator, came from a devout Episcopalian family. Mary Caroline probably transferred her ties to the Protestant Episcopal Church when they married. Robinson Cator grew up on the family farm in Dorchester County on Taylor's Island, a large island in the Chesapeake Bay, and moved to Baltimore in 1841 at age fifteen. Both the Pattison and Cator families had strong connections to Dorchester County, especially Taylor's Island, and probably met there. Mary Caroline was the daughter of Nancy LeCompte Hooper and Jerimiah L. Pattison (d. 1814) of Dorchester County. It is apparent that quiltmaking was an established tradition in the Cator/LeCompte/Pattison families; two more album quilts are associated with the Dorchester branch of the LeCompte family, and a chintz quilt, circa 1820, made by Ann B. Cator of Taylor's Island, is in the collection of the Maryland Historical Society.[3]

Robinson Cator had a distinguished career in the mercantile firm Armstrong, Cator and Company of Baltimore. The firm was the oldest commercial house in Baltimore and by 1856 the largest millinery jobbing business of its kind in the country. By 1873 the firm had expanded into white goods, laces, embroideries, piece white goods, and ladies' fancy and staple neckwear. A contemporary historian deemed Robinson Cator "the dominant spirit of the business for more than half a century." Cator was a member of the Baltimore Board of Trade, organizer of the Merchant's and Manufacturers Association, and a director of the Merchant's Bank of the Eutaw Savings Bank.[4]

80. *Mary Caroline Hooper Pattison (1830–99).* *(Photograph courtesy of Jeanne P. Dobson)*

Robinson and Mary Caroline raised eleven children, some of whom went on to distinguish themselves in the family business. The Cator family summered on Taylor's Island, maintaining ties with their extended family. Both Robinson and Mary Caroline are buried on Taylor's Island. The quilt descended in the family through the eldest daughters.

1. Members of the Haslup family are primarily located in two counties of Maryland in the 1850 federal census: Anne Arundel and Baltimore counties. The name Mary C. Haslup is not found in either county.
2. MAFCE used a square (second row, second from right) from this quilt as part of its documentation logo. Much appreciation goes to Cindy Edinberg, graphic artist and quilt show chairman, for designing the logo for this project.
3. Jennifer Faulds Goldsborough, *Lavish Legacies: Baltimore Albums and Related Quilts in the Collection of the Maryland Historical Society* (Baltimore: Maryland Historical Society, 1994), 56. Dena Katzenberg, *Baltimore Album Quilts* (Baltimore, MD: Baltimore Museum of Art, 1981), 78. See also William Rush Dunton Jr., *Old Quilts* (Catonsville, MD: n.p., 1946), 55, for an early album quilt with the name "Deliah LeCompte/Aged 65/Septem. 27, 1842."
4. Clayton Hall, *History of Baltimore*, vol. 3 (New York: Lewis Historical Publishing, 1912), 675–78.

BALTIMORE ALBUM QUILT, 1849

Made for Mary Caroline Pattison (1830–99)
Baltimore City
Cotton, silk embroidery, cross-stitched inscriptions
103 x 103 inches
Owned by Jeanne P. Dobson

Mary Brown's Quilt

ONE OF THE MOST VIsually exciting quilts located by the Maryland project, and documented on the Eastern Shore in Cecil County, has the unusual feature of a framed central diamond design surrounded by two borders of album blocks; the inner border has figurative and floral blocks, the outer border has more geometric blocks.[1] Many of the appliquéd areas are inlaid or worked in reverse appliqué. The sophisticated style of this quilt—as well as the pictorial appliqué, the wide selection of printed fabrics, and the elaborate quilting—suggests a Baltimore origin. Conveniently for the researcher, the quiltmaker took pride in her accomplishment and signed her work (81). In the center of the quilt to the right of the parrot she worked in cross stitches:

Mary Brown
Made in the 75th year of her
age 1851

In one corner she stitched the initials "I.R." and in another corner "I.R.1852."

Mary B. Brown, daughter of Jesse and Rebecca Brown, probably grew up in Cecil County, but she may have spent several years residing in Baltimore City.[2] During her later years she lived with a younger brother, or nephew, in the East Nottingham area of Cecil County. The 1850 census recorded Mary living with Lydia and Daniel Brown and their young daughter, Anna Mary. The child died

within the year, the second of the Brown's children to die in infancy. In 1860, Mary still was living with the childless Brown family, who in the intervening years had lost a third child. At age eighty-three Mary gave her occupation to the census taker as dressmaker. The Browns, like many of their neighbors in northern Cecil County, were Quakers and attended services at the East Nottingham or, as it was usually called, the Brick Meeting House (84). The family, including Daniel, Lydia, their three children, and Mary, is interred in the old part of the meetinghouse cemetery. A few graves away are the remains of Israel and Elizabeth Mearns Reynolds (1822–68).

Close in death, the Reynoldses and Browns also were close in life: they attended the same Quaker meeting, and they evidently shared the same love of nature. Mary Brown made her appliquéd quilt, with its array of flowers, fruit, leaves, birds, and animals, for Israel Reynolds between 1851 and 1852. Israel probably commissioned the quilt and paid Mary for her work. According to family memory, the quilt was made to order by a local seamstress who studied

81. Detail of center of Mary Brown's quilt showing areas of inlaid fabric. (Photograph courtesy of ESPRIT Quilt Collection, San Francisco, photographer, Sharon Risedorph)

nature and transformed the shapes she saw into cloth.

Members of the Reynolds family were also longtime residents of rural Cecil County and part of an extended Quaker kinship network that encompassed Cecil County, Maryland, and Chester County, Pennsylvania. In 1850 the household included their four children, Israel's mother, a farmhand, and two servants. By 1860, three more children had been born to Elizabeth and Israel, whose farm was prospering. Their third oldest daughter, Harriet, was ten at the time; she would eventually inherit her father's quilt.

The Reynolds quilt is interesting not only for its visual appeal but also for its connection to several other bedcovers. A granddaughter of Harriet Reynolds Ewing was the last family owner of the quilt. She recalls seeing at a cousin's home in Chester County five or six appliquéd quilt squares identical to those on the Reynolds quilt. These squares, presumably made by Mary Brown because of design similarity, were donated to a local hospital group whose members assembled them into a small quilt and sold it to benefit the hospital.[3]

An album quilt that was published in the *Quilt Engagement Calendar* in 1981 and attributed as "possibly Pennsylvania, ca. 1845," has more than a dozen squares identical to squares on the Brown/Reynolds quilt.[4] Quite possibly, Mary Brown made this quilt in its entirety or, at least, contributed the more intricate figural blocks. The quilt, which has four larger album blocks in the center surrounded by three rows of smaller album blocks, lacks the design sophistication of the Brown/Reynolds quilt. Geometric and pictorial blocks are interspersed, rather than confined to separate borders, and the four central blocks are not large enough to provide a focus. There are no inscriptions on this quilt and no evidence of inlaid work.

Two blocks on the above album quilt—an appliquéd owl surrounded by branches and a

APPLIQUÉD QUILT, 1851–52

Made by Mary B. Brown (1777–1861) for Israel
Reynolds (1809–91)
East Nottingham, Cecil County
Cottons, cross-stitched inscriptions
101 x 102 inches
Owned by the ESPRIT Quilt Collection, San Francisco
(Photograph courtesy of ESPRIT Quilt Collection,
photographer, Sharon Risedorph, San Francisco)

pieced Seven Sisters or seven-star block—do not appear on the Brown/Reynolds quilt but do appear on an album quilt signed by Martha and Adaline Pierson of East Nottingham in 1847 and 1848.[5] Other blocks, reflecting different skill levels, contain additional signatures. This album quilt, sold at the same Christie's auction as the Brown/Reynolds quilt but by a different consignor, came from Mary Brown's East Nottingham community and, in part, may reflect her work.

A counterpane in the collection of the Shelburne Museum also bears a resemblance to the Brown/Reynolds quilt.[6] This bedcover is inscribed in cross-stitch, "Mary Jane Carr's Quilt Completed in 1854." Mary Jane Carr lived in Lancaster County, Pennsylvania. No kinship connection between the Carrs and Reynoldses has been established, but the bedcovers share many design features. Both are composed with a central diamond format, and both have a flat decorative appearance with sharply defined dark leaves and brightly colored flowers. Many similar motifs enliven both quilts; the exotic birds on branches, the squirrels, and the dogs all suggest a common design source.

The above examples imply that Mary Brown, a seamstress by profession, may have designed a number of quilts and sold basted or completed squares that quiltmakers could incorporate into album quilts. It is possible that Mary Brown worked in much the same

82. Detail showing the parrot and squirrel blocks in the inner border. These motifs are reversed and combined on the c. 1845 album quilt, published in The Quilt Engagement Calendar 1981; they are separate motifs on the Shelburne Museum counterpane. (Photograph courtesy of ESPRIT Quilt Collection, San Francisco, photographer, Sharon Risedorph)

way as Mary Simon, who designed and basted the elaborate squares found on a number of Baltimore album quilts.[7]

An additional bedcover is related to the Reynolds quilt by family association, rather than by design. A forty-nine-block friendship quilt presented to twenty-two-year-old Mary L. Mearns in 1853 contains the names of Israel and Elizabeth Reynolds and five of their children.[8] Elizabeth, who was Mary Mearns's older sister, inscribed her name and "When this you see/ Remember Me/ March 5 1853" in a block placed to the right of her sister's central block. The blocks of three other Mearns sisters are in the same horizontal row, whereas the blocks of Mary's two deceased sisters and father are placed above,

below, and catty-corner to her block. Israel Reynolds's block, to the upper left of Mary's block, corresponds to Mary's mother's block placed to the upper right. Israel's block was given unusual status in that it is the only block not belonging to a member of the immediate Mearns family placed within the central nine blocks. Alternating floral bouquets and crossed bell flowers, cut from small-figured red, green, and yellow prints, resemble the flat decorative appliqué style of Mary Brown, who possibly took responsibility for the design and assembly of this quilt—although her name is not inscribed on it.

When the Israel Reynolds quilt was auctioned at Christie's in 1991, the cataloguer enthusiastically described Mary Brown's proficiency as a quiltmaker.[9] "The intricacy of the appliqué work, the composition, and the bold graphic nature of this piece rival the very finest work achieved in Baltimore at this time."[10] The authors of A Maryland Album concur.[11]

83. Detail showing a block with a dog barking at birds in a tree, flanked by two sunflower blocks. A condensed and reversed version of the dog and bird block is in the outer border of the c. 1845 album quilt; a sunflower block is in the inner border of the same quilt. Similar dogs, with raised heads and tails, are appliquéd to the Shelburne counterpane. (Photograph courtesy of ESPRIT Quilt Collection, San Francisco, photographer, Sharon Risedorph)

1. A Baltimore album quilt top, c. 1845, in the collection of the Maryland Historical Society, has a large central motif surrounded by album blocks. It bears a resemblance to Mary Brown's quilt but does not appear to be her work. See Jennifer Faulds Goldsborough, *Lavish Legacies: Baltimore Album and Related Quilts in the Collection of the Maryland Historical Society* (Baltimore: Maryland Historical Society, 1994), Catalogue no. 22.

Another quilt, in the Smithsonian's collection, has a similar central diamond motif with album blocks in the four corners. Somewhat coincidentally, as Mary Brown was a professional seamstress, this quilt is referred to by Doris Bowman of the National Museum of American History as the "Seamstresses' Quilt." It is thought to have been made by two seamstresses residing with the Slothower family of Baltimore. Doris M. Bowman, *The Smithsonian Treasury: American Quilts* (Washington, DC: Smithsonian Institution Press, 1991), 49.

2. Brown is a Cecil County name and can be traced back to William Penn's Nottingham Lots. The 1783 *Tax List* for Cecil County records a Jesse Brown living on 150 acres in the East Nottingham township. His household contained eight white inhabitants and probably included Mary Brown. The names "Jesse" and "Rebecca Brown" also can be found in Baltimore City tax records for the early 1800s, so it is possible that Mary spent those years in Baltimore.

3. The former owner of the Brown/Reynolds quilt has kindly shared this information with us. The present location of the quilt is unknown.

4. Cyril I. Nelson, comp., *The Quilt Engagement Calendar 1981* (New York: Viking Studio Books, 1981), fig. 1. We are grateful to Julie Silber, of the Quilt Complex, for bringing this quilt to our attention.

5. Julie Silber also has brought this quilt to our attention. Christie's auction, January 26, 1991,

no. 160. The 1850 federal census for Cecil County lists twenty-two-year-old Martha and ten-year-old Adaline as the daughters of Joseph and Ruth Pierson.

6. Celia Oliver, "Electra Havemeyer Webb and Shelburne's Quilt Collection" in *On the Cutting Edge: Textile Collectors, Collections, and Traditions*, edited by Jeannette Lasansky (Lewisberg, PA: Oral Traditions Project, 1994), 4.

7. The quilts cited are known to the authors only through photographs. A comparative study of the artifacts would reveal similarities and differences in materials and techniques.

8. This quilt was not documented by MAFCE. It is privately owned and was brought to the attention of the DAR Museum in 1991.

9. The former owner of the Brown/Reynolds quilt has shared with us her reasons for sending

84. Brick meeting house as it looks today. (Photograph courtesy of Gloria Seaman Allen)

her family heirloom to auction: she hoped her quilt would find its way to a safe environment where it would be professionally cared for yet made available for others to enjoy and study. Having been hidden away in a storage box, the quilt was seen only on special occasions by members of her family.

10. Christie's auction, January 26, 1991, no. 196.

11. The former owner related to us that the Brown/Reynolds quilt was not always highly valued. Several years ago it was displayed at a county fair where it failed to receive even honorable mention; it was said to be too elaborate!

Wreath of Roses Quilt

HEN MARY JANE WARE-ham made her album quilt, she varied the design from those of her contemporaries by choosing to appliqué each square in a variety of rose wreaths, plus one tulip wreath, including a different floral or bird decoration in the center of each square. She cleverly bordered each block with thin red cotton piping, a method of separating the squares by piping that is found on at least one other album quilt top made in Montgomery County in 1849.[1] The three-dimensional roses decorating some of the squares are formed by gathering the fabric together and sewing it in place, a method called "ruching."[2]

A similar rose wreath quilt is in the collection of the DAR Museum. All of its roses are ruched. It also was made in Howard County, Maryland. Dated 1860, it may have taken its inspiration from this earlier album quilt (85).

86. *The Talbott Lumber Company as it appears today in Ellicott City. (Photograph courtesy of Martha Clark Crist)*

Mary Jane Wareham was born on the Eastern Shore in Talbot County. She married Edward Alexander Talbott (1818–90) of Anne Arundel County in 1841 and moved to Ellicott's Mills, Howard County. Edward was listed as a blacksmith by the federal census taker in 1850 and was probably in partnership with John N. Clark, one of two blacksmiths residing in the Talbott household. Many years later, John Clark's son, John Lawrence Clark, married Mary Jane's youngest daughter, Mary (1855–1918). But by 1850 only four children had been born to the couple.[3]

Edward Talbott was the sixth generation of Talbotts to own Talbott's Last Shift, the original Talbott family estate located in Anne Arundel County and first surveyed in 1732. He possessed title from 1848 to 1850. According to family tradition he wished to pursue a career of his own making; thus he and his wife moved to Howard County and settled in the mill town, Ellicott's Mills, known today as Ellicott City. Edward and his wife operated a store, selling products such as

85. WREATH OF ROSES QUILT, 1860, made by the Sheetz sisters for Winfield Augusta Sheetz Robb, Cooksville, Howard County. The roses in eight-year-old Winfield Robb's quilt are entirely worked by ruching. (DAR Museum, Friends of the Museum Purchase, photographer, Mark Gulezian)

lumber, building supplies, and tools. The store was called E. A. Talbott and it continued to be operated by descendants of the family until 1945 (86). Edward and Mary Jane were buried in Oella cemetery in Ellicott City. The quilt was bequeathed to the present owner in 1979 by her great-aunt, a granddaughter of the maker.

1. Jennifer Faulds Goldsborough, *Lavish Legacies: Baltimore Album and Related Quilts in the Collection of the Maryland Historical Society* (Baltimore: Maryland Historical Society, 1994), 64.
2. The earliest reference to "ruching" known to the authors is in an 1827 trade dictionary.
3. Federal census for Maryland, 1850, Howard County.

WREATH OF ROSES ALBUM QUILT, c. 1850

Made by Mary Jane Wareham Talbott (1820–83)
Ellicott's Mills, Howard County
Cottons, wool, silk
102 x 102 inches
Owned by Martha Clark Crist

Somerset County Album Quilt

ALBUM QUILTS MADE ON Maryland's Eastern Shore are uncommon, and those that do appear usually were made after the fad for such quiltmaking had subsided. Although Mary Berry lived all her life on the Eastern Shore, her husband, George H. Berry

87. Mary Berry and Dr. George Berry with their granddaughter, Mary E. Long. Standing to the right in the background is grandson, Edwin Ralph Long. (Photograph courtesy of Barbara Ann Carter and Harry Brown)

(1824–1909), was born in Baltimore (87). George Berry graduated from the University of Maryland School of Medicine in 1844. He began his practice on the Eastern Shore at Tangier Island, moving to Smith Island after several years, then settling permanently in Hopewell, where he specialized in obstetrics. His reasons for choosing this area to practice are unknown. He married Mary Ann Travis Coulbourne, the daughter of Isaac and Leah Coulbourne around 1855. She was born to a distinguished family whose forefathers were among the original settlers of Somerset County in the seventeenth century. Her ancestor, Col. William Coulbourne, bought property near Coulbourne's Creek, which was named for him; he held the original land grant for Pomfret, a 1,400-acre estate.[1]

Mary and George Berry had eleven children and lived close to the church they attended, St. Peter's Methodist Church in Hopewell. Descendants of the family, some living on the original Berry land, have been active in this church for more than 150 years and are buried in its cemetery. The quilt was passed on to George and Mary's daughter Edith, from granddaughter to granddaughter thereafter.[2]

Family tradition maintains that Mary made this album quilt while pregnant with daughter Edith in 1869, more than twenty years after the fashion for such quilts had passed. Although it is possible that this oral tradition is accurate, a more likely story is that it was made for the couple's marriage in 1855. The fabrics and style of the quilt place it with other 1850s album quilts. A similar quilt was made for another Somerset County woman—Sallie Coulbourne (1817–85)—in 1859. Now in the collection of the Newark Museum, this quilt is inscribed, "Sallie Coulbourne/Pomfret Md./ March, 16 1859 and Carrie Briggs/Melrose/ 1859."[3] Mary Coulbourne Berry and Sallie

Coulbourne, probably cousins and only eight years apart in age, both lived in the vicinity of Hopewell. Sallie Coulbourne also was a member of St. Peter's Methodist Church.

The Coulbourne and Berry quilts differ in some design and construction features. Sallie's quilt combines the block and medallion format, while Mary's is made of blocks only. The Coulbourne quilt uses a buttonhole stitch to fasten down the appliquéd areas and includes more wool-embroidered embellishments in the blocks and on the rose vine border. The similarities between the two quilts, however, are unmistakable: the same colors and fabrics appear on both, various appliquéd designs in the squares and on the border are almost identical, the techniques of layering some of the flowers is identical, and the quilting patterns are both geometric. These two quilts represent the enduring nature of friendship over many years and the strength of female community and social networks that existed in nineteenth-century American life.

1. Woodrow T. Wilson, *Thirty-Four Families of Old Somerset County, Maryland* (Crisfield, MD: n.p., 1974), 169.
2. Another interesting object also has been passed through generations of the Berry family: Dr. George Berry's large unopened safe, whose combination is long lost and contents remain a mystery. In 1994, it was inherited by yet another generation of curious descendants!
3. See Gloria Seaman Allen, *Old Line Traditions: Maryland Women and Their Quilts* (Washington, DC: DAR Museum, 1985), 23. West Virginia-born Carrie Briggs (d. 1877) was Sallie Coulbourne's sister-in-law. She taught school in Marion, a small community in the vicinity of the Pomfret plantation.

APPLIQUÉD ALBUM QUILT, c. 1860

Made by Mary Ann Travis Coulbourne Berry
(1825–1903)
Hopewell, Somerset County
Cottons, silk, and wool embroidery
85 x 84 inches
Owned by Mary Elizabeth Brown and Barbara Anne
Carter

Mid-Shore Album Quilts

*A
Present by
Mary A. Rhodes
To
W L H. Rhodes
1856*[1]

MARY A. TAYLOR Rhodes's genealogical album quilt records in red embroidery her birth and 1850 marriage date, the birth date of her husband, Benjamin (1822–69), and the age of her six-year-old son, William Levy Hooper Rhodes. Mary Rhodes also inscribed a square with her intention for the quilt (88). In another square she recorded that she quilted her bedcover in 1857.

Mary and Benjamin Rhodes, both originally from Wicomico County, resided near the Dorchester County town of Brookview, where Benjamin was postmaster and kept a general store.[2] His brother Richard gave land for the railroad station, freight house, and cattle pen; in return, the neighboring town of Rhodesdale was named for him. On December 20, 1869, Benjamin Rhodes was brutally murdered by Cyrus Stack, who confessed to his crime before fleeing the country.[3] His widow, Mary, remained in Dorchester County to raise her son, William, and his sister, Rebecca. It is believed that Mary also made a genealogical quilt for her daughter, Rebecca.

Although Eastern Shore album quilts are uncommon, the Dorchester County quilt survey documented another quilt almost identical to Mary's. The quilt was made by Sarah Elizabeth English Bradley about the time of her marriage in 1857. Though Sarah's quilt lacks embroidered inscriptions, she employed the same technique of coarse buttonhole stitching around areas of highly stuffed appliqué work. In each quilt the sixteen appliquéd blocks are separated by pieced sashing: in Mary's, a barber pole design; in Sarah's, a chevron. Both quilts are bordered by the same twisting grapevine with scattered grapes and chained-stitched tendrils. Eight of the blocks, drawn from the standard lexicon of album motifs, are identical in design and scale (89). Originally both quilts were appliquéd from vibrant dyed red, green, and yellow fabrics. On the Bradley quilt, the reds have now faded to tan.

Although no obvious connection between the makers is known, some relationship must have existed.[4] Sarah Bradley lived near Mardela Springs in Wicomico County; her mother's maiden name was Taylor. Mary Rhodes, also a Taylor, was orig-

APPLIQUÉD AND STUFFED GENEALOGICAL ALBUM QUILT, 1856–57

*Made by Mary A. Taylor Rhodes (1824–1903) for her son William L. H. Rhodes (1851–1919)
Brookview, Dorchester County
Cottons, embroidered inscriptions
91 x 91 inches
Owned by Rebecca Rhodes Saunders*

inally from Wicomico County. Her parent's farm bordered the Mardela-Sharptown Road. Mary Rhodes's quilt, which she presented to her son, William Levy Hooper, passed to his son, John, and then to John's daughter, the present owner. Sarah Bradley's quilt is owned by her great-granddaughter.

1. Presentation block on Mary Rhodes's album quilt.
2. The Rhodes's family connection with the postal service has continued to the present day.

88. *Detail of presentation block of Mary Rhodes's quilt. The stuffed appliqué areas are secured by buttonhole stitches, and small cherries are appliquéd to the blocks where the barber pole sashing crosses. Someone added gingham and muslin patches at a later date.*

89. *This block from Mary Rhodes's quilt is not typical of Maryland album quilts; it may have been her original creation.*

William Levy Hooper Rhodes was postmaster of Brookview during the 1880s. His granddaughter, the quilt owner, works in the Rhodesdale post office.

3. Benjamin Rhodes's tombstone reads "Born July 3, 1821, was murdered by Cyrus Stack Dec. 20, 1869." While his birth date on the tombstone is given as 1821, Mary stitched 1822 on her quilt.

4. The present owners know each other but were unaware of their nearly identical quilts.

APPLIQUÉD AND STUFFED ALBUM QUILT, c. 1857

Made by Sarah Elizabeth English Bradley (1837–1910)
Near Mardela, Wicomico County
Cottons
94 x 93 inches
Owned by Victoria W. Todd

Cecil County Album Quilt

ALBUM QUILTS USUALLY are not found on the upper Eastern Shore. By the 1850s, however, the Philadelphia, Wilmington, and Baltimore Railroad was providing much expanded communication between Cecil County and Baltimore City. A rural quilt-maker could have received inspiration from quilts she saw on beds while visiting in Baltimore homes, or she may have borrowed patterns from her urban friends.

This elaborate album quilt is attributed to Eliza Jane Benjamin Alexander, who resided on a farm at Alexander's Cross Roads near Charlestown in central Cecil County.[1] Eliza Jane was the daughter of Sarah Taylor and Revolutionary War veteran George Benjamin (90). She married John Washington Alexander (1810–75), a carpenter, in 1836. The Benjamins and Alexanders had emigrated to Maryland from Scotland, Ireland, and England and were longtime Cecil County residents. Traditionally the men in the Alexander family were trained as carpenters. Eliza Jane and John Washington

Alexander raised eight children. This quilt passed to her youngest son and favorite, John Washington Alexander Jr., and from him to his oldest surviving son, father of the present owner.

Eliza Jane is remembered not only for her skill in creating an album quilt in the fashionable style of the Western Shore but also for her fortitude during the Civil War. According to family tradition, two of Eliza Jane's sons, Nathan and Matthew, had joined the Union army. Matthew deserted his regiment and returned home, possibly to visit a lady friend. When the Federal troops came looking for him, they were met at the front porch of the homestead by Eliza Jane and seven-year-old John Washington Jr. While Matthew hid in the root cellar, Eliza Jane barred the door with her double-barreled flintlock gun and refused to let anyone in to search the house. A bribe of candy offered to young John produced the response that Matthew had left two days earlier on a swift horse. Eventually Matthew was located. Disciplinary action was taken, and after a short time he returned to his regiment.[2]

Eliza Jane Alexander's quilt contains many of the same classical motifs—wreaths, vases of flowers, lyre, and cornucopia—found on album quilts made in Baltimore and Carroll counties. The very classical swagged and tasseled border set off by rows of applied sawteeth also is common to the Western Shore. This quilt, in which the appliquéd motifs are simply conceived in bold heavy shapes and cut from a limited number of dyed and printed textiles, illustrates the diffusion of a popular style slowly outward from the cultural hearth, or style center, of Baltimore City.

90. Photograph of Eliza Jane Benjamin Alexander (1816–99), copied from an original tintype provided by the late W. Emerson Wilson. (Photograph courtesy of Lorain E. Alexander)

1. This quilt is known in the owner's family as the Catholic Quilt and was thought to have been made by Anna Frederick Alexander, born in 1862 to Catholic immigrant parents. The style of the appliqué and the type of fabrics, however, are more typical of quilts made in Maryland between 1850 and 1870.
2. We are grateful to Lorain E. Alexander for sharing this family story with us.

APPLIQUÉD ALBUM QUILT, c. 1860

Made by Eliza Jane Benjamin Alexander (1816–99)
Alexander's Cross Roads, near Charlestown, Cecil
County
Cottons
86 x 86 inches
Owned by Jean Daugherty

Montgomery County Quilting Patterns

TWO EXTRAORDINARY QUILTS, related by quilting style and kinship of the makers but separated over time, have come together as a result of the Maryland quilt documentation project. Both the Mariner's Compass variation and the eight-pointed star are finely quilted at thirty-four to thirty-six stitches to the inch. The white reserves between the pieced designs are filled with quilted floral bouquets, bountiful cornucopiae, exotic birds, fluttering butterflies, swimming fish, hunters on horseback, trees covered with birds, trailing grapevines, and numerous flowers and leaves. Dates and signatures of the makers are quilted on each. On the Mariner's Compass quilt the inscription "S.M. Dorsey/1852" is quilt-

91. Quilting patterns used on the Woodbourne and star quilts. A drawing for a long-tailed bird is compared with the quilted motif on Mary Waters's quilt. (Courtesy of the Montgomery County Historical Society)

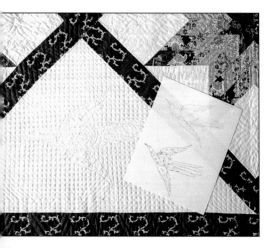

ed in the center and "H.W. Blunt" in the lower-right corner. On the star quilt "Mary M. Waters/1853" is quilted above the center block.

The quiltmakers were members of the Dorsey and Waters families, both well known in Montgomery County. The two families were "particular with whom they married" and therefore frequently intermarried.[1] Harriet Woodward Dorsey Blunt was the daughter of Henry Woodward Dorsey and his first wife, Mary Macubbin. In 1816 Harriet married Samuel Blunt. After her father's death in 1840 she inherited the family home, Woodbourne (94).[2]

Susan Maria Waters Dorsey, the other maker of the Woodbourne Quilt, as the compass quilt has become known, was the daughter of Ignatius and Elizabeth Dorsey Waters. In 1844 she married her widowed brother-in-law, the younger Henry Woodward Dorsey. Henry was Harriet Dorsey Blunt's half-brother, the son of their father's second marriage. The Dorseys moved to the New Market district of Frederick County prior to 1850; however, Susan remained in close contact with her husband's family through her collaboration on a quilt with his sister.[3]

Mary Macubbin Waters Waters, the maker of the star quilt, was also a member of this complex family and closely related to both makers of the Woodbourne Quilt. She was the daughter of Nathaniel Magruder Waters and Achsah Dorsey. Achsah Dorsey Waters and Harriet Dorsey Blunt were sisters, so Mary was Harriet's niece. In 1848 Mary Waters married Dr. Washington Waters, her second cousin and a prominent local physician and Whig politician. Dr. Waters had been married first to Ann Dorsey, Harriet Dorsey Blunt's youngest sister and Mary's aunt. He was also the brother of Susan Maria Waters Dorsey, Harriet's co-quiltmaker.

Mary and Washington Waters's home, now known as Sycamore Hollow, is set on rolling farmland outside the village of Goshen less than two miles from Woodbourne. In the 1850s there were probably no other property owners between the home places of the two families. The close location of the properties must have

92. One of several quilting patterns of hunters in pursuit of prey. (Courtesy of the Montgomery County Historical Society)

played a role in the sharing of interest and technique.

Stylistically the Dorsey/Blunt and Waters quilts are very similar. While the pieced designs are different, they are both complex and rendered with great skill. The compass pattern is composed of three layers of directional pointers, a technique seen on several Maryland quilts of the period.[4] The classically inspired swag and bowknot border is another traditional Maryland motif usually seen on album quilts.[5] The ribbon ends change direction, creating lively movement and an element of surprise in the otherwise symmetrical design.

93. Detail of Mary Waters's quilt showing her signature and date.

On the star quilt, the eight-pointed stars of several different brown and tan prints are enclosed by a grid of rainbow blue sashing. The dark and light tones of the pieced fabrics forming the stars are carefully placed so that the outer nine stars end in dark points and the middle four stars end in light points. The central star, above which Mary Waters has quilted her name and date, is pieced from a warmer range of printed fabrics (93).

The elaborate quilting motifs, however, are what best show the close relationship between these two quilts. Both are covered with a variety of original motifs drawn from the same source. Many of these designs are based on one or more of the fifty-two quilting patterns that accompanied the

PIECED STAR QUILT, 1853

Made by Mary Macubbin Waters Waters (1817–64)
Near Goshen, Montgomery County
Cottons, quilted inscriptions
103 x 105 inches
Owned by Joyce Hawkins

94. *Woodbourne, home of the Dorsey family.* *(Photograph courtesy of the Montgomery County Historical Society)*

be determined, Harriet obviously knew them.[10] The 1850 federal census for Montgomery County lists Harriet as living on the property next to Mary and Washington Waters. Harriet Hobbs (1837–1911) was thirteen at the time and the daughter of Rezin and Elizabeth Hobbs. In 1858 she married another neighbor, Charles T. Purdom, and moved to Frederick County. It is quite possible a third quilt exists, elaborately quilted in figural motifs and signed in tiny stitches by Harriet Blunt Hobbs. This quilt would probably date c. 1856, the latest date on the paper patterns.[11]

Sources for these quilting designs have not been found in ladies' magazines of the period, although formulae for drawing simple leaves and rosettes appeared in the June 1854 edition of *Godey's Lady's Book.* Many of the subjects illustrated by the quilting pat-

Woodbourne Quilt when it was donated by Dorsey descendants to the Montgomery County Historical Society in 1984 (91).[6] The matching of the quilted motifs in the Waters quilt to the paper patterns, in addition to working out the family relationships, conclusively established that the Waters quilt was made by someone intimately connected with the Woodbourne Quilt (95).[7]

The patterns, which the Historical Society has reproduced and published, are interesting social documents of the mid-nineteenth century in themselves.[8] Some are sketched on thin paper while others are drawn on recycled paper, including a cotillion invitation from 1856, a business letter dated 1854, an announcement from a dentist dated 1850, and an undated envelope still retaining its wax seal. On the inside of the envelope Mary Waters wrote her name and the date, 1853, in the same style she would use in quilting her signature. "HB-b-lu-n" is also written on the envelope (96).[9]

In addition to the Blunt and Waters names on these patterns, a third name appears on the pattern with a fish motif used on both quilts. The name "Harriet Blunt Hobbs" is carefully drawn in the same upper-case and lowercase style as the other two names. Although her relationship to the Blunt, Dorsey, and Waters families cannot

PIECED AND APPLIQUÉD MARINER'S
COMPASS QUILT, 1852

Made by Harriet Woodward Dorsey Blunt
(1794–1862) and her half-sister-in-law, Susan Maria
Waters Dorsey (1817–82)
Woodbourne, near Goshen, Montgomery County
Cottons, quilted inscriptions
95 x 93 inches
Owned by the Montgomery County Historical Society

95. *Quilting patterns used on the Woodbourne and star quilts. One of the cornucopiae designs and two pages of floral designs rest on Mary Waters's quilt next to her quilted cornucopiae motif. (Courtesy of the Montgomery County Historical Society)*

96. *Quilting patterns used for the Woodbourne and star quilts. An envelope with Mary Waters's and Harriet Blunt's names sits on top of a pattern page with Harriet Hobbs's name. This page also includes the fish motif found on both quilts and the leafless tree used for the bird tree on Mary Waters's quilt. Another pattern page shows a few of the many leaf designs included with the donation of quilting patterns. (Courtesy of the Montgomery County Historical Society)*

terns—hunters with raised guns and racing dogs, cornucopiae, urns of flowers, scrolling grapevines, and exotic long-tailed birds—are similar to those block printed on chintz fabrics of the early to mid-nineteenth century (92).[12] The same motifs cut from small-figured prints are found appliquéd on high-style Maryland album quilts of the 1850s. According to family tradition, several women in the Dorsey family gave art lessons, so the quilting designs may have been their own interpretations of the popular and classical design aesthetics of their times.[13]

1. Anne Simpkinson, *Heirloom Quilting Designs from the Woodbourne Quilt* (Rockville, MD: Montgomery County Historical Society, 1985), 5.

2. Ibid., 6. Harriet Dorsey Blunt's father had stipulated in his will that his son-in-law was to have no part in the inheritance of his house or estate. As a result Harriet left a sizable estate at the time of her death. Her inventory listed thirty slaves and was valued at $5,405. Montgomery County *Inventories, List of Sales & Accounts,* J.S.W. no. 5 (1860–63).

3. According to family tradition, Susan Dorsey started the Woodbourne Quilt, and Harriet Blunt finished it.

4. An almost identical Mariner's Compass quilt, worked from red and green printed fabrics, was made in Alleghany County c. 1850 and documented as MO-176. It is finely quilted in clamshell and crosshatch patterns. The border has a quilted feather swag.

5. Dunton illustrates several album quilts with swag and bowknot borders. They date from c. 1850 to 1854. William Rush Dunton Jr., *Old Quilts* (Catonsville, MD: n.p., 1946), plates 18, 22, 26, 27.

6. The Woodbourne Quilt donation also included the wooden frame upon which it, and perhaps the Waters quilt, had been quilted.

7. The owner of the Waters quilt is not directly related to the maker's family. Mary and Washington Waters had no children, so Mary's quilt passed to Harriet, his second daughter by his first marriage. Harriet Waters was only nine when her father married Mary Waters. The quilt descended in Harriet Waters's family to Virginia Bell, who willed it to her niece by marriage, the present owner.

8. The patterns are published in *Heirloom Quilting Designs from the Woodbourne Quilt,* cited above.

9. Finding Mary Waters's name among the patterns was additional evidence for linking the two quilts.

10. Harriet Blunt Hobbs's mother was Elizabeth Ramsauer so the source of Harriet's middle name is uncertain.

11. A detailed pattern of a dog, with crosshatch background, has the date 1851 worked into the design. Because the two known quilts date 1852 and 1853, there may be an earlier quilt.

12. See Dilys Blum and Jack Linsey, "Nineteenth-Century Appliqué Quilts," *Philadelphia Museum of Art Bulletin,* vol. 85 (Fall 1989), 363–64. Along the border of the illustrated bedcover, attributed to Maryland or Pennsylvania, top-hatted hunters with fowling pieces and dogs pursue oversized pheasants and other exotic birds in a pastoral landscape of palms and passion flowers. The motifs have been cut from a variety of printed fabrics popular in the 1820s and 1830s. Many of these same prints appear on Maryland chintz appliqué quilts.

13. This information is summarized from the introduction by Anne Simpkinson to *Heirloom Quilting Designs* and from an earlier publication of the Woodbourne Quilt; see Gloria Seaman Allen, *Old Line Traditions: Maryland Women and Their Quilts* (Washington, DC: DAR Museum, 1985), 34.

Maguire-Evans Family Quilts

T HREE WOMEN OF THE Maguire-Evans family, who spanned two generations in time and who lived in both Baltimore and on the rural Eastern Shore of Maryland, made a number of quilts over a period of nearly 100 years. Louisa Cecelia Banks, the daughter of Jane Harrison and Edmund Banks, was probably born in Fruitland, Wicomico County, and lived for short periods of her youth in Baltimore. Prior to 1849 she married Uriah Maguire of Madison, Dorchester County, and spent the rest of her life on the lower Eastern Shore. Ten children, from eighteen

97. Alice Maguire Evans (1851–1940) in the 1930s. (Photograph courtesy of Nannette T. Berberich)

pregnancies, survived to adulthood, including the oldest daughter, Alice, born in 1851. A neighbor once remarked that he never saw Louisa when she wasn't "in the family way." In addition to bearing children and creating lovely quilts, Louisa Maguire is remembered as an accomplished baker and an industrious lady. She once received a card with a quotation from Proverbs 31:27, which she took as her model: "She looketh well to the ways of her household and eateth not the bread of idleness."[1] Louisa Maguire died from a ruptured appendix at age sixty-two. Her son Frank, a respected physician, diagnosed his mother's illness but was unable to operate in time to save her.[2]

Alice Maguire dearly loved her mother and revered her memory (97). Growing up in Dorchester County, Alice also spent time with her maternal grandmother on Federal Hill in Baltimore. Probably during one of these visits, she met her future husband. In 1879 she married George Nelson Evans (1849–1914) and moved permanent-

PIECED AND APPLIQUÉD CRADLE QUILT, 1850–60

*Made by Louisa Cecelia Banks Maguire (1831–92)
Madison, Dorchester County
Cottons
43 x 43 inches
Owned by Nannette T. Berberich*

98. Esther Aydlotte Evans (1820–93) around 1880. (Photograph courtesy of Nannette T. Berberich)

ly across the bay to settle in Baltimore. In later years she lived with her daughter and family and shared with them tales of her past. Alice is remembered by her granddaughter as being very proud of her family lineage. Her outlook, however, was parochial: she considered people born on the Eastern Shore to be a little better than those born in other parts of the state; people born outside the state she considered "foreigners."[3]

George Evans was the son of William and Esther Evans of Baltimore. His mother, Esther Aydlotte Evans, was born on the Eastern Shore, in or near Snow Hill in Worcester County (98). The Aydlottes were descended from Huguenots who fled France for England after the revocation of the Edict of Nantes in 1685. Three Aydlotte brothers purchased land in 1687 in what is now Worcester County. Esther Aydlotte married William Evans, a carpenter, and moved to a

PIECED MARINER'S COMPASS QUILT, 1850–60

Made by Louisa Cecelia Banks Maguire (1831–92)
Madison, Dorchester County
Cottons
93.5 x 90 inches
Owned by Nannette T. Berberich

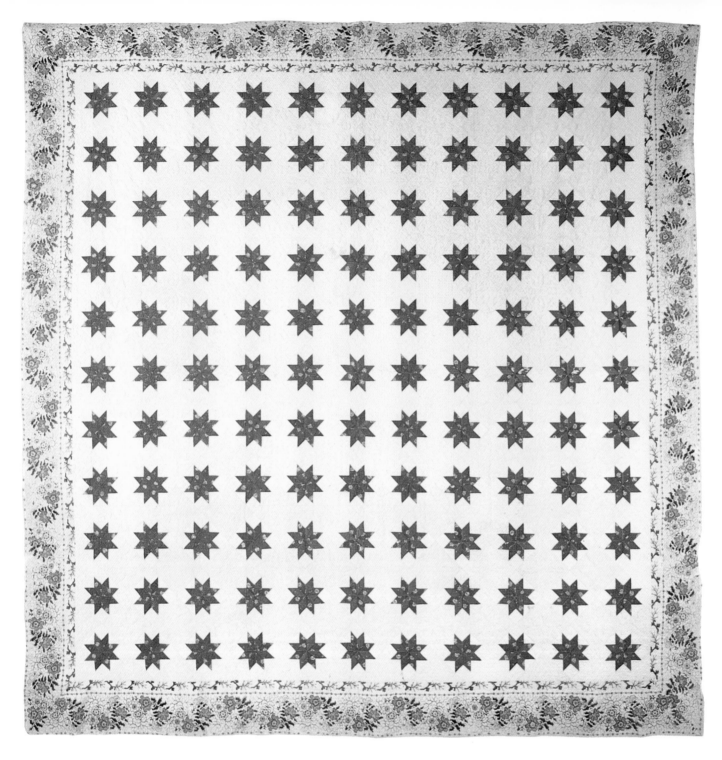

house owned by William's mother in the 100 block of East Montgomery Street in Baltimore. Here William and Esther raised seven children, George being their third child and first son. Esther died tragically at age seventy-three, while working at her wood stove; her dress caught fire. She was burned severely and died the next day. Many of her possessions, which included her quilts and a pine cupboard crafted by her husband, now belong to her great-granddaughter.

Louisa Maguire, Esther Evans, and their daughter/daughter-in-law, Alice Maguire Evans, were all proficient quiltmakers. Louisa Maguire's quilts were made on the Eastern Shore and date from the 1850s. She favored intricate piecing and the red and green palette. In addition to the red, green, and yellow Mariner's Compass quilt with its double saw-tooth border, Louisa also made a cradle quilt with a pieced checkerboard field and an unusual appliquéd bird and branch border. She pieced a red and white Prairie Star quilt, which

PIECED STAR QUILT, 1840–45

Made by Esther Aydlotte Evans (1820–93)
Baltimore City
Cottons
102 x 100 inches
Owned by Nannette T. Berberich

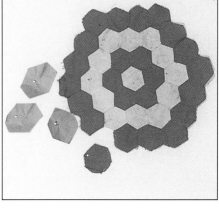

mother liked, in the border. Alice began piecing her last quilt for her grandson in 1928, but it was not quilted until forty years later. This quilt combines a bright red fabric with many examples of pastel printed fabrics that became popular in the 1920s and were stocked by Baltimore dry-goods merchants. These cotton fabrics resemble but predate the printed feed sacks that many Eastern Shore farm women would cut and piece for their quilts in the 1930s and 1940s.

Quiltmaking in the Maguire-Evans family stopped with the death of Alice. Her only child, a daughter, did not make quilts nor does her granddaughter, the present owner. Her granddaughter has preserved the family's textile legacy, however, and recorded their genealogy and anecdotes that she has, in turn, passed on to her grandchildren.

was quilted sometime later, and she started, but did not finish, another red and white quilt with tiny diamond piecing (99).

Esther Evans's surviving quilts date from the 1840s. She also worked in the red and green palette that was so popular in Maryland around the middle of the nineteenth century. Her illustrated quilt, with eight-pointed stars pieced from red and green block prints, has a border cut from a sophisticated red and green roller-printed fabric that probably was more readily available to Baltimore quiltmakers than to those living on the remote lower Eastern Shore.

Alice Maguire Evans made quilts in the traditional style of her mother and mother-

PIECED BLAZING SUN QUILT, 1928, quilted in 1968

Made by Alice Maguire Evans (1851–1940) for her grandson, Samuel Evans Trott
Baltimore City
Cottons
71 x 81 inches
Owned by Nannette T. Berberich

in-law. Her quilts date from the early twentieth century but continue the use of nineteenth-century pieced patters. She also favored the red and green color combination and pieced a hexagon quilt in those colors (100). For that quilt and the one illustrated here she used the solid red fabric, that her

1. Narcissa L. Erwin Black, a skilled seamstress involved in all aspects of textile production on her Mississippi plantation, recorded the same quotation in her diary. On August 27, 1870, her sixtieth birthday, she wrote, "My verse in proverbs is she Looketh well to the ways of her household and eateth not the Bread of Idleness. I have got My Living By the sweet of My face as the Lord has commanded." Quoted by Mary Edna Lohrenz and Anita Miller Stamper in *Mississippi Homespun: Nineteenth-Century Textiles and the Women Who Made Them* (Jackson, MS: Mississippi Department of Archives and History, 1989), 5.
2. We are grateful to Nannette Berberich for sharing with us stories of her family.
3. See "Maryland Women and the Civil War" for additional recollections by Alice Maguire Evans.

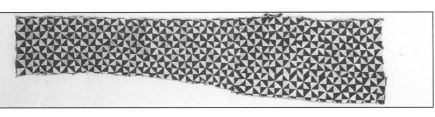

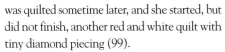

Amanda Doub's Dowry Quilts

ACCORDING TO A LETTER written in 1959 by Amanda Doub's daughter, Laura Remsburg, sisters Malinda and Sarah Koogle made three quilts as part of Amanda's dowry when she married John Henry Routzahn on March 18, 1858.[1] Neighbors of the Doub family, the Koogle sisters were the eldest daughters of local carpenter Christian Koogle and his wife, Frana. Christian was the son of one of five Koogle brothers who emigrated from Darmstadt, a province of Germany, in the latter half of the eighteenth century. Many of the Koogle brothers first settled in Frederick or Washington counties and from there moved west to Kentucky and Kansas. The Christian Koogle family attended the Zion Evangelical Lutheran Church in Middletown; their childrens' baptisms were dutifully recorded in church records.

101. The Doub family home as it appears today. (Photograph courtesy of Nancy Gibson Tuckhorn)

Shortly before 1850, Malinda Koogle went to live on the neighboring farm of Enos and Elizabeth Doub (101). The couple were the parents of six young children, all boys except thirteen-year-old Amanda. Two teenage sisters were left at home to help Frana Koogle with household chores, thus Malinda was available to help the Doub household with their growing family. Malinda may have been sought after by the Doub family to assist with sewing garments for their five active boys or to simply help Amanda with her needlework and household chores. In any case, it was customary in large families for the female help (paid or unpaid) to share a bed with the daughters in the family and to help with the sewing. In 1832, Lydia Maria Child wrote in her book, *The American Frugal Housewife*, about this practice: "Two or three years with a mother, assisting her in her duties, instructing brothers and sisters, and taking care of their own clothes . . . this is the way to make them happy as well as good wives, for being early accustomed to the duties of life, they will sit lightly as well as gracefully upon them."[2] The quilts made for Amanda's wedding by Sarah and Malinda document the bonds of friendship that developed between the sisters and Amanda during the years Malinda lived in the Doub household. In rural Maryland this custom of using a young girl from a good family to assist a mother with her household duties was practiced well into the early twentieth century.

The family has preserved three quilts (two are shown here) made by Malinda and her sister Sarah, and perhaps Amanda. All three quilts show evidence of being made by experienced hands. Malinda Koogle quilted her own name along one side of a Rose of Sharon quilt (not shown) and Amanda Doub's name near the center. Quilting was probably a popular activity the girls shared, and possibly other quilts were made that are now lost.[3] Amanda was an experienced needlewoman as the sampler she worked in 1857 and the crazy quilt she made thirty-five years later in 1892 show (102). Possibly Malinda taught Amanda these needlework skills during the time she resided in the Doub home.[4]

No marriage or death record has been located for either Koogle sister. Both are listed in the federal census for Frederick County in 1880 as living with their eighty-five-year-old mother, Frana. Frederick County cemetery records, which are amazingly complete through 1920, contain no burial record of either sister.

Malinda and Sarah supplied Amanda with a quilt in the Flower of Paradise or Democratic Rose pattern, one of the most popular appliqué designs with mid-nineteenth-century quiltmakers. Descendants of the Doub family always referred to this quilt as being made in the Flower of Paradise pattern. The New York State documentation project recorded a similar quilt made in 1862 with a history of being called Flower of Paradise.[5] The MAFCE project documented another virtually identical but unattributable quilt. Now in a private collection, it was formerly owned by the late Maryland antiques collector Mrs. Frederic Leiter.

The design similarity of the two quilts led to a search for a published pattern or design inspiration. The search did not locate a published pattern but did discover two more quilts similar in design, color, and fabric composition. Documented by the Kansas Quilt Project both are privately owned.[6] Almost identical to each other, they differ slightly from the two Maryland quilts. Each has an additional row of half-rose appliqués on all four sides, missing on the Maryland examples. However, the sawtooth borders surrounding the field and the

102. Sampler stitched by Amanda Doub in 1857, one year before her marriage. (Courtesy of Carol Remsburg Bare)

outer appliqué rose vine on all four quilts are identically laid on; the corners are remarkably similar.[7]

The family histories passed down with the two Kansas-documented Flower of Paradise quilts are tantalizing; one has a direct link to western Maryland and the other has a possible connection. The maker of the Kansas-documented quilt (#Dd088), Sarah Snively Warner (1832–1929), was born in Hagerstown, Maryland, a large town in Washington County not far from the Koogle and Doub homes in Frederick County. By 1880 Sarah Snively had married Zebadee Warner and was living in West Virginia. She may have been a childhood friend of the Koogle sisters, as she was near them in age, or could be a distant relative.

APPLIQUÉD TULIP QUILT, c. 1858

Made by Malinda Koogle (b. 1827) and Sarah Koogle (b. 1833) for Amanda Doub (1837–1914)
Frederick County
Cottons
85 x 82 inches
Owned by Margaret R. Miller

A possible explanation for the similarity may lie in an old tradition still followed by quiltmakers in the mountains of western Maryland. Unexpectedly, the authors have identified a square in the same pattern and fabrics as these Flower of Paradise quilts (103). It remains with the descendents of Washington County quiltmaker Elizabeth Huyett (14). It was listed in the household inventory taken after her death in 1878. The square may be a pattern or template used to make a full-size quilt. Twentieth-century quiltmakers from this part of Maryland favored this method of transferring patterns and have kept the tradition alive.

103. QUILT SQUARE, 1858–78, probably a fabric pattern or template meant to be used for making a full-size quilt. It represents a method of transferring patterns before the popularity of publishing patterns and kits in newspaper and magazines took hold. In 1878 this particular square was listed in the household inventory of quiltmaker, Elizabeth Huyett of Washington County. (Courtesy of the estate of Helen E. Gladhill)

FLOWER OF PARADISE QUILT, c. 1858

Made by Malinda Koogle (b. 1827) and Sarah Koogle (b. 1833) for Amanda Doub (1837–1914)
Frederick County
Cotton
93 x 93 inches
Owned by Betty Remsberg DeColigny

The similar Kansas-documented Flower of Paradise (#Dd221), is attributed to a Kentucky woman, Martha Gorin (b. 1846). Coincidentally, this quilt's owner brought another nineteenth-century quilt to be documented with an oral tradition of originating with a Gorin ancestor living in Frederick, Maryland. The present owner may have confused the makers of these two quilts. In any event, all four Flower of Paradise quilts are remarkably similar, and the evidence points to a single, yet, unidentified source.

1. All three quilt owners have copies of Laura Remsburg's letter.
2. Lydia Maria Child, *The American Frugal Housewife* (Boston: n.p., 1832), 92. For more on this topic, see Jane C. Nylander, *Our Own Snug Fireside: Images of the New England Home, 1760–1860* (New York: Knopf, 1993), 41–53.
3. The fragile condition of this quilt made it impossible to photograph for inclusion in this book.
4. Family history has remembered Sarah Koogle's name as one of the makers of the Doub wedding quilts, in spite of the fact that her name is not recorded on the quilts themselves.
5. Jacqueline M. Atkins and Phyllis A. Tepper, *New York Beauties: Quilts from the Empire State* (New York: Dutton Studio Books, 1992), 112. The name Flower of Paradise is inscribed on the quilt.
6. Barbara Brackman, Jennie A. Chinn, Gayle R. Davis, Terry Thompson, Sara Reimer Farley, and Nancy Hornback, *Kansas Quilts and Quilters* (Lawrence: University Press of Kansas, 1993). The authors thank Barbara Brackman for bringing these two quilts to their attention and sharing her documentation notes with them. The authors also are grateful to Nancy Hornback for sharing her notes, spending many hours digging into archival records, and, most important, reinterviewing the owners of the quilts.
7. Two other similar quilts are in the collections of the Museum of American Folk Art in New York City and of Franklin and Marshall College in Lancaster, Pennsylvania. Both quilts were published with a Pennsylvania attribution, makers unknown.

Eagle Quilt

TWENTY-YEAR-OLD MAR-
garet E. Buckey appliquéd this
eagle quilt in 1857, a year before her marriage to Elhanan Englar (1833–92), and it is
the only surviving textile attributed to
Margaret's hand," according to Joanne
Manwaring, textile scholar and former director of the Historical Society of Carroll
County. Manwaring's research on the
Buckey quilt is the basis for the following
interpretation.[1]

Margaret, the daughter of Ezra (1803–
58) and Susannah Root Buckey (1808–41),
spent the first years of her life on a farm in
the Mount Pleasant district of Frederick
County. Her ancestors settled in Frederick
County during the early eighteenth century,
but by the time Margaret was born, some
members had moved to Carroll County.

Margaret's mother, Susannah,
died in 1841, at the age of thirty-
three, leaving a husband and
four children. Soon after
Susannah's death Ezra married
his sister-in-law, Ann Root
(1797–1868).[2] Sometime before
1850, Ezra moved his family to
the Root farm near Johnsville, in
Frederick County. Johnsville is
only a few miles from Union
Bridge and New Windsor, small
towns in neighboring Carroll
County. Manwaring states, "The
Buckey family probably came to
these towns for goods and services, and the fact that Margaret
married Elhanan Englar, a farmer
from New Windsor, provides evidence that the family traveled
across this political boundary."

Margaret Buckey's quilt is one of only two
documented in the MAFCE project that features an eagle as its primary design element.[3]
Manwaring asks, "What was Margaret's
motivation for using this particular eagle in
her quilt? Was it a response to the political
tenor of the times? Were women motivated
by politics, and did this show up in their
daily lives through their needlework?"

Ironically, Maryland has become identified
with several types of eagle quilts. Recent
research has concluded that almost all of the
so-called Maryland eagle quilts were produced by two women, Anna Catherine
Hummel Markey Garnhart (1773–1860) and
Susan Strong (b. 1809). Catherine Garnhart
made at least eleven quilts, four of which contain an eagle in the center. Three more eagle
quilts are attributed to her but are as yet not
proven.[4] Another famous and much-repro-
duced eagle quilt in the collection of the
Smithsonian Institution is attributed to
Maryland-born Susan Strong. Susan and her
husband left Maryland for Ohio sometime
after their marriage in 1831; thus, her eagle
quilt may have been made outside the state.[5]

A group of eagle quilts was recorded in the
Pennsylvania Documentation Project and

*104. Detail of inscription stitched on Margaret Buckey's
quilt.*

published in the 1986 book *In the Heart of
Pennsylvania*. The project uncovered about
three dozen eagle quilts, all of which are sig-
nificantly different than Margaret Buckey's
in composition and age. The Pennsylvania
eagles are laid-on in each corner at an angle
to the center; Margaret placed the eagle in
the middle of the design.[6] The Pennsylvania
eagle quilts date from the centennial period
and later.

Manwaring suggests that Margaret's eagle
might have been inspired by the symbol of
the antislavery party, the Know-Nothing or
American Party, which was popular in
Carroll County in the 1850s. Events sponsored by this party were advertised in Carroll
County's newspaper, *The American Sentinel
and General Advertiser* during the weeks leading up to the 1856 election.[7] The eagle on
Margaret's quilt features characteristics of
two eagles available as printer's woodcuts
and used by the newspaper publisher to represent the Know-Nothings (105 and 106).
These blocks were widely available for use in
newspapers and magazines across the country. The smaller of the two eagles is most like
Margaret's; it holds a shield in its mouth,
while Margaret's eagle holds a ribbon with
the phrase "E Pluribus Unum."

Although Manwaring's theory cannot be
proved, it is clear that eagles as patriotic symbols had been familiar to Marylanders for
many years. Eagles decorate furniture, silver, and ceramics made
and/or used in the state during
the Federal period. Catherine
Garnhart probably based the
eagle on her quilts on the design
of a transfer-printed Liverpool
pitcher, which has descended in
her family. Quiltmakers including Margaret Buckey and
Catherine Garnhart used everyday objects as sources for quilt
designs.

According to Margaret's obituary, she was a member of the
Brethren Church for sixty-eight
years. Elders of the church were
politically active against slavery, especially Margaret's uncle,
Daniel P. Saylor, leader of the
congregation at Beaver Dam

EAGLE QUILT, 1857

Made by Margaret E. Buckey (1837–1925)
Frederick County
Cottons, embroidered inscriptions
91.5 x 91.5 inches
Owned by the Historical Society of Carroll County, Inc.

105. Advertisement for the American Mass Meetings being held across the state by the American State Central Committee of the American Party. Note the printer's cut eagle is similar to the eagle decorating Margaret's quilt. This advertisement was one of two used to promote this political event by the American Sentinel and General Advertiser.

where Margaret worshipped while she was single. After her marriage she and her husband joined the congregation at the Pipe Creek Brethren Church. Both are buried in the church cemetery. Manwaring writes, "Margaret certainly would have embraced the teachings of her church and been affected by her uncle's views."[8]

Margaret's eagle quilt descended to her grandaughter, who bequeathed it in 1981 to the Historical Society of Carroll County, where it exhibits a not-so-subtle statement of one woman's political leanings in the tumult leading to the Civil War.

1. Joanne S. Manwaring, "The Margaret E. Buckey Quilt: Patriotic Sentiment or Political Statement," unpublished paper, 1990. The authors are grateful to Joanne Manwaring for allowing them to quote extensively from her paper.
2. Two almost identical alphabet samplers are in the collection of the Historical Society of Carroll County: one was made by Susannah Root and signed, "Work Done in Margaret Corcoran's School"; another made by Ann Root is signed and dated "Ann Root, 1816."
3. This statistic does not include album quilts in which an eagle is appliquéd in a single block.
4. Nancy Gibson Tuckhorn, who mounted an exhibition of the Garnhart quilts at the DAR Museum in 1990, hopes to publish more on the quilts and their maker.
5. Doris Bowman, *American Quilts* (Washington, DC: Smithsonian Institution Press, 1991), 30. An eagle quilt similar to Susan's with a Frederick County attribution was sold in 1994 to an unidentified Japanese collector.
6. Patricia T. Herr, "What Distinguishes a Pennsylvania Quilt?", *In the Heart of*

106. Advertisement for the "Grand Mass Meeting, Procession And Barbecue! Of The American Party At Westminster, Maryland," in the American Sentinel and General Advertiser, *October 1856. This printer's woodcut eagle was referred to as "the big eagle" by the writers working for that newspaper.*

Pennsylvania: Symposium Papers (Lewisburg, PA: Oral Traditions Project, 1986), 35.
7. Even though party candidate Millard Fillmore lost, he received all eight of Maryland's electoral college votes.
8. Manwaring, "Buckey Quilt."

A Quilt for Gootee

ON NOVEMBER 27, 1858, Violetta Stevens Lyden of Caroline County gave birth to her second son, Gootee Stevens. Shortly after his birth she completed a full-size fleur-de-lis quilt on which she stitched her son's name and the date "March 14, 1859" along the bottom edge (107). The exact significance of the date is unknown; it may record the day Gootee was christened or the day Violetta completed the quilt.

Violetta Lyden's quilt resembles others made on the Eastern Shore of Maryland during the mid-nineteenth century. She chose the popular fleur-de-lis pattern, often used for friendship quilts, and cut her motifs from a variety of Turkey red prints (pp. 103–07). The Garden Maze sashing and applied stepped border, cut from a small-figured green/black/yellow print frequently used in conjunction with Turkey red fabrics, also are

107. Detail of Violetta Lyden's quilt showing the stitched inscription and date. The pencil lines are still visible.

common to Maryland quilts of the period. The quilt is finely stitched at twenty-four stitches to the inch in clamshell, swag, and circular patterns.

Violetta Stevens Lyden was the daughter of Elizabeth and Gootee Stevens of Denton, Caroline County.[2] On September 11, 1855, she married William Edward Lyden (1838–1916), son of Sarah and Edward Williams Lyden, also of Caroline County.[3] Both the Stevens and Lyden families earned their livelihood through farming. Unlike some of their neighbors who were slaveholders, they hired laborers, both white and black, to work their fields.[4]

After their marriage the Lydens settled at the family homestead, Lyden's Grant, near Smithville. The land was part of a 1,000-acre tract granted to two Layden, or Leyden, brothers by King Charles II in 1684 in return for their services of transporting settlers and supplies to North America. Richard Layden's descendant, Shadrack Lyden, commanded the local militia during the Revolution; he also acquired additional land.[5] His great-great-grandson, William Edward Lyden, took over the farming operation, improved the eighteenth-century dwelling with the addition of a second story in 1867, and later surrounded two earlier structures with a frame building.[6] Lyden also participated in local politics as a judge of the orphans' court. His and Violetta's different political affiliations led to many heated discussions.[7]

Gootee Stevens was the second of their seven children (108). At age twenty he married Nancy Henrietta Adams of Sussex County, Delaware. He followed his father in

farming but expanded his operation to include a sawmill that provided lumber for the local community. He added a veneering machine that produced thin wooden strips for the manufacture of baskets and fruit containers. The baskets were intended for large fruits and vegetables, and the pint- and quart-sized containers were used for strawberries and other small fruit. After a fire in 1916 destroyed his mill, veneering plant, and basket factory, Gootee relocated to Federalsburg and opened one of the earliest gas stations in the area.[8]

Gootee's quilt, which has seen very little use, descended in the male line to his grandson, the present owner.

1. The family name is spelled "Lyden" in the 1850 and the 1860 federal census but "Liden" in birth and marriage records. According to Conrad Liden, the names Layden, Lyden, and Liden were used interchangeably through the family history. He refers to his great-grandfather as Lyden and to his grandfather as Liden. The name, Leyden, is associated with members of the family who migrated from England to Leyden, Holland, in the seventeenth century.
2. The unusual name of Gootee or Gouty was also given to Violetta's brother. Mary Gouty, possibly a cousin, lived with the Stevens family, and other Goutys lived in the area. The name is spelled Gouty or Gootee in different records.
3. After Edward Williams Lyden's death, his

108. The Lyden family, in front of their house on Lyden's Grant, about 1888. William Edward and Violetta Lyden are in the center; Gootee is diagonally behind his father, to the left; his wife, Nancy, and two daughters are in front of him. The family members include William Edward and Violetta's other children, their spouses, and grandchildren. (Photograph courtesy of Conrad Liden)

widow, Sarah, married Gootee Stevens, Violetta's father; thus, William Edward Lyden and Violetta Stevens were stepbrother and stepsister as well as husband and wife.

4. According to the 1850 federal census for Caroline County, Gouty Stevens employed three white and two black farm laborers in addition to his son William. Edward Lyden employed two white farm hands.

5. Communication from Conrad Liden.
6. Maryland Historical Trust, *Inventory of Historic Sites in Caroline County* (Annapolis: Maryland Historical Trust, 1990), 70.
7. Their son, Gootee, recalled their arguments and related this story to his grandson Conrad.
8. Conrad Liden has fond memories of staying with his grandfather, Gootee, and being allowed to pump gas—at twelve cents a gallon.

APPLIQUÉD AND PIECED QUILT, 1859

Made by Violetta Stevens Lyden (1833–1921) for Gootee Stevens Liden (1858–1943) [1]
Lyden's Grant, Smithville, Caroline County
Cottons, quilted inscription
85 x 87 inches
Owned by Marjorie and Conrad H. Liden

Maryland Women and the Civil War

THE CIVIL WAR TOUCHED THE LIVES OF Maryland women in different ways: many lost husbands and sons and faced economic ruin or a postbellum lifestyle totally different from any they had known previously.

Maryland was a border state and shared cultural, economic, and political characteristics with its northern and southern neighbors, Pennsylvania and Virginia. In 1860 Maryland was both urban and rural, industrial and agricultural; both wage and slave labor supported the economy. The population of Maryland doubled between 1830 and 1860. Disproportionately large numbers of German and Irish immigrants found employment in new industries and in building the transportation network that would link Baltimore with western lands.[1] When the states of the Confederacy seceded, Maryland remained in the Union to safeguard the Federal City from a Southern invasion. Many people in rural southern Maryland and on the lower Eastern Shore, however, sympathized with the Southern cause, and maintained a traditional agrarian way of life sustained by the "peculiar institution of slavery."[2] In Baltimore little enthusiasm existed for the continuation of slavery. The city had strong economic ties to the North, a large immigrant population, and a free black citizenry that outnumbered slaves by almost six to one.[3]

The first real bloodshed of the Civil War occurred on the streets of Baltimore. On April 19, 1861, the Sixth Massachusetts Volunteer Infantry, en route to Washington to defend the capital, fired into a local mob that tried to impede their march between the city's northern and southern train stations; sixteen people died and scores were injured. By 1863, 53,000 Marylanders had joined the Union army, and 18,000 the Confederate army.[4] As a writer for the *Baltimore American* recalled years later, "Thousands of her [Maryland] sons, not a few of the very flower of her youth, rushed across the border to join hands with her brothers of the South."[5] Many families were divided in their loyalties. John Willson Magruder Jr., whose name is inscribed on the quilt on page 94, grew up in a slave holding family. He became a prominent surgeon in the Union army. According to tradition, he warned his family, while home on leave, "Y'all know I am in the Union Army, and all the rest of you are copperheads [Southern sympathizers], and I don't want to hear any Rebel talk from any of you while I'm home."[6] Alice Maguire was in her teens when the war started. She grew up on the Eastern Shore but attended school in Baltimore City during 1862 (p. 149). Her father was a secessionist, so she must have encountered conflicting sentiments during her stay with relatives in Union-occupied Baltimore. Alice often spoke to her grandchildren of her memories of the "Great War." She told them of hearing distant cannon fire during one of the battles, and she recalled sewing on a Confederate flag that was displayed in her house.[7] Maggie Mehring, who was about Alice's age, kept a diary during part of 1863. Living in New Windsor, Carroll County, to the north of Baltimore, she was closer to the war zone. Maggie recorded her excitement at seeing Union troops and supplies as they passed through New Windsor on their way north to Gettysburg, Pennsylvania.[8] Women living in the western counties of Maryland were close to some of the fiercest encounters of the war. During the Battle of Antietam in Washington County, more than 20,000 men were killed, wounded, or captured in one day, September 17, 1862—"the bloodiest day in American military history."[9]

Maryland women responded to the war in different ways. With their men folk away from home, some took over their husbands' businesses; some ran their farms. Women who had been dependent on slaves were now faced with operating large plantations without laborers.[10] Women became planters, millers, merchants, manufacturers, and managers. Many returned to spinning and handweaving and other forms of domestic manufacture to supplement increasingly scarce necessities.

While rural women remained isolated, middle-class women in Baltimore joined together in organizing soldiers' aid societies and other ladies' groups to provide clothing, bedcoverings, and bandages for the Union

UNION FLAG BED QUILT AND SHAMS, *probably Washington County; quilt 88 x 69 inches, pieced cottons, stitched in a running feather motif and appliquéd with initials and date—".S.1861.B." Owned by Gladys Fahrney.*

army. Some women served as nurses, whom wounded soldiers referred to as the "Crinoline Brigade."[11] Others staged fairs to raise money for the troops. The Baltimore Sanitary Fair was held at the Maryland Institute in April and May 1864, to support "the defenders of the Union."[12] As a local newspaper reported, "It [was] now fashionable to be loyal to the government."[13] The fair opened on April 18, a day short of the third anniversary of the massacre in Baltimore, and was attended by 3,000 people including President Abraham Lincoln.[14] The fair ran for more than three weeks and took in more than $60,000; the proceeds went toward supplying Union army hospitals in Annapolis.[15]

Different counties sponsored fancy tables and raffled or sold blankets, quilts, and other household articles. The New England Kitchen, where costumed workers served baked beans, applesauce, and other old-timey foods, attracted many visitors and earned favorable comments in the press.[16] During the evenings, the kitchen was the scene of "old fashioned quilting parties." The ladies of Baltimore, dressed in colonial costumes, stitched away at a quilting frame.[17] A reporter for the *Baltimore American* commented, "Last evening the 'Quilting Party' was placed before us in a manner that brought the thrifty doings of our grandmothers vividly before us."[18]

Many years after the war had ended, Baltimore women again joined together, this time in support of impoverished Civil War veterans and widows. In April 1885, women who were "the leaders in society and fashion" worked side by side with women of lesser means to put on the Confederate Relief Bazar at the Fifth

Baltimore Sanitary Fair at the Maryland Institute. Woodcut from Frank Leslie's Illustrated Newspaper, May 14, 1864. (Photograph courtesy of The Peale Museum, Baltimore City Life Museums)

Regiment Armory.[19] "Those whose sympathies were with the Union during the war worked . . . with the greatest enthusiasm with those who sent sons, husbands, and lovers to the Confederate cause."[20] The intention of the bazar was to raise funds for the relief of the Confederate soldiers of Maryland. Unlike Union veterans, Confederate veterans received no pensions or other financial aid from the federal government, and many were "broken down by wounds, disease, and hard fortune."[21] The arrangement of the bazar included a dozen or more tables named after Southern states and Confederate heroes, where women sold numbered paddles to be used in raffling off cigars, cakes, quilts, and other donated household goods of small size. The South Carolina and Tennessee tables both raffled off crazy quilts—one was valued at $125.[22] The Murray Association table—which honored the memory of Capt. William H. Murray, killed at Gettysburg while commanding the Second Maryland Infantry—attracted a great deal of attention. The raffle items included "a beautiful silk quilt marking all the battles Captain William Murray's command was engaged in." The quilt had been presented by the ladies of West River, Maryland, Murray's birthplace; it was ultimately won by a member of the Murray family.[23]

The Women's Industrial Exchange was founded in Baltimore in 1880, but its roots go back to the days following the Civil War "when impoverished old Maryland families made a little extra money by discreetly selling heirlooms, needlework, cakes, and cookies to acquaintances in the parlor of wealthy Mrs. G. Harman Brown."[24] When the enterprise outgrew Mrs. Brown's home, a shop was opened on Charles Street. There, "gentlewomen [could] find a way to support themselves protected from the publicity from which a sensitive nature shrinks."[25] The exchange's restaurant, bakery, and salesroom provided genteel employment for ladies, and its sales of food, baked goods, needlework, and quilts provided income for the consignors and funds for the upkeep of the exchange. In its first decade of operation, sales exceeded $283,000.[26]

MAFCE documented a number of quilts that can be dated in the 1860 to 1870 range, but only one appears to have been directly inspired by the Civil War. A bed quilt, two pillow shams, and one bolster sham, with pieced red and white stripes and white stars appliquéd to blue borders, resemble flag quilts made during the 1860s. Barbara Brackman has identified the source. In June 1861, Peterson's Magazine printed a color illustration of "A Patriotic Quilt" in the form of a flag. Both the MAFCE quilt and the quilt design in Peterson's have thirty-four stars in the border—representing the thirty-four states in the Union, including those that had seceded. Peterson's quilt also has a central diamond with an additional thirty-four stars. Brackman notes that these flag quilts were political as well as patriotic. The inclusion of stars to represent all the states expressed Union, rather than Confederate, sentiments.[27] In some localities flag bed quilts were made by sewing groups and given to families of soldiers sent to war.[28] The Maryland quilt, which is associated with Washington County, has the appliquéd inscription, ".S.1861.B.," but the identity of S. B., whether maker, recipient, or honoree, remains unknown.[29]

Gloria Seaman Allen

1. Maryland had the highest number of foreign born residents of any eastern slave state. Robert J. Brugger, Maryland: A Middle Temperament 1634–1980 (Baltimore: Johns Hopkins University Press, 1988), 255.
2. This phrase was popularized by historian Kenneth Stampp. He wrote The Peculiar Institution: Slavery in the Antebellum South (New York: Knopf, 1956).
3. Figures from Suzanne Ellery Greene Chappelle et. al., Maryland: A History of Its People (Baltimore: Johns Hopkins University Press, 1986),

148. In contrast, St. Mary's County in southern Maryland had almost six times as many slaves as free blacks; blacks also outnumbered whites in the total population of the county. Overall, Maryland had more "free people of color" than any other state in the Union.

4. Ibid., 166–67.

5. *Baltimore American*, April 8, 1885.

6. Reported in an undated article by Montgomery County historian Roger Farquhar Sr. Vertical place name file, Montgomery County Historical Society Library. The Copperheads, an anti-Lincoln faction, opposed his attempts to free the slaves in the South; they favored compromise with the Confederate states to end the war.

7. We are grateful to Nannette Berberich for sharing with us her recollections of her grandmother, Alice Maguire Evans.

8. Frederick Shriver Klein, ed., "A Little Girl's Wartime Journal" in *Just South of Gettysburg: Carroll County, Maryland in the Civil War* (Westminster, MD: Historical Society of Carroll County, 1974), 211–16.

9. *New York Times*, September 16, 1994, A16. The *Times* article reported on the recent archaeological and anthropological study of the remains of four soldiers killed during the Battle of Antietam.

10. Chappelle, *Maryland*, 166–67.

11. Ibid.

12. *Baltimore American and Commercial Daily Advertiser*, May 2, 1864. Virginia Gunn has made a thorough study of the U.S. Sanitary Commission and the sanitary fairs for her excellent article "Quilts for Union Soldiers in the Civil War" in *Uncoverings* 1985, edited by Sally Garoutte (Mill Valley, CA: American Quilt Study Group, 1986), 95–122. She notes that sanitary fairs, held in cities across the country between 1863 and 1865, raised a total of $4.5 million for the cause. Gunn, 106.

13. *Baltimore American and Commercial Daily Advertiser*, May 2, 1864.

14. Ibid., April 19, 1864.

15. Ibid., May 12, 1864.

16. The Kitchen was also a moneymaker with daily receipts averaging $2,000. *Baltimore Daily Gazette*, April 22, 1864. Virginia Gunn has observed that the New England Kitchen was a popular attraction at the Brooklyn and Long Island Fair. Gunn, 109.

17. Ibid., April 28, 1864.

18. Ibid., April 25, 1864. It is curious that with the strong tradition of quiltmaking in Baltimore, the quilting party was a novelty. Unfortunately, the reporter did not note the designs of the quilts worked on during the fair.

19. *Baltimore American*, April 8, 1885. Julie and James Kappler have kindly brought to our attention a series of articles on the Confederate Relief Bazar. They have collected memorabilia associated with the bazar.

20. Ibid., April 11, 1885.

21. Ibid., April 8, 1885. The Confederate Soldiers Home was not opened until 1888.

Interior of the Woman's Exchange from The Baltimore American, *February 29, 1896. (Photograph courtesy of the Maryland Historical Society)*

22. Ibid., April 11 and April 15, 1885.

23. Ibid., April 10 and April 17, 1885.

24. *Baltimore Sun*, November 29, 1959.

25. *Baltimore American*, February 29, 1896.

26. Ibid.

27. Barbara Brackman, *Clues in the Calico* (McLean, VA: EPM Publications, 1989), 23.

28. Jacqueline Marx Atkins, *Shared Threads: Quilting Together—Past and Present* (New York: Viking Studio Books, 1994), 92. Atkins found evidence in a Canandaigua, New York, diary that the Young Ladies Sewing Society made a flag bed quilt for each of its members who sent a soldier to war.

29. In addition to flag quilts, Maryland women made numerous flags and other textile items to express their political support for the Union. The James Cramer and Dean Johnson Collection of patriotic textiles includes a child's apron in the design of a thirty-four-star flag. It is said to have been worn to a Maryland parade in the mid-1860s.

Child's Album Quilt

WHEN CATHARINE ANNA Poole finished her pink and green album quilt, she proudly stitched her name, age (twelve), and the date completed in pink and red cotton thread (109). Her quilt is the only one documented by MAFCE attributed with certainty to a child. Quilts made by children in the nineteenth century are not uncommon. The "Catalogue of Articles" at the 1851 Maryland Institute Fair listed a "Henry Clay Cradle Quilt called Star of the West, made and deposited by Miss Anne McDonald, ten years old."[1] In 1852 the Maryland Institute added a category; Class No. 10 was designated "Juvenile, very aged, and Infirm Persons." A number of young girls and women in their seventies and eighties entered articles in the "Needlework, Quilts, and Embroidery" category. A "quilt made and deposited" by four-year-old "M.L. Fowler" was entered. Presumably she had help from her mother.[2] In 1853 a quilt was "made and deposited" by five-year-old Elizabeth Dixon who entered a Child's Quilt.[3]

Catharine Poole made her album quilt in a style popular with quiltmakers twenty years earlier. She fashioned squares similar in design to those found on mid-century album quilts but used cotton fabrics and colors favored by quiltmakers after the Civil War. The appliquéd designs are heavy and rudimentary, and her modest quilting designs in diagonal and parallel lines are simply worked at twelve stitches to the inch. Nevertheless, the quality is high for a twelve-year-old attempting the challenge of an appliquéd album quilt.

Catharine appliquéd her squares with several designs associated with the Odd Fellows fraternal organization: the heart and hand placed in a five-pointed star surrounded by crossed axes; the three linked rings representing friendship, love, and truth, containing an ax; and the intersecting triangles that form a six-pointed star, surrounding an hour glass. The eagle with three linked rings in the quilt center brings together two American symbols, one patriotic and the other fraternal. Catharine probably knew the symbols from the social activities of her parents, Conrad and Mary. Conrad Poole (b. 1803), a laborer, was probably a member of the Odd Fellows Lodge, and Mary Poole (b. 1803), might have been a member of the Rebekah Lodge, the women's branch of the Odd Fellows order.[4]

Catharine lived her entire life in Frederick County. She married local carpenter Robert Conrad (1854–1920) in 1882 at the German Reformed Church in Frederick (110). She bore seven children, three of whom died in infancy.

Catharine's granddaughter, the present owner of the quilt, remembers her grandmother as a warm, pleasant woman who truly adored children. She has no recollection of her grandmother sewing but does remember that her own mother liked to work samplers. The present owner never had much interest in sewing, but passed the quilting tradition to her two daughters, who today are prolific Maryland quiltmakers.

110. Catharine Anna Poole Conrad and her husband, Robert Conrad. (Photograph courtesy of Catherine Anna Ramsberg Hildebrand)

1. *The Book of the Exhibition: Fourth Annual Exhibition of the Maryland Institute, Baltimore, 1851* (Baltimore, 1852), 459.
2. *Fifth Annual Report of the Board of Managers and Treasurers of the Maryland Institute for the Promotion of the Mechanic Arts* (Baltimore, 1853), 18.
3. *The Book of the Exhibition, Sixth Annual Exhibition of the Maryland Institute for the Promotion of the Mechanic Arts* (Baltimore, 1853), 21.
4. In 1848 at the Maryland Institute Fair an "Odd Fellows Quilt" was entered. *Catalogue of the First Annual Exhibition of the Maryland Institute for the Promotion of the Mechanical Arts Held October 31st, 1848, at Washington Hall, Baltimore* (Baltimore, 1848), 112.

MADE BY CATHARINE ANNA POOLE   AT THE AGE OF 12   FINISHED APRIL 1 1867

109. Detail of Catharine Anna Poole's album quilt with embroidered inscription, "Made by Catharine Anna Poole at the age of 12 Finished April 1, 1867."

APPLIQUÉD ALBUM QUILT, finished April 1, 1867

Made by Catharine Anna Poole (1855–1934)
Frederick County
Cottons
74 x 71 inches
Owned by Catherine Anna Ramsberg Hildebrand

Irish Chain Quilt

QUILTS MADE IN THE Irish Chain pattern are found in Maryland as early as the first two decades of the nineteenth century. The popularity of this pattern peaked in the 1840s, slowly diminishing as the century wore on but never quite disappearing.[1] The pattern regained popularity during the colonial revival period (1876–1940), when quiltmakers sought to reproduce quilts in the style of their colonial ancestors. This simple geometric pattern is still popular with quiltmakers today.

This green/yellow and pink Double Irish Chain quilt covered the black walnut spool bed in which Frank Newcomer Sands was

112. Cecilia Barry Jessop (1800–40), c. 1820, possibly painted by Sarah M. Peale, Baltimore. There has been some discrepancy over the attribution of this portrait. In 1951 scholars attributed it to Jacob Eichholtz. (Courtesy of F. Sands Kiser)

born in 1871. He cherished the quilt his entire life as a comforting reminder of his mother, who gave it to him. The condition is pristine, without visible signs of wear despite its continuous use for more than 100 years. A green and yellow discharge-printed cotton and a double-pink roller-printed cotton, both found frequently on Maryland quilts in the mid-nineteenth century, make up the alternating rows of small pieced squares. The tightly woven, white cotton ground cloth and the lining are cut from the same bolt of fabric. A meandering grapevine, showing the skill of experienced hands, is quilted on the border, twenty-six to thirty stitches per inch.

The maker, Florence Jessop Sands, was the daughter of William and Cecelia Barry Jessop of Vaux Hall, Baltimore County.[2] The Jessop family was prominent in the area, residing there since 1748.[3] Florence's grandfather, Charles Jessop, established a Methodist church in Baltimore County. The Jessop church still stands, although most of the family land was flooded in the early 1930s to form Loch Raven, the present-day source of Baltimore city and county drinking water.

Cecelia died the year Florence was born, possibly from complications of childbirth (112). Her deathbed wish was for her infant daughter to be raised by her best friend, Mary Ann West (1800–82) (113). Family tradition records that William Jessop offered his hand in marriage to Mary Ann but was rejected. Although he soon married another, Mary Ann stayed on in the house to raise Florence. In fact, she spent the rest of her life with Florence, helping to raise her eight children. Even today, descendants of Mary Ann's family and the quilt's present owner keep in touch.

Florence married William Bell Sands in October 1864 at Vaux Hall (111). A prominent young Baltimorean, William was the first person to receive a bachelor of arts degree from the Maryland Agricultural College, now the University of Maryland at College Park. After graduation he became a clerk in the office of U.S. Secretary of War Edwin M. Stanton. William's courtship letters to Florence in 1863 and 1864 recount "musical evenings and visits with friends"

111. Photographs of Florence Jessop Sands, William Bell Sands, and their son, Frank Newcomer Sands, placed on Florence and William's marriage certificate.

113. Mary Ann West (1800–82), c. 1830, painted by Sarah M. Peale, Baltimore. Family history relates that there was "great intimacy" between Sarah Peale and members of the Jessop-Gorsuch-Barry families. Mary Ann West raised Florence after the death of her mother and lived out her adult life with the Jessop/Sands family. (Courtesy of Mary Read Cooper)

and other aspects of the social life of the capital. He joined the Army of the Potomac soon after his marriage, leaving Florence to spend the first year of married life in a boarding house on Garden Street in Baltimore, waiting for the war to end. Obviously devoted to her, William continued to write frequently. Even while on a fishing trip, he flagged a passing boat to deliver a letter to her in Baltimore.[4]

William and Florence had eight children, seven sons and one daughter. Their fourth child, Frank, and his siblings grew up in the large, rambling family home on Lake Roland in Baltimore County. Frank later became a successful banker and stockbroker in Baltimore City. The quilt descended to Frank's daughter, Margaret Sands Kiser Crebbin. She was an avid collector of quilts from the 1930s through the 1940s, amassing a large number. She sold the quilts in 1985 just before she died. She already had presented Florence Sand's Irish Chain quilt to her daughter, the present owner, in 1953.

1. Jennifer Faulds Goldsborough, *Lavish Legacies: Baltimore Album and Related Quilts in the Collection of the Maryland Historical Society* (Baltimore: Maryland Historical Society, 1994), 17. Goldsborough quotes from a diary in the manuscripts division of the Library of Maryland History at the Maryland Historical Society: ". . . I saw one the pattern of the Irish Chain which was quite pretty. . . ." Hannah Mary Trimble Papers, MS2517, diary entry, February 1, 1850. Although quilts in the Irish Chain pattern are known that date prior to 1850, this is the earliest written reference to the pattern known to the authors.
2. The Smithsonian Institution owns a quilt top attributed to Cecilia Barry Jessop (1800–40) and her mother-in-law, Mary Gorsuch Jessop (1767–1832), between 1800 and 1840. The daughter of the donor questions this attribution. After examining family documents she feels this top was made by Cecilia's mother, Jemina, and

sister Mary. The laid designs on the Smithsonian Institution top are cut from fabric manufactured at the printworks of the noted Philadelphia textile printer John Hewson. Hewson prints show up on another quilt made in Baltimore now in the collection of the DAR Museum. Correspondence with Mary Read Cooper, April 15, 1994.
3. William Jessop arrived in Maryland by 1748, marrying Margaret Walker in Baltimore on June 25 of that year. They had six children; the fourth was Florence's grandfather. "Florence's two grandmothers were sisters, Mary Gorsuch Jessop, mother of her father, William, and Jemina Gorsuch Barry, mother of her mother, Cecelia. Thus William and Cecelia were first cousins."

PIECED QUILT, c. 1871

Made by Florence Jessop Sands (1840–1910) for her son Frank Newcomer Sands (b. 1871)
Hollins Station, Lake Roland, Baltimore County
Cottons
101.5 x 103 inches
Owned by Mary Read Cooper

Correspondence with Mary Read Cooper, April 15, 1994.
4. The authors are grateful to Mary Read Cooper for allowing us to quote from her article on her grandfather published in *Maryland Today*, May 1984.

Mezick-Houston Wedding Quilt

WHEN SARAH ELIZA-beth Mezick married Levin James Houston (1841–1906) on July 7, 1870, she received as a gift a Mariner's Compass quilt (114). Probably made by her mother, Anne B. Stevenson Mezick, this striking quilt combines bright blue rainbow prints from the 1840s with more recently purchased fabrics. The slender points of the compass are set off by fine diamond quilting (116). The blocks are defined by pieced Garden Maze sashing and enclosed by an appliquéd and fully stuffed rosevine border. Both the Mariner's Compass pattern and the Garden Maze sashing were popular in Maryland for many decades. In this instance, the compass motif was especially appropriate; Levin Houston had been a sea captain on the Chesapeake Bay before his marriage.[1] Stuffed roses, which give the quilt dimension, were frequently used by

114. Sarah Elizabeth Mezick Houston and Levin James Houston. (Photographs courtesy of Mary Lou Justice)

Maryland quiltmakers on album, Rose of Sharon, and other floral appliqué quilts.

Before her marriage Sarah Mezick lived with her family in Newtowne, now Pocomoke City, Worcester County. Sarah's father, Francis Mezick, was a trader, who also owned a hat business, introducing the first silk hats into the area. Sarah met her future husband while taking singing lessons in Pocomoke, where both had joined the Presbyterian church choir. After a successful career at sea during the Civil War years, Levin Houston started a business in Stockton in 1869. Eventually he acquired most of the land around the town. He combined grain farming with the operation of a general store, sawmill, and grist mill.[2]

Sarah and Levin's six children included Cecelia Polk.[3] During World War I, Cecelia, a nurse, was in charge of a hospital in Marseilles, France (115). After the war she supervised the nursing staff at Johns Hopkins University Hospital in Baltimore. During the Great Depression she was drafted by Worcester County to be the county nurse. She inherited her mother's wedding quilt, which she in turn left to her favorite niece, Josephine.

Josephine Houston Justice was the keeper of the family records. Her home, and now those of her descendants, was filled with family heirlooms. She treasured her grandmother's quilt; she instilled in her son and his family the importance of keeping the past alive. In 1989, the year before her death, Josephine wrote in her family album, "If we do not honor the achievements of our ancestors, it is unlikely that we shall accomplish anything by which our descendants will remember us."

1. Barbara Brackman has determined that this pattern motif was not known as Mariner's Compass in the nineteenth century. The earliest published reference with pattern and name combined comes from a 1929 Oklahoma farmers' publication. A signed and dated quilt in this pattern from 1878, documented in Kansas, had the name "Virginia Beauty" written on the back. Over the years, the motif has been referred to by many names, more often astronomical than nautical. Barbara Brackman, *Clues in the Calico* (McLean, VA: EPM Publications, 1989), 167. MAFCE recorded eight quilts identified by maker or owner as Mariner's Compass. No maker or owner referred to her quilt pattern as Mathematical Star, yet that name was used by judges at the Maryland Institute Fair for a number of quilts made in the late 1840s and 1850s.
2. Mary Lou Justice has kindly supplied the authors with information on her husband's family.
3. Cecelia Houston added "Polk" to her name. According to family tradition, she was a great admirer of Leonidas Polk, Episcopal bishop and Confederate general. Polk was killed in battle at Pine Mountain, Georgia.

116. Detail of one compass block.

PIECED, APPLIQUÉD, AND STUFFED
MARINER'S COMPASS QUILT, c. 1870

Probably made by Anne B. Stevenson Mezick
(1813–80) for her daughter, Sarah Elizabeth Mezick
Houston (1846–1930)
Pocomoke City, Worcester County
Cottons
101 x 101 inches
Owned by James Harold Justice

Sophia's Star Quilt

SOPHIA RUTH PECKHAM Reid probably made her colorful star quilt shortly before the 1872 marriage of her daughter Sophia Jane Reid to John T. Buxton (117). Using a star pattern popular in Maryland for a number of decades, she pieced together a selection of printed fabrics from the 1860s and 1870s and added a border cut from a fashionable paisley-style print. Eight-pointed stars are applied around a large central star and to the wide

inner border. The placement of stars recalls a quilt made almost thirty years earlier by an Eastern Shore woman (p. 66). Like Sarah Woolford, to whom the earlier quilt is attributed, Sophia Reid also used a different number of points for the star directly below the large central star. Both quilts are finely quilted at twenty stitches to the inch; this one is embellished with flowers and leaves, the earlier with pineapples and rosettes.

Although no other quilts by Sophia Ruth Reid are known, she was undoubtedly an accomplished seamstress. She grew up on F Street in Washington City, where her mother, Sophia LaBille Peckham, a French Catholic immigrant, conducted a dame school for young boys and girls. One of Mrs. Peckham's former students recalled years later that the girls who attended the school were taught to sew in addition to learning the "three R's." She reminisced, "When I left Mrs. Peckham I could stitch and do overcasting as well as I can now, and in those days when man's shirt bosoms were stitched by hand those things counted."[1]

Sophia Ruth Peckham was teaching with her mother at the time she met Thomas Reid, a graduate of Georgetown University and a teacher in a school on L Street. According to family tradition, Reid had intended to enter the priesthood, but his plans were derailed when he met and fell in love with Sophia Ruth. They were married in 1844 in St. Matthew's Catholic Church in Washington City and shortly thereafter moved about thirty miles outside the city to a farm between the villages of Boyds and Cloppers in Montgomery County. Calling their home the Bear's Den, there they farmed the land and raised eight children (118).[2] Sophia Jane Reid was their second daughter and the first to marry. Her older sister, Mary Agnes, joined the Sisters of Charity, and another sister joined the Sisters of the Holy Cross. Sophia Jane Reid and

John Buxton had two daughters who remained single, so the quilt descended in the family of another sister, Frances Reid Van Doren, to her granddaughter, the present owner and keeper of the family record.[3]

In addition to her talents as a seamstress, Sophia Ruth Peckham Reid is remembered as "a remarkable woman" and for "her devotion to her church and to her friends; her kindly advice and her never failing Christianity . . . "[4]

1. Recalled by Miss Louisa Weightman in the 1930s and published in a *Washington Star* article written by John Proctor and compiled in John Clagett Proctor, *Proctor's Washington and Environs* (Washington, DC: 1949), 284.
2. The Reid farm was probably part of a 200-acre tract surveyed in 1729 as Bear Den; T.H.S. Boyd, *The History of Montgomery County, Maryland from Its Earliest Settlement in 1650 to 1879* (Baltimore: Regional Publishing, 1968), 44.
3. We are grateful to Helen Elizabeth Van Doren for supplying us with information on her fascinating and well-documented family.
4. Obituary of Mrs. Sophia R. Reid published in the *Washington Evening Star*, about May 5, 1902.

PIECED AND APPLIQUÉD MATHEMATICAL
STAR QUILT, c. 1872

Made by Sophia Ruth Peckham Reid (1819–1902) for
her daughter Sophia Jane Reid (1848–1922)
Bear's Den, near Cloppers, Montgomery County
Cottons
90 x 88 inches
Owned by Helen Elizabeth Van Doren

Garden of Eden Quilt Top

IN SPITE OF THE PRESENCE OF the name "John Adkins" and date "1874" on this unusual quilt top, very little is known about it. Passed down in the Miller/Anderson family of Baltimore County for several generations, the present owner has a faint memory of her mother attributing the quilt top to a great-aunt, Josephine Miller. According to family history, the Miller family operated a dry-goods store in Baltimore City in the 1870s. The 1872 city directory for Baltimore lists Daniel Miller & Co., wholesale dry-goods merchants at the corner of Baltimore and German streets, and Roger Miller & Co., also wholesale dry-goods merchants, located several stores away.[1]

Although the design of this quilt top is called Garden of Eden, it does not contain the figures Adam and Eve but is composed of four appliquéd squares joined together by a large eight-pointed star. A fabric-covered wooden button anchors the design elements in the middle of the central star. Open-weave appliquéd baskets hold stuffed flowers in all four corners of each square. Stuffed animal and bird figures surround a small star in each square, while two squares contain a snake and an apple tree. Padded heart, leaf, butterfly, and fish motifs are interspersed among the larger figurative designs. Many of the padded designs are laid on by wool embroidery in a style that harks back to the exotic album quilts made around 1850 (p. 124), and precedes the embellished crazy quilts that became popular in the 1880s. The seven-inch-wide green scalloped border surrounding the squares places the appliquéd field in relief, adding to the uniqueness of the design.

Several quilts exist identified by the authors that are similar to this one. The Smithsonian Institution is home to a quilt purchased in a church bazar in Fort Smith, Arkansas, around 1900. This quilt has a central star and corner baskets holding flowers, as does the Maryland quilt. Both also feature leaves, birds, butterflies, trees, and a scalloped border. Although the quilt at the Smithsonian Institution is not dated, it probably was made during the last quarter of the nineteenth century.[2]

Another Garden of Eden quilt is pictured in *American Quilts* by Jennifer Regan and attributed to Abby F. Bell Ross of Irvington, New Jersey.[3] It is dated 1874, the same year as the quilt shown here. Both are approximately the same size and share such common images as animals, birds, butterflies, trees, snakes, and fish. The quilt pictured in Regan's book has a medallion format unlike the Maryland block configuration.

Although the design source for the Garden of Eden quilts is unidentified, the inspiration probably grew from the conflict between science and religion that was raging in the second half of the nineteenth century (119). In 1859 Charles Darwin published *Origin of Species* and proposed the idea of biological evolution and natural selection. His theory of evolution took western society by storm. It was debated in Europe during the years the United States was preoccupied by the Civil War. Darwin published *The Descent of Man* in 1871 and a year later, *The Expression of the Emotion in Man and Animal*. Both of these books explored Darwin's theory in greater detail. The years when the Garden of Eden quilts were being made were the years evolutionary theory was being debated in newspapers and pulpits across the United States. A grass roots movement begun by the American Protestant Orthodoxy's annual Bible conferences dealt with issues relating to liberalism and criticism against the Bible. Darwin's theory was an obvious and popular target.[4] The Garden of Eden quilts probably were made to show support for the literal interpretation of the Bible. The maker of this quilt was following in the footsteps of those quiltmakers who had gone before who used the needle to illustrate their political leanings.

119. Cartoon, Harper's Bazar, "A Pretty How-de-do," September 30, 1876. Illustrated in this satirical cartoon is a farm family gathered around "Aunt Perlina's bedquilt" and judging it "not suitable for exhibition at the Centennial." Just a few weeks before this cartoon appeared in Harper's Bazar another was featured satirizing Darwin's theory of evolution. (Photograph courtesy of the Library of Congress)

A PRETTY HOW-DE-DO.
AUNT PERLINA'S BED-QUILT IS RETURNED AS NOT SUITABLE FOR EXHIBITION AT THE CENTENNIAL.

1. Baltimore City Directory, 1872.
2. Doris M. Bowman, *The Smithsonian Treasury: American Quilts* (Washington, DC: Smithsonian Institution Press, 1991), 63.
3. Jennifer Regan, *American Quilts: A Sampler of Quilts and Their Stories* (New York: Gallery Books, 1989), 29–30. Several Garden of Eden quilts are illustrated in this book.
4. Many thanks to Renee Bomgardner at the DAR Museum for sharing her unpublished paper on the impact of Darwinism and the Scopes trial in American

APPLIQUÉD GARDEN OF EDEN QUILT TOP,
1874

Made for John Adkins
Probably Baltimore City
Cottons, wool, embroidered inscriptions
87 x 80 inches
Owned by Verna Walter

Amish and Mennonite Log Cabin Quilt

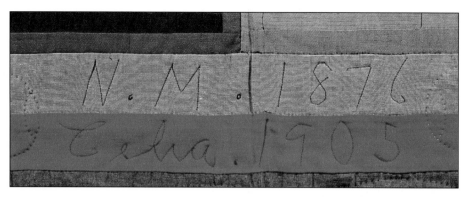

NANCY MILLER AND HER husband, Elias J. Miller, resided in a small Amish and Mennonite community in the mountains of Garrett County in western Maryland (120). Elias worked as a cabinetmaker and undertaker near Grantsville, Maryland, a town just a few miles from his birthplace, Springs, Pennsylvania. He probably served clients on

120. Nancy Miller (d. 1922). (Photograph courtesy of Rhoda Hummel)

both sides of the state line as did most other business owners in the area.

Nancy and Elias were the parents of three daughters, one of whom assembled and then quilted this bedcover (121). Celia Miller was born in 1884, eight years after her mother pieced the quilt top (122). Although she was raised in an Amish home, Celia became a Mennonite when she married Irvin Shoemaker from nearby Pennsylvania. She and Irvin settled on a small farm in Shade Hollow, Garrett County. Irvin supported the family as a day laborer and at times worked as a coal miner in Niverton. Celia, raised five children, was a prolific needlewoman, making at least one quilt for each child and later for her grandchildren.[1] The patterns Celia preferred included Log Cabin, Double Wedding Ring, Devil's Puzzle, and Dutch Babies. She obtained these patterns, which she traced onto heavy brown paper, from friends and relatives in a way that documents the sharing of a tradition as well as social and religious bonds: using a finished pieced or appliquéd square obtained from another quilter as a pattern for a larger quilt. Celia would incorporate the square into the quilt, along with other squares she made herself. This practice of sharing patterns may have been common among religious sectarians in the county as well as a longstanding tradition.[2]

121. Detail of quilted initials and dates on Nancy Miller and Celia Shoemaker's log cabin quilt.

1. Interview with the owner, August 1994.
2. This is the only mention of this method of sharing patterns documented by the MAFCE project. An informal survey of quilt publications led the authors to conclude that this quilt narrative may present the only published account of this method of pattern transmission.

122. Celia Miller Shoemaker (1884–1981). (Photograph courtesy of Rhoda Hummel)

PIECED LOG CABIN QUILT, 1872–1902

Made by Nancy Miller (d. 1922) and Celia Miller
Shoemaker (1884–1981)
Shade Hollow, near Grantsville, Garrett County
Wool, cotton
89 x 89 inches
Owned by Rhoda Hummel

Quaker Log Cabin Quilt

THE REYNOLDS FAMILY OF Cecil County traces its ancestry to the early eighteenth century. In 1702 Henry Reynolds (b. 1655) settled on two of the thirty-seven Nottingham Lots of 500 acres granted by William Penn to eighteen Quaker families who had migrated from New Castle, Delaware, the preceding year. Originally territory claimed by Pennsylvania, the land is now part of Cecil County, Maryland.

In 1861 Stephen J. Reynolds (1832–1926), a descendant of Henry and son of Jacob and Ann Moore Reynolds, married Anna Amelia Phillips in a Quaker ceremony at the home of her parents, David and Ann Amelia Holcomb Phillips (123).[1] The wedding, joining two families prominent in the milling business, was witnessed by relatives and friends, all members of the Nottingham Meeting.[2] The young couple initially went to housekeeping in Lancaster County, Pennsylvania, but a few years later returned to the Reynolds family homestead. There Stephen achieved recognition as an "energetic and progressive agriculturalist,"[3] and his wife, Anna Amelia, gained respect as a Public Friend or minister in the Quaker faith.[4] A local history describes her role in the Nottingham Meeting:

She was a most estimable lady, beloved by all who knew her, and a faithful member of the Society of Friends, taking an active and prominent part in the work of that church, and for a number of years was a prominent minister in the society to which she belonged.[5]

Through her official recognition as a Quaker minister, Anna Amelia Reynolds moved into a public leadership role in her community and gained respect usually afforded to male leaders.[6]

The Reynoldses' first two children were born in the 1860s; their third child and only son, William, was born nearly twenty years later in 1881. Two pieced quilts made by Anna Amelia date from this period and have descended in the male line. The Barn Raising quilt illustrated here is pieced from colorful small-figured prints popular in the 1870s and 1880s. The red, green, and yellow color combination is varied with the introduction of different prints in the four corners. Two additional printed fabrics were used for the lining and binding. Anna Amelia's other quilt is a nine patch in a predominantly green and brown color scheme that recalls the hues of Quaker dresses. Except for the colors of these printed fabrics, the Reynolds quilts cannot be distinguished as Quaker. They are in the mainstream of late-nineteenth-century American quilt-making traditions.

A family member owns Anna Amelia's marking sampler, worked in 1852, and her mother's sampler, worked in 1816 (124).

124. Sampler worked in 1852 by Anna Amelia Phillips. (Courtesy of Mrs. William Reynolds)

The earlier sampler is especially characteristic of samplers made in schools organized by the Society of Friends.

1. Most of the Reynoldses in the Cecil County area descend from Henry Reynolds. Henry and Haines Reynolds, whose names appear on a friendship quilt (p. 107), were great-grandsons of Henry Reynolds.
2. Alice L. Beard, *Births, Deaths and Marriages of the Nottingham Quakers* (Westminster, MD: Family Line Publications, 1989), 91, 228.
3. *Biographical Record of Harford and Cecil County Maryland* (Westminster, MD: Family Line Publications, 1989), 262.
4. In the Quaker faith, ministers were "recorded" or designated by the monthly meeting. They were particularly gifted men and women, unusually inspired by the spirit of God, who practiced lay ministry and provided most of the vocal messages in the meeting. We are grateful to Elizabeth T. Brown of the Quaker Collection, Haverford College, for this information.
5. *Biographical Record*, 262.
6. Joan M. Jensen, *Loosening the Bonds: Mid-Atlantic Farm Women, 1750–1850* (New Haven: Yale University Press, 1986), 147. Jensen includes an informative chapter on the historical role of women in the Quaker faith.

123. Stephen J. and Anna Amelia Phillips Reynolds. (Photograph courtesy of Mrs. William Reynolds)

BARN RAISING QUILT, c. 1880

Made by Anna Amelia Phillips Reynolds (1841–93)
Cecil County
Cottons
88 x 88 inches
Owned by Mrs. William Reynolds

Sampler Quilt

"Mother, Wast mild and lovely - gentle as the summer breeze."

Tombstone inscription, 1897
Anna Stover

ALTHOUGH THIS COMplex sampler quilt was made in Maryland, it resembles closely several sampler quilts made in neighboring Pennsylvania. Quilt patterns and design ideas crossed state lines as easily as farmers' wagons and family carriages visiting relatives on Sunday. Descendants of the quiltmaker, Anna Stover, who was a first generation German-American, entered the quilt in the York County Fair in Pennsylvania for several years in the 1920s. One year it took first prize, and the owners were awarded free admittance to the fair.

Anna Stover and her husband, Absalom (1825–1906), resided on a farm in New Midway, a small community in Frederick County located just a few miles from the Pennsylvania border (125). The Stovers and their fourteen children were members of the Rocky Ridge Church of the Brethren; many of them are buried in the church cemetery. Amanda, Anna and Absalom's daughter, inherited the quilt and passed it to her daughter, who then gave it to her son and daughter-in-law. They are presently storing the quilt safely for another generation of the family.

The quilt, although relatively small, is composed of 100 six-inch pieced squares, each an example of a different quilt pattern that was popular with quiltmakers at the end of the nineteenth century. The quilt's colors—indigo, yellow, green, and red—were very popular during this period with middle-class farm women such as Anna Stover.

The current name for this type of quilt is Sampler quilt, indicating that it is a sampler of different quilt patterns. Though sometimes patterns are repeated, in many quilts of this type all squares are different. Historian Jeannette Lasansky states in her article "The Colonial Revival and Quilts, 1864–1976" that the few extant sampler quilts from this period probably were inspired by the single-block quilt patterns published between the 1880s and the 1920s by such catalogue companies as the Ladies Art Company of St. Louis, Missouri.[1]

125. *Anna Elizabeth Buzzard Stover with her husband, Absalom Stover. (Photograph courtesy of Martha Brose Swapp)*

1. Jeannette Lasansky, "The Colonial Revival and Quilts 1864–1976," in Jeannette Lasansky, ed., *Pieced by Mother: Symposium Papers* (Lewisburg, PA: Oral Traditions Project, 1988), 97–105. Two sampler quilts (one is used as the cover illustration) are pictured in this article.

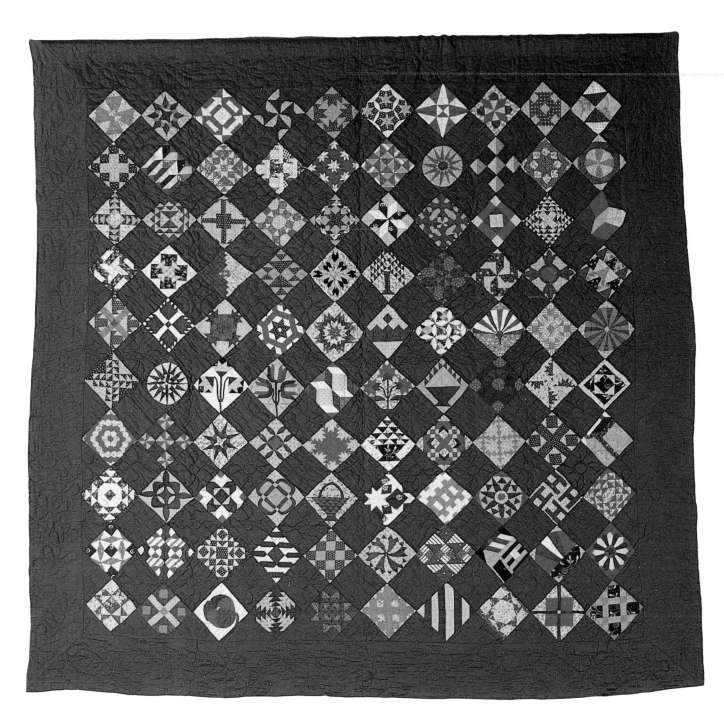

PIECED SAMPLER QUILT, 1880–97

Made by Anna Elizabeth Buzzard Stover (1828–97)
New Midway, Frederick County
Cottons
69 x 71 inches
Owned by Martha Brose Swapp

Leaf Quilt

VIRGINIA ELLEN BASSETT married Isaac W. Nock (1852–96) in 1873 and went to live at the Nock farm outside of Newark in Worcester County, where Isaac grew corn and wheat and Virginia raised their three children and helped with farm chores. During the third winter of their marriage and before their first child was born, Virginia Nock had some unexpected leisure time. To occupy herself during long days confined indoors, Virginia decided to make a quilt. Lacking patterns and any other quilts to copy, Virginia took a walk in the nearby woods and selected two leaves to use as templates for her original design.[1] The large oak leaves and smaller walnut leaves and hearts are cut from chrome orange and white cloth and appliquéd to a deep blue ground.[2] The large quilting stitches, done in orange, white, and blue thread, echo the contours of the leaves.

Quiltmakers frequently took inspiration from their environment and copied directly from nature. Leaves were especially favored because they came in a variety of interesting shapes, could be easily traced,[3] and were always available when printed patterns were not. A former slave woman recalled that ". . . she got the pattern [for her quilt] by goin' out into the woods an' gettin a leaf to cut it by. The two parts of the pattern is cut from the bull-tongue leaf and the gopher grass."[4] The son of a Maryland African-American quiltmaker also related that he used to pick up oak leaves on his way home from school in rural Charles County for his mother to use as patterns for her c. 1930 oak-leaf quilt.[5]

Unidentified Eastern Shore lady at her needlework, c. 1870. Carte-de-visite taken by R. Clay Crawford, Chestertown. (Photograph courtesy of the Maryland Historical Society)

In a collection of reminiscences by Worcester County residents, many farm women recalled sewing and quilting activities at the end of the nineteenth century. Virginia Nock probably knew some of the women who contributed to the oral history of her community; her experiences may have been similar. Gertrude Truitt Collins remembered that her mother made all their underwear: "Drawers, flannel petticoats in winter. Red for school. For Sunday, sometimes blue and sometimes white . . . and of course our dresses were all gingham and calico."[6] Mrs. Fred Cherrix told of using clothing scraps for rag rugs: "We tore up rags. Any kind of clothes we had, tore it in little strips, sewed it together. They would fasten the rags to this [shuttle] and give it a fling across this loom . . . we made carpet for a good bit of the house."[7] Mary White reminisced about quiltings: "They used to have quilting parties. Whole great big crowds would gather . . . and make homemade ice cream and make a party out of it. The men would come sit in one room, and the women in the other room, quilting. We used to have a good time."[8]

1. The authors are grateful to Virginia Sturgis for sharing with us this family tradition.
2. Red oak and black walnut trees are native to the Eastern Shore. Virginia's heart shape may have been inspired by the heart-shaped leaf of the mulberry tree. During the 1830s, as part of the "silk craze," many mulberry trees were planted up and down the Eastern Shore.
3. Leaf motifs are found on many mid- to late-nineteenth-century Maryland quilts. Women who had the opportunity to travel collected leaves and flowers and pressed them in their albums and scrapbooks. Other women found a variety of leaves closer to home. Quilting patterns drawn in the early 1850s for the Woodbourne and Waters quilts included several dozen leaf designs, some identified by species (pp. 142–45).

Also in the mid-nineteenth century, Elizabeth Huyett of Frederick County made a leaf quilt; it was described as such in her 1878 estate inventory and valued at $6 (p. 49). Mary Brown of Cecil County was inspired by the forms she found in nature, cutting out a number of leaf shapes for the quilt she made for Israel Reynolds in 1852 (p. 131).
4. Quoted from a Mississippi slave narrative by Gladys Fry, *Stitched from the Soul: Slave Quilts from the Ante-Bellum South* (New York: Dutton Studio Books, 1990), 46.
5. Although the family history suggests otherwise, the authors (having seen other quilts in a similar pattern) believe the design of the oak-leaf quilt came from an as-yet-to-be identified published pattern.
6. Victoria J. Heland, *Worcester Memories 1890–1933* (Snow Hill, MD: Worcester Heritage Committee, 1984), 9.
7. Ibid.
8. Ibid., 108.

APPLIQUÉD LEAF QUILT, c. 1876

Made by Virginia Ellen Bassett Nock (1852–1939)
Nock Farm, near Newark, Worcester County
Cottons
94 x 75.5 inches
Owned by Virginia T. Sturgis

Aunt Liz's Twenty-Day Quilt

A PROLIFIC AND ENER-getic quiltmaker, Amanda Elizabeth Dryden may have made this vibrant Whig Rose quilt in only twenty days. In one corner she embroidered in chain stitch her initials and a beginning date, "March 11th 1885," and in the opposite corner the completion date, "April 1th 1885."[1] She repeated the date "1885" in the other two corners. The rose blocks, pieced in pie-shaped sections, are outlined by quilting of eighteen stitches to the inch and meet at small corner blocks, creating a four-patch effect that contrasts with the curvilinear flowers.[2] The pieced sawtooth border is enclosed by a blue-green border, edged with orange binding applied front to back and cut into five-eighths-inch high triangles or saw-teeth (126). According to family memory, Amanda did the piecing, appliquéing, and fine stitching by herself on the family farm near Furnacetown in Worcester County. A niece recalled her always doing needlework. One of her great-nephews mentioned that she quilted all the time; another remembered that she was never without her tatting and crocheting.

The Dryden family settled near Eden on the lower Eastern Shore of Maryland between 1695 and 1700. George Johnson Dryden (1830–1905), Amanda's father, married Catherine E. Jones (1829–94) in 1855 and moved from Eden in Somerset County to Furnacetown, where they raised nine children. Amanda Elizabeth grew up on the family farm. After her youngest brother married, she moved to the town of Newark to join her sister, Annie.[3]

Amanda Elizabeth, or Aunt Liz as she was usually known, never married but left many examples of beautiful handiwork as her legacy.

Amanda's Whig Rose quilt passed to her brother George's daughter, and then to her son, Bennett. She gave another quilt, remembered as a lovely crazy throw, to the daughter of her youngest brother, Putnam.

126. *Amanda Elizabeth Dryden (1857–1946), around 1890. Her photograph is shown against a corner of her quilt where she has embroidered her initials and the date she started work. The large sawteeth are pieced, and the small sawteeth are brought from back to front and appliquéd to the blue-green border. (Photograph courtesy of Mimi F. and A. Bennett Boulden Jr.)*

PIECED AND APPLIQUÉD WHIG ROSE QUILT, 1885

Made by Amanda Elizabeth Dryden (1857–1946)
Near Furnacetown, Worcester County
Cottons, embroidered inscriptions
89 x 88 inches
Owned by Mimi F. and A. Bennett Boulden Jr.

1. The date is spelled incorrectly on the quilt, "April 1th," rather than April 1st. It is not clear whether the dates refer to the total time Amanda worked on the quilt or to the time it took for her to do the quilting. Family members believe the twenty-day span refers to the quilting period.
2.. Bets Ramsey has observed that some rose blocks that we assume to be appliquéd are actually pieced. She, Cuesta Benberry, and others have documented about twenty-five examples of pieced-rose construction in a variety of styles. Most of these date from the mid-nineteenth century. Bets Ramsey, *Old and New Quilt Patterns in the Southern Tradition* (Nashville: Rutledge Hill, 1987), 33–35, and personal communications, January 2 and 11, 1995.
3. Dryden family history courtesy of the Bouldens and Virginia Dryden Moore.

Carpenter's Wheel Quilt

EVA ELIZABETH HILL GREW up on a farm near Snow Hill in Worcester County (127). When Eva was six months old, her mother died, and Eva went to live on the nearby farm of Levin Causey, farmer and herb doctor, and his wife, Hetty, who had seven unmarried children of their own.[1]

Around 1895 Eva Hill became the second wife of Thomas Cornelius Dunlap (1851–1932), a Scottish-Irish baker who had emigrated to the United States as a young man. Eva kept busy raising Annie, Thomas's daughter by his first wife, and Mabel, her own daughter, and tending to their large garden.

Snow Hill was a good location for a bakery at the end of the nineteenth century. The town, settled in 1642 and twice burned, could boast a railroad station, bank, lumber mill, two shirt factories, several clothing and dry-goods stores, a drugstore, two ice cream parlors, and a barber shop.

Eva Hill made several quilts before her marriage; she had capable assistants among the daughters in the Causey family. Priscilla, the second oldest Causey daughter still living at home in 1880, earned her living as a seamstress and probably encouraged Eva in her needlework.

The vibrant Carpenter's Wheel quilt, with its Flying Geese sashing, was pieced from solid-colored orange, green, and reddish-brown cottons. The striking use of chrome-orange fabric in this quilt, and in other appliquéd and pieced quilts made in Worcester County and neighboring Wicomico County during the last quarter of the nineteenth century, indicates the local availability and popularity of this brightly dyed fabric.[2] Though favored by quiltmakers at this time, chrome-orange fabrics were rarely used for clothing.[3]

1. The 1850 federal census records fifty-two-old Levey Causey living in Snow Hill with his wife, seven children, and two-year-old Eva Hill.
2. Of the quilts researched for this book, not all of which could be included, the authors found chrome-orange fabric in three made in Worcester County (pp. 178, 180) and in one made in Wicomico County.
3. The owner of this quilt and the owners of two of the quilts cited above mentioned clothing scraps as the source for their quilts' fabrics, but this seems unlikely. For a discussion of orange

PIECED CARPENTER'S WHEEL QUILT, 1875–95

Made by Eva Elizabeth Hill (1859–1930)
Near Snow Hill, Worcester County
Cottons
92 x 93.5 inches
Owned by Annilin Buppert

fabrics in nineteenth-century dress goods, see Ricky Clark, George W. Knepper, and Ellice Ronsheim, *Quilts in Community: Ohio's Traditions* (Nashville: Rutledge Hill, 1991), 75–76. The authors conclude that the color orange, considered unflattering to Caucasian skin tones, was little used for dress fabrics. Solid-colored orange, red, and green cottons, found in appliqué quilts from the 1840s on, were not found in existing cotton dresses of the same period. The brightly dyed fabrics may have been manufactured specifically for quiltmaking.

127. Eva Elizabeth Hill Dunlap, 1859–1930, in a photograph taken when she was in her early fifties. (Photograph courtesy of Mabel D. Hudson and Ann L. Hudson)

St. John's Chapel Tithing Quilt

PIECED AND APPLIQUÉD CRAZY
FUNDRAISING QUILT, 1895–96

*Made by members of St. John's Chapel Methodist
Episcopal Church South*
Tilghman Island, Talbot County
Cottons, silks, painted and embroidered inscriptions
86 x 84 inches
Owned by John C. Millican

BETWEEN 1895 AND 1896, more than 400 members and friends of St. John's Chapel, Tilghman Island, Talbot County, donated money to their new church. Their names, initials, and, in some cases, the amounts contributed were embroidered in twenty blocks of this "crazy" style quilt. The tithing quilt, which is tied rather than quilted, is now owned by the grandson of the church's minister at the time it was made.

Rev. Charles Kitchens Millican (1864–1934) was born in northwest Georgia. After receiving his seminary training at Emory University in Atlanta and ministering in Virginia, he was assigned in 1893 to serve the Methodist Episcopal Church South parishes of St. John's Chapel and Royal Oak, both in Talbot County, Maryland.

The Methodist Episcopal Church South had broken from the pro-Union parent church in 1846. Members sympathizing with the Southern cause founded new churches, locating many of them in the same towns with their former churches.

St. John's Chapel was organized in 1890 and its building completed in 1891 at a cost of $2,000. Local residents still recall the story of the church's lumber, which had been transported from North Carolina to Tilghman Island on a skipjack. While anchored in Black Walnut Cove, the boat—either by a storm or malicious intent—was overturned and the lumber set adrift. Islanders salvaged most of the wood and construction proceeded as planned.[1] In 1893 the Rev. Charles Kitchens Millican, along

with his wife, Lucy Keister Millican (1865–1924), and their three-year-old son, Smithson, came to St. John's Chapel as its first regular minister (130). The Millicans stayed until 1895 when church leaders assigned him to another circuit.

St. John's Chapel still stands on a barren tract of land more than halfway down Tilghman Island and several miles from the bridge connecting the island with mainland Talbot County (128). The island always has been somewhat cut off from the rest of the county, and the people have kept to themselves. However, in the words of a local historian, "On Tilghman . . . life bloomed in the 1880s and 1890s" as the island community reinforced its bonds of kinship and occupation through husking bees, oyster roasts, berry pickings, "straw" rides, and box socials.[2] Oystermen, sailors, and boat builders made up the majority of the island's population, who made a living in

the traditional ways of the Chesapeake Bay.[3] Many shucked and packed oysters at local island firms; by 1891 they were among the 32,000 people across Maryland who worked in oyster-related jobs.[4] Bay oysters were packed by a steam-canning process and shipped by refrigerated rail cars from St. Michaels, Talbot County, directly to consumers in Philadelphia and New York City, and from there across the United States.

The Reverend Mr. Millican's parishioners fit the demographic profile of the island. Of

128. St. John's Chapel as it looks today. (Photograph courtesy of Elizabeth Hughes)

129. Detail showing the Kinnamon family tree and the names of Rev. Charles Millican and his wife.

animals, fans, and Christian symbols. The block to the upper right of the center fan block, which includes the names of Charles Millican and his wife, also includes the Kinnamon family tree or Tree-of-Life (129). Many, but not all, of the Kinnamons inscribed on the tree can be located in the 1900 census; some of the names may memorialize deceased family members or represent relatives living off the island.[6]

The quilt was worked and assembled totally by hand even though in 1887 Margaret Sinclair, kin to the numerous Sinclair "signers," became the proud owner of the first sewing machine on Tilghman Island, an event sufficiently noteworthy to merit mention in a history of Talbot County.[7]

the seventy-two men whose entire names were embroidered or painted on the quilt and who could be located in the 1900 federal census, forty-one were oystermen or sailors. These watermen, noted for their independence and rugged endurance, braved the winter winds and ice storms to harvest oysters from September to April. Many of their wives, usually described in the census as "keeping house," probably were responsible for the artistry on the tithing quilt. They raised donations ranging from $2 to $7 and recorded in stitches many of the amounts. They presented the finished quilt to their minister as a remembrance of his short stay on Tilghman Island.[5]

Typical of crazy quilts of the 1890s, the St. John's Chapel quilt includes a variety of fancy fabrics and artistic techniques. Names and initials were both painted and embroidered; individual areas have pieced, appliquéd, and painted designs of flowers,

1. The authors are grateful to Elizabeth Hughes, William Bodenstein, and Anne Pettit for sharing with us their wealth of information and documentary evidence for Tilghman Island and Talbot County.
2. Dickson J. Preston, *Talbot County: A History* (Centerville, MD: Tidewater Publishers, 1983), 243. "Straw" ride was the local term for hayride.
3. Ninety-eight out of 162, or 61 percent, of the heads of households listed in the 1900 census for Tilghman Island made their living from the Bay.
4. Suzanne Ellery Greene Chapelle et al., *Maryland: A History of Its People* (Baltimore: Johns Hopkins University Press, 1986), 204.
5. Jacqueline Atkins refers to this type of fundraising quilt as a tithing or revenue quilt where church members pledged varying amounts for specific projects or church upkeep. She notes that sometimes the amount donated was embroidered along with the name. Jacqueline Marx Atkins, *Shared Threads: Quilting Together—Past and Present* (New York: Viking Studio Books, 1994), 69.
6. Although the total membership of St. John's Chapel in 1895 is unknown, it is unlikely that members alone accounted for the large number of signatures on the quilt.
7. Preston, *Talbot County*, 244. Preston also recorded that the first washing machine arrived on the island in 1895 and the first phonograph in 1898.

130. Rev. Charles Kitchens Millican and Lucy Keister Millican with their son, Smithson, photographed in Baltimore around 1893. The Millicans are shown against a quilt block covered with embroidered initials and motifs. (Photograph courtesy of John C. Millican)

Wesley Chapel Name Quilt

I N 1917 THE REVEREND C. E. McCullough, pastor of Wesley Chapel in Rock Hall, Kent County, suggested to members of the Ladies Aid Society that they undertake as a project a "name quilt" to raise money for new carpeting for the church (131).[1] Each member of the society attempted to fill one or more of the fifty-six squares of embroidered daisies with seventeen names at ten cents apiece. The members' efforts resulted in raising $241.15. The subscription quilt included names of nearby and distant relatives and friends of the society's members, business and professional people in Kent County and Baltimore, all the former pastors of Wesley Chapel (1866–1917), and eight presidents of the Maryland Annual Conference of the Methodist Protestant Church.[2] Several ladies embroidered the daisy petal outlines in red, and Mary Leary carefully wrote the names in India ink.

Wesley Chapel traces its beginnings to a camp meeting held near Rock Hall in September 1829. A frame structure was erected shortly thereafter, and Wesley Chapel became part of the Kent Circuit of the Methodist Protestant Church. In 1852 the present brick structure was built (132). The chapel then shared a minister with another church on the Chesapeake Circuit.

The Ladies Aid Society began early in the church's history as a vehicle to provide care for the parsonage. In addition to the name quilt their fundraising endeavors included bake sales, suppers, fish fries, and the Maryland tradition of "beaten biscuit bakes."[3] In 1983 members of the Margaret Tucker Memorial Class (adult Sunday school class) created another fundraising quilt in exactly the same design as the 1917 quilt. Allowing for inflation, they sold names for one dollar apiece and raised $1,221.35 to offset the debt on the new church hall. A number of names appear on both quilts, as children and grandchildren purchased space in memory of early church members. Both quilts remain the property of Wesley Chapel United Methodist Church.

132. Photograph of Wesley Chapel on a postcard dating from the 1920s or 1930s. (Photograph courtesy of Ida Mae Dulin and Wesley Chapel United Methodist Church)

1. We are grateful to Ida Mae Dulin, longtime member of Wesley Chapel, for sharing with us the history of her church's two fundraising quilts. The 1917 quilt was published along with a list of all contributors in *A Heritage of Faith* (Easton, MD: Economy Printing, 1978).
2. Jacqueline Atkins defines a subscription quilt as one where monetary subscriptions in small amounts are received from individuals and businesses. Jacqueline Marx Atkins, *Shared Threads: Quilting Together—Past and Present* (New York: Viking Studio Books, 1994), 69.
3. Beaten biscuits are small, hard biscuits made from flour, water, and lard. They are traditional to the Eastern Shore but were made in other parts of the state as well. The dough is beaten on a wooden block with the back of an ax head—or more recently, with a baseball bat—until it starts to blister. Men frequently do the beating, but women take credit for the preparation. Recipes for beaten biscuits were treasured and handed down from mother to daughter. Montgomery County diarist Roger Brooke Farquhar noted with pride on September 8, 1880, that his daughter's sewing and his wife's beaten biscuits took premiums at the Rockville Fair. *The Montgomery County Story*, vol. 4, no. 8 (May 1961), n.p.

131. Detail of center block—"C.E. McCullough, Pastor/ The plan of this quilt/ Was suggested by/ Rev. C.E. McCullough/ And adopted by/ The Ladies Aid Society/ For the purpose of/ Raising funds to/ Redecorate Church/ The names in the/ Squares represent/ The contributors/ Amount raised $241.15/ Wesley Chapel/ Methodist Protestant Church/ Ladies Aid Society/ February 22d, 1917"

EMBROIDERED FUNDRAISING QUILT, 1917

Made by the Ladies Aid Society of the Wesley Chapel
Methodist Protestant Church
Rock Hall, Kent County
Cotton, ink inscriptions
89 x 82 inches
Owned by Wesley Chapel United Methodist Church

Homemakers' Bedcover

THE LESLIE HOMEMAKERS Club was founded in 1926 and initially attracted members from around Marysville and Leslie, farm communities in Cecil County.[1] The Homemakers Club was advised by the Maryland Cooperative Extension Service in Elkton. Club members met once a month with the home demonstration agent who instructed them in baking, canning and preserving, furniture refinishing, upholstery and caning, doll-making, artificial flower-making, rug braiding and crocheting, quilting, and other useful and ornamental arts.

The Homemakers put their needlework skills into raising money to cover the costs of club activities. Charging three dollars a quilt, they quilted tops for other women. In

133. Alvia Benjamin and her daughter, Marian Benjamin Walbeck, in 1946. (Photograph courtesy of Marian Walbeck)

1928 they undertook a more ambitious project to raise money for their organization (134). They made a red and white fundraising bedcover in the embroidered Sunflower pattern. Club members sold spaces for signatures at ten cents a piece as well as ten-cent chances on the finished bedcover. (It was never quilted.) Different members took responsibility for selling and embroidering individual blocks, although all the club members are listed together in the upper-right corner block. Another block contains the names of women from the area who attended the Rural Women's Short Course offered by the Home Demonstration Department of the Extension Service at the University of Maryland in College Park.[2] The women paid a nominal amount to attend the weeklong course where they "were introduced to the finest in culture, and arts and crafts."[3]

At least two club members turned blocks over to their daughters to embroider.

EMBROIDERED FUNDRAISING BEDCOVER, 1928

Made by the Leslie Homemakers Club
Near North East, Cecil County
Cotton, embroidered inscriptions
84 x 84 inches
Owned by Ronald and Kathy Gray

Mildred Logan Hudgins recalls that she was sixteen and recuperating from surgery when her mother suggested embroidering names as an activity to keep her occupied. She placed her eighty-three-year-old grandmother's name at the center of her block. Her mother, Elizabeth, made another block with her own name at the center and the names of local organizations in the petals. Her block also contains the name "Colonel Lindbergh" in honor of the recent completion of Charles A. Lindbergh's solo transatlantic flight. Marian Benjamin Walbeck was seventeen at the time she embroidered a block for her

134. Detail of center block of the Leslie Homemakers Club fundraising bedcover.

135. Mary Etta Gray, winner of the raffled bedcover, and her husband, Warner Gray, with their daughter, Dottie, in 1923. Their photograph is shown against the block made by Mary Gray, president of the Leslie Homemakers Club. (Photograph courtesy of Kathy Gray)

mother (133). She placed her mother's name, Alvia, in the center and embroidered the name of her boyfriend and future husband on one of the petals. Marian joined the Leslie Homemakers Club two years later, and since that time has worked on numerous needlework projects as an accomplished quilt and dollmaker.

When the Homemakers' bedcover was finished and raffled off, the winning chance belonged to Mary Etta Gray (1891–1977), sister-in-law of club president, Mary Gray (135). Mary Etta, the wife of Warner Gray, lived in nearby North East and ran a board-ing house for school teachers. She was not a member of the Leslie Homemakers, and her name was not among those embroidered on the bedcover. Her grandson found the raffle prize in a trunk of his grandmother's belongings. Only recently has the family pieced together the bedcover's history from conversations with surviving members of the Leslie Homemakers Club.

1. The first Cecil County Homemakers Club was organized in 1919 with 41 members. By 1924 the county supported eight clubs. Jeanette Green, *"Today's Home Builds Tomorrow's World": Maryland Extension Homemakers Council* (College Park, MD: 1982), 49.
2. Ibid., 5–6, 8. The first Rural Women's Short Course was offered in 1923 and attracted 241 women from twenty counties who attended lectures and demonstration classes. "Subject matter for the program included clothing, food, household management, house furnishing, landscaping, gardening, parliamentary law, millinery, home dairying, poultry, and health." By 1931 enrollment had jumped to 750; a large number of Maryland women thus were provided with the opportunity to share new knowledge with their families, clubs, and communities.
3. George H. Corddry, *Wicomico County History* (Salisbury, MD: Peninsula Press, 1981), 105.

Tree-of-Life Counterpane

*I*N 1933 THE ADULT WOMEN'S Sunday School Class Number Nine of the Ayres Methodist Episcopal Church of Pittsville came up with a novel way to raise money for their pastor's support. They solicited donations for a "name quilt," inscribed in a tree-of-life design, that also created a record of the church's history.[1]

The roots of the tree are embroidered in green with names of the church's founders, charter members, and trustees, along with those responsible for major donations to the original church building. The bedcover records that "Geo. T. Truitt [a lumberman] furnished lumber," and "Z.P. Richardson [a carpenter] gave labor." Neither man was a church member at the time, but they later converted. The trunk represents the church, and on the limbs are the names of the twenty-four pastors who served between 1888 and 1933. Surviving pastors were solicited; one dollar was donated for each pastor's name. Running off each limb, in the form of branches, and along the two sides are the names of church members.

According to the church's published centennial history, "Every person who joined church was invited to come to church to pay ten cents for his name on the spread."[2] Both men and women supported Class Number Nine's project; some are listed in family groups while other members are scattered about on the tree or along the sides. Martha Stubbs is credited with all the embroidery. She was the mother-in-law of Rev. William H. Kohl, the pastor of Ayres Church at the time the bedcover was made. While the amount of money raised is not known, the Reverend Mr. Kohl was no doubt grateful for

the financial support. Due to hard times, declining attendance, and delays in payments from members, his annual salary had fallen from $1,600 to $1,400 and then to $1,200.

Methodists began holding meetings in the Pittsville area of Wicomico County in the 1830s. After worshiping in several small churches and splitting over the issue of slavery, they organized Ayres Methodist Episcopal Church in 1888. The church's first minister, Rev. George W. Bowman, preached every fourth Sunday as part of the Parsonburg Circuit. He conducted revivals and dedicated himself to converting the unfaithful and raising money for a building to replace the crowded tabernacle. In 1889 the church could celebrate a new building, costing $1,490, and a membership of 150 people (136). Mr. Bowman also is remembered for his crusade to abolish the town's three saloons. He offered local working men the sober alternative of Saturday afternoon fellowship. Saturday noon was payday for many men in town, and the afternoon and evening traditionally were spent in alcoholic relaxation. Bowman's plan succeeded in closing down the saloons.[3]

The women's Sunday school classes used a number of means to raise money for their church. Classes often competed with each other to see which could raise the most money. During the year they organized church suppers and picnics with homemade lemonade, ice cream, and cakes. One group presented plays in Pittsville and nearby communities while others sold vanilla and lemon extracts.

In the 1970s members of Class Number Eleven (formerly Class Number Nine) still offered their needlework services for the quilting of tops. Charging from $25 to $100, they raised $2,544 from 1973 to 1976. The women of Class Number Nine are remembered in their church history as "dedicated Christians [who set] a good example that motivated the congregation, young and old."[4] Their tree-of-life bedcover, which always remained church property, had been missing for years. Fortunately it was found, folded up on a shelf in the parish hall, in time to be displayed for the Ayres United Methodist Church Centennial in 1988.

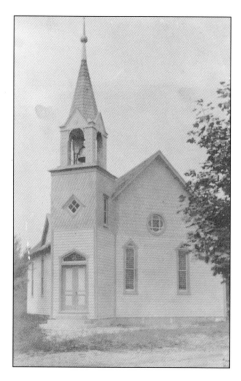

136. Ayres Methodist Episcopal Church, 1906. (Photograph courtesy of Doris Farlow and Ayres United Methodist Church)

1. The tree-of-life was an appropriate spiritual symbol for a church project. Chapter 2, verse 9 of Genesis mentions the tree-of-life in the Garden of Eden, "the tree of life is also in the midst of the garden, and the tree of knowledge of good and evil." In nineteenth-century needlework the tree-of-life was occasionally used on genealogical samplers as a framework for family lineage. In the late eighteenth century the motif, inspired by Indian palampores, was block-printed on linens and cottons.
2. *History of Ayres United Methodist Church, Pittsville, Maryland, 1888–1988* (Pittsville, MD: n.p., 1988), 9.
3. Rev. George Bowman's actions predated by a few years the work of the Anti-Saloon League, organized in 1895. Maryland would ratify the Eighteenth Amendment in 1918.
4. *History*, 10.

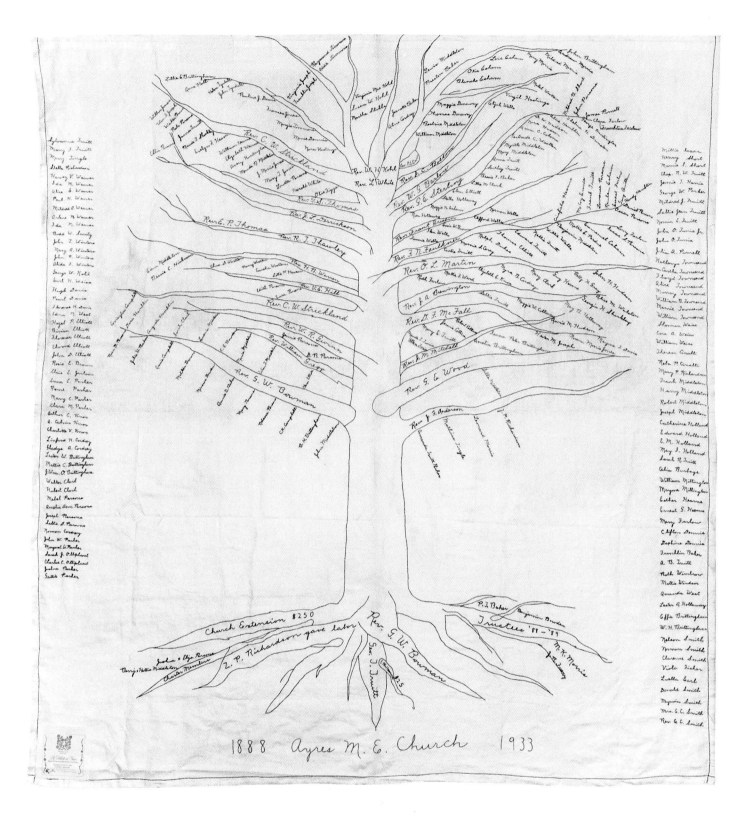

EMBROIDERED FUNDRAISING BEDCOVER,
1933

Made by Sunday School Class Number Nine, Ayres
Methodist Episcopal Church
Pittsville, Wicomico County
Linen, embroidered inscriptions
91 x 85 inches
Owned by Ayres United Methodist Church

Walter's Quilt

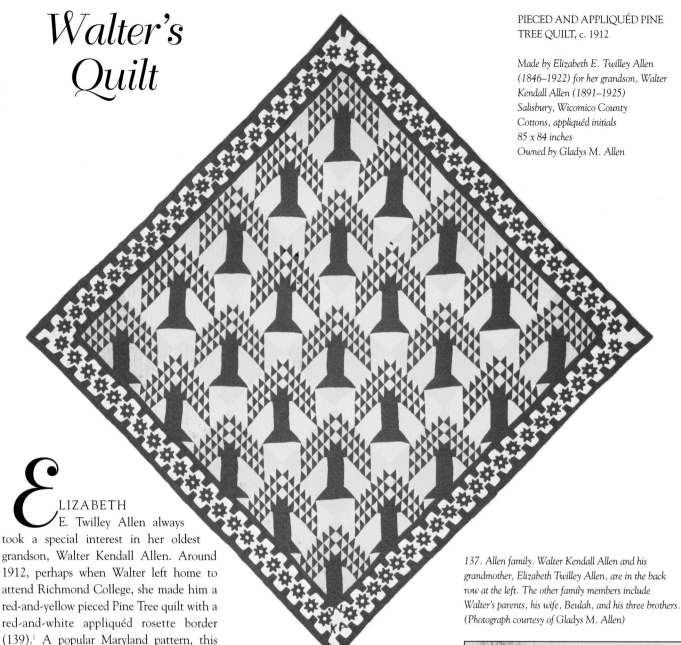

PIECED AND APPLIQUÉD PINE
TREE QUILT, c. 1912

Made by Elizabeth E. Twilley Allen
(1846–1922) for her grandson, Walter
Kendall Allen (1891–1925)
Salisbury, Wicomico County
Cottons, appliquéd initials
85 x 84 inches
Owned by Gladys M. Allen

ELIZABETH E. Twilley Allen always took a special interest in her oldest grandson, Walter Kendall Allen. Around 1912, perhaps when Walter left home to attend Richmond College, she made him a red-and-yellow pieced Pine Tree quilt with a red-and-white appliquéd rosette border (139).[1] A popular Maryland pattern, this dramatic example with twenty-five blocks pieced from dyed fabrics has a more elaborate border than most.[2] The initials "WKA," appliquéd in the lower-right corner, identify the recipient and create the illusion that the quilt should be viewed as a diamond rather than as a square or rectangle.

A red-and-green Double Irish Chain quilt, owned by the Allen family and marked on the back with Walter's name, probably was made by his grandmother Allen as well.[3] This quilt, with its early- to mid-nineteenth-century pattern, suggests that Elizabeth Allen took inspiration for her quilting designs from sources that spanned a number of decades.

Walter Kendall Allen elected to go into the Baptist ministry after graduation from Yale Divinity School. In 1918 he married Beulah Nock and in 1921 he went to Assam, India, as a missionary with the American Baptist Mission Board (137). Four years later, thirty-four-year-old Walter Allen died from typhoid fever, leaving a young wife and two daughters. The Division Street Baptist Church in Salisbury was renamed the Allen Memorial Baptist Church to honor his memory. A number of years later his younger daughter, Gladys, returned to India as a

137. Allen family. Walter Kendall Allen and his grandmother, Elizabeth Twilley Allen, are in the back row at the left. The other family members include Walter's parents, his wife, Beulah, and his three brothers. (Photograph courtesy of Gladys M. Allen)

138. *Picking strawberries on the north side of the Allen home. William Francis Allen's commercial strawberry operation surrounded the Allen homestead. This land is now part of the campus of Salisbury State University. (Photograph courtesy of Gladys M. Allen)*

1. This pattern is also called Tree of Life, an appropriate design for a future minister. Several late-nineteenth- and early-twentieth-century quilts made in the Pine Tree/ Tree of Life pattern were documented in Maryland. William Rush Dunton Jr. devoted a whole chapter to this motif. In Chapter IV, "Tree of Life and Others," Dunton described and illustrated the pieced Tree of Life and its variations, Pine Tree and Tree of Paradise, as well as the traditional appliquéd Tree of Life or flowering tree type. William Rush Dunton Jr., *Old Quilts* (Catonsville, MD: n.p., 1946), 219–33.

140. *Residence of William Francis Allen, from a postcard of around 1910. (Photograph courtesy of Gladys M. Allen)*

medical missionary. She treasures another remembrance of her father, his personalized quilt.[4]

The Allen family is well known in Wicomico County for its many accomplishments. The town of Lower Trappe was renamed Allen in 1884 after its postmaster, Joseph S. C. Allen. Albert James Allen, brother of Joseph and husband of Elizabeth Twilley Allen, raised and sold strawberries. His only son, William Francis, at age fifteen borrowed $15 to invest in strawberry plants in order to produce enough for sale. He issued his first catalogue in 1885 under the name W. F. Allen Company (140). Of his four sons, all but Walter Kendall followed him in the thriving business that raised, sold, and shipped strawberry plants to destinations across the United States (138).[5]

2. By comparison, a Baltimore County Tree of Temptation quilt (BC-309), made in the 1930s or later, has only nine blocks separated by blue sashing and bordered by strips of green and red fabric. The leaves on this quilt, however, are pieced from an array of colorful solid and printed fabrics.

3. The Allen family owns a number of quilts thought to have been made by Elizabeth Twilley Allen, Martha Byrd Nock, Walter's mother-in-law, or other family members. One additional quilt has "W. K. Allen" written on the back.

4. Dr. Allen has kindly shared her family history and photo albums with us.

5. Raising strawberry plants for market was a thriving industry on Maryland's lower Eastern Shore from the late nineteenth century up until World War II. Many of the quiltmakers from this part of Maryland had a connection with strawberry growing.

139. *Elizabeth Twilley Allen and Walter Kendall Allen in photographs taken about the time Elizabeth made Walter's quilt. His appliquéd initials are beneath the photographs. (Photographs courtesy of Gladys M. Allen)*

Scraps from Shirts

A NUMBER OF EARLY-TWENTIETH-century quilts from Maryland's Eastern Shore contain striped and small-patterned white ground fabrics similar to those used for men's shirts. Several owners remarked that their quilts had been made out of scraps from local shirt factories. These two observations suggested a preliminary investigation into the location, operation, and output of Eastern Shore shirt factories.[1]

Women's work—that of sewing clothing—has taken many forms over the years. Originally women sewed to meet the needs of their families. The 1817 account book from William Willson's Montgomery County store recorded numerous purchases for cloth, thread, and buttons (pp. 50–51). For example, Zadok Magruder bought "25 yds Cambric Shirting at .55 [per yard], 1½ doz. shirt buttons at .18¾ [per] doz., 24 skeens thread at .02 each."[2] From his purchased articles Magruder's wife, or one of the slave women on his plantation, could cut and stitch several men's shirts.

In the 1830s, a number of urban women along the Eastern Seaboard gained employment sewing precut garments in their homes on an outwork basis. A man's shirt might require 20,000 stitches, for which a New York City seamstress received 12½¢.[3] This system of outside production with low wages paid to the worker and low capital investment on the part of the owner was known as "sweating."[4]

Between 1830 and 1860, the invention of the sewing machine, standardization of measurements and patterns, and declining prices for cloth led to centralization.[5] Work was gathered in one place—a factory—where it could be closely supervised. Many farm women eagerly sought factory work and the opportunities offered by urban living. Working in a clothing factory was a suitable "genteel trade" for an unmarried woman, and factory work paid better than home work.[6]

By the 1880s the industrialization of the garment industry was complete. A change in manufacturing site, however, occurred when the traditional movement of workers from farm to city reversed. Company owners began to move their factories out of cities and into the countryside where taxes were lower, land was cheap, labor was plentiful, and laws to protect the rights of workers were unenforced or non-existent.

Baltimore can trace its reputation as a center for large-scale clothing production back to the American Revolution. In August 1780, Mrs. Smith and the "Ladys of the Town" received a commission to make 260 shirts from "Country made Linnen" for the soldiers of the Continental army. When the ladies delayed in filling the order, Mr. William Smith, a local merchant, came to the rescue with a loan of 200 "Ready made" shirts to be used by the soldiers only until their shirts were ready.[7]

The systematic manufacturing of ready-to-wear clothing began in Baltimore in 1838; it was a major industry by 1859.[8] As historian Philip Kahn Jr. has noted, "The coincidence in time of stronger sea and land transportation, peak immigration, and the invention of the sewing machine played a vital role in the establishment of Baltimore's needle trades."[9] Women from rural Maryland, then Jewish immigrants from Germany and later eastern Europe, worked twelve to fourteen hours a day, first in their homes and then in

Advertisement for the Jackson & Gutman Co. from the Tatler, 1919 yearbook from Wicomico County High School. (Courtesy of Gloria Seaman Allen)

THE JACKSON & GUTMAN CO.

Manufacturers of the Well Known.

Salisbury Shirts
TRADE MARK

OFFICES:

Salisbury, Md.

Boston, Mass.   Philadelphia, Pa.
Chicago, Ill.   New York, N. Y.

East Baltimore sweatshops.[10] Many of these women were employed to sew men's shirts out of northern cotton fabrics, which—when completed—were shipped to the South and Midwest.[11] Eventually these outside shops were joined by "inside" shops where cutting, sewing, pressing, and finishing were done in factory buildings owned by the manufacturers.[12]

From 1860 to 1916, men's clothing generated the greatest income and employed the most workers of any industry in the state. Maryland's clothing trade ranked fourth in the United States between 1880 and the start of World War I.[13] By 1920, Baltimore ranked second, after New York City, in total dollar value of its clothing manufactures.[14]

The Baltimore shirt industry, in particular, flourished as men took a growing interest in dress. A freshly laundered white shirt conveyed gentility and the economic where-with-all to keep it clean. Conversely, colored shirts, which required less frequent laundering, denoted a lower social class or a "blue collar" working man.[15]

In 1890, Baltimore industries started to move out to less populous regions in the state. The depression of 1893–94 and the strikes by Baltimore clothing workers for shorter hours and higher wages in 1892 and 1893 accelerated the move to the countryside.[16] A network of rail lines, many built since the Civil War, increased access to the more remote parts of the state. Worn-out farms provided inexpensive land with ample space for airy, well-lighted factories. A report published in 1892 by the Maryland Bureau of Industries, Statistics, and Information recognized the rural migration:

> Many of the manufactures of Maryland have during the past years, sought more advantageous locations in the rural districts for the conduct of their business, notably in the towns of . . . Havre de Grace, Cambridge, Easton and Salisbury in the east. In many of these towns new factories have been erected and many hands have been given employment to the great advantage of the rural population.[17]

Salisbury on the lower Eastern Shore was, by 1890, a town of 3,000 people, a terminus on the Philadelphia, Dover, Salisbury Line, and supplied by electrical power.[18] During the next several decades, Salisbury attracted numerous businesses from Baltimore, New

Factory building of the Wicomico Shirt Manufacturing Co., Salisbury, in a photograph taken shortly after its founding in 1907. Most garment factories had long narrow buildings lit by rows of windows. (Photograph courtesy of Gloria Seaman Allen)

York, and other northern cities. By 1910 its population had more than doubled. The Salisbury Shirt Company was established in 1897; it became known as Jackson and Weisbach, and later Jackson and Gutman, as Jewish capitalists joined in ownership with Wicomico County businessmen to bring new money into the company. At least thirteen shirt factories set up operation within the town limits of Salisbury or neighboring Fruitland.[19] Many of these companies also carried the names of German and East European Jews—Stein, Jacobson, and Liebovitz.

The Manhattan Shirt Factory, although larger than most, was fairly typical of factories opened in Salisbury by out-of-state entrepreneurs.[20] The Manhattan Factory was founded in New York City in 1857. Initially the firm employed the "home sewing system" in which precut shirts were distributed to women to sew at home by hand. The first factory was erected in Patterson, New Jersey, in 1867. Patterson's ample supply of water allowed the factory to produce a laundered shirt. Prior to that time shirts were sold unwashed. In 1929 Manhattan opened its Salisbury factory; by 1949 it employed 500 people and produced 50,400 shirts per week, becoming the largest of Manhattan's ten factories.

Six miles west of Salisbury, the crossroads of Hebron grew into a thriving town in the early twentieth century as industrialists discovered it rural attractions. By the mid-1920s, Hebron was the fastest-growing town on the Delmarva Peninsula; it could boast of five shirt factories

employing 200 people. A laudatory article published in 1926 noted that the shirt factories had contributed to the growth and prosperity of the town and had greatly increased the earning capacities of its families.[21] Workers were kept busy year round, and there were "no strikes . . . no labor trouble from any source." The writer of the article went on to note that "no foreign element in labor or capital has been necessary to take care of all sides of the business of the town."

In contrast to factories in Baltimore and the North with their predominantly immigrant work force, the shirt factories of Salisbury, Hebron, Sharptown, Mardela Springs, Berlin, Rock Hall, and other small towns relied on local woman who had lived all their lives in the farming communities of the Eastern Shore. Rural women could combine factory work with their duties on the farm. Agricultural work was seasonal, and farm women were no longer as essential to the operation as farms became consolidated and farm work partially mechanized. A second job gave farm women the opportunity to contribute to their family's support during the depression years or when farm prices were otherwise low.[22] Wives and daughters of watermen found that factory work also helped to occupy the long days when their menfolk were at sea and to supplement family income when oysters were in short supply. Female operatives were paid by the piece. Unlike their urban coun-

terparts, there were no wage or hour laws for women and children working outside of Baltimore prior to 1920.[23] Reform legislation of the Progressive Era, which mandated factory inspections and otherwise improved working conditions for Baltimore workers, was slow in coming to the rural parts of Maryland. Supervised by relatives, friends, or people they had known all their lives and lacking any type of labor organization, Eastern Shore farm women did not follow the lead of their Baltimore sisters in striking for higher wages and shorter hours. A passive female labor force with strong ties to the local community, together with low land prices, low taxes, and low utility rates, must have been very appealing to businessmen looking for an economical location for a shirt factory.

Women made up the majority of the work force in shirt factories. Usually only a handful of men supervised a large number of female operatives. In 1928, for example, the Hayman Shirt Company of Salisbury employed 43 women and 2 men; Jackson & Jackson, also located in Salisbury, employed 275 women and 40 men, who were mainly in supervisory and maintenance positions.[24] Using the "Boston system," or part work, the women performed a number of simple, low-skill operations. The majority ran sewing machines and were assigned to stitch one part of the garment before it was passed along to the next operator. A collar alone might require four to six steps and, thus, pass through the hands of four to six women. Using this method of manufacturing, a worker could develop proficiency in a specific task.[25]

Elma Thomas Cornelius, who worked for the Rock Hall Manufacturing Company, a shirt company founded in the 1920s in lower Kent County, recalled what it was like in her factory during the 1950s.[26] The Rock Hall Manufacturing Company made Marboro shirts.[27] The shirts came from Baltimore to the Rock Hall factory already cut and sized. Because cutting involved the highest stage of risk and therefore demanded the greatest skill, incorrectly cut fabric was waste most companies could not afford. In Rock Hall the pieces of shirting were stitched and trimmed, and then the shirts trucked back to Baltimore to be pressed and folded. Elma Cornelius noted that her factory employed about 80 local women and girls, wives and daughters of farmers and watermen, who were supervised by the owner and his son. Two other men looked after the machines. As a "floor lady," Elma Cornelius was paid by the hour; she was responsible for half the floor or 30 to 40 workers, who were paid by the piece and who frequently put in a nine- or ten-hour day. Elma examined the bins of completed work to check stitch tension and to look for missed stitches and puckers. She also trained new girls on the machines, giving them rags to practice stitching on so none of the valuable fabric would be ruined by inexperienced operators. There was little waste.

Given the precautions against waste taken by the Rock Hall Manufacturing Company and other shirt factories, it is surprising that a number of Maryland quilts contain scraps from shirt factories. Neither Elma nor her mother, both quiltmakers, used shirt scraps, but women in other factory towns, especially in the Salisbury-Hebron area, did. Mary Virginia Ellis Downing and Cora Lowe Taylor both made quilts from fabric used in Hebron shirt factories, and Sadie Collins made a crazy quilt with scraps from the factory in Powellville.[28] Sadie also was employed for a time by the factory as a seamstress.[29] The family of Edna Downes of Pittsville recalled that during the 1930s she bought

Detail of an early-twentieth-century Double T quilt made by Lillian Nelson Wimbrow (1878–1938), of Hebron, Wicomico County. Many of the striped fabrics are typical of those used in shirt factories in the Hebron-Salisbury area. As the sister of a factory owner, Lillian had ready access to fabric scraps left over from the shirt manufacturing process.

scraps at the local shirt factory by the bundle. Her six quilts, documented in Wicomico County, confirm her extensive use of shirt scraps.[30]

Quiltmakers who lived in towns where shirt factories did their own cutting and sizing had access to small scraps of fabric left over from the cutting process. Always with an eye to profit, factory managers found a way to avoid waste. Scraps were saved, bundled up, and sold. Female factory employees may have been allowed to keep certain scraps for their own use or they may have helped themselves to scraps when the supervisor was out of sight. Regardless of how they obtained their scraps, Eastern Shore women found an inexpensive source for quilting fabrics. The small-figured patterns and stripes printed in a limited palette on white ground and cut in small irregular shapes, in turn, influenced their designs and distinguished their quilts from more typical rural Maryland quilts with their pastel calico and feed-sack piecing.[31]

Gloria Seaman Allen

Pieced Double T quilt, 1900–25. Made by Lillian Wimbrow. Cottons. 84.5 x 84 inches.

1. The database indicated that several Western Shore quilts contained fabrics from shirt factories, and one entry specified a factory in Carroll County; however, the majority of entries suggested Eastern Shore sources. No quilts with shirting fabric were documented in the Baltimore area where the majority of shirt factories were located. The lack of data may signify that Baltimore quiltmakers had a wide selection of new fabrics to choose from and did not need to resort to using shirt scraps.

2. William Willson's *Day Book*, 1817. Collection of the Montgomery County Historical Society Library.

3. Brooke Hindle and Steven Lubar, *Engines of Change: The American Industrial Revolution 1780–1860* (Washington, DC: Smithsonian Institution Press, 1988), 208. The amount paid for stitching shirts did not increase substantially over the years. A chronicler of Mardela Springs, Wicomico County, recalled that women in the late nineteenth century would stitch seven shirts a day at the rate of 18¾¢ a piece. Sylvia S. Bradley, *Mardela Springs, Maryland: A History* (Salisbury, MD: Mardela Springs Heritage Festival), 15.

4. Hindle and Lubar, *Engines*, 208.

5. Ibid.

6. Ibid., 212.

7. Bernard C. Steiner, ed., *Journal and Correspondence of the State Council of Maryland 1780–1781* in *Archives of Maryland*, vol. XLI (Baltimore: Maryland Historical Society, 1927), 16, 64, 65, 120.

8. Richard Walsh and William Lloyd Fox, *Maryland: A History, 1632–1974* (Baltimore: Maryland Historical Society, 1974), 413.

9. Philip Kahn Jr., *A Stitch in Time: The Four Seasons of Baltimore's Needle Trades* (Baltimore: Maryland Historical Society, 1989), 19.

10. Walsh and Fox, *Maryland*, 410.

11. Ibid., 414.

12. Kahn, *Stitch in Time*, 77.

13. Walsh and Fox, *Maryland*, 403.

14. Kahn, *Stitch in Time*, 131.

15. Ibid., 81.

16. Walsh and Fox, *Maryland*, 449. Suzanne Ellery Greene Chapelle, et al., *Maryland: A History of Its People* (Baltimore: J. H. Press, 1986), 117.

17. Maryland Bureau of Industrial Statistics and Information, *1890–91 Report* (Baltimore, 1892), 6.

18. Chapelle, *Maryland*, 181.

19. This number reflects the thirteen companies from the Salisbury area identified to date by the author from business directories, local histories, advertisements, and the like.

20. The information that follows has been extracted from an article that appeared in the *Salisbury Daily Times* in 1965, describing the opening of the Manhattan Shirt Company's new air-conditioned factory. At that time all the executives were from northern cities and most had eastern European surnames. Local people supervised the cutting, sewing, and assembly departments. Vertical Files, Wicomico County Public Library.

21. The following information comes from an essay written by Emma Marks, one of the 1926 graduates of Hebron High School. Her essay won a five-dollar gold piece and was published in the local newspaper. Vertical Files, Wicomico County Public Library.

22. Farm women, unlike urban women, had limited local opportunities for employment. Some left home and moved to the cities to join the thousands who entered the office work force after World War I. The resulting reduction in available urban garment workers further contributed to a need to seek employees in rural areas. Kahn, *Stitch in Time*, 153.

23. Walsh and Fox, *Maryland*, 658.

24. R. Beach, *Industrial Brief* (Salisbury, MD, 1928), 12.

25. Kahn, *Stitch in Time*, 77.

26. Personal interview, July 22, 1994.

27. Baltimore's Marboro Shirt Company, under the direction of Isadore E. Rosenbloom and Soloman Silverman, became one of the nation's largest shirt manufacturers. Kahn, *Stitch in Time*, 141.

28. Documented as WI-058, CO-070, CO-071.

29. Her quilt was documented as WO-209.

30. Documented as WI-087, WI-092 through WI-096.

31. Brackman, from her extensive investigation of dated quilts, has determined that quiltmakers were fond of using shirting fabrics between 1870 and 1925. This use seems to have continued longer on Maryland's Eastern Shore where shirt factories remained in operation through the 1960s and 1970s. Barbara Brackman, *Clues in the Calico* (McLean, VA: EPM Publications, 1989), 74–75.

Colonial Revival White Quilt

The beautiful white quilts that are treasured as relics of past industry by their fortunate owners deserve special mention. They are rare because nowadays no on will expend the large amount of time necessary to complete one.

Marie Webster, 1915

LILLIAN SHIPLEY (1890–1989) made a white wholecloth quilt in 1926 at the age of thirty-six (141). The second child of Dr. Daniel F. and Laura Lambert Shipley, Lillian spent her childhood in Westminster in a house her father built on the corner of East Main and Center streets. She had an idyllic childhood filled with Sunday afternoons walks in the country with her brothers and sisters studying the local plants and animals and traveling through the rolling countryside with her father as he visited patients. These travels fostered in her a love and appreciation of local history. Lillian attended the Baltimore Millinery School and opened the Hat Shop on Main Street in Westminster and operated it for several years.

Lilidan, a poultry farm and hatchery, was her next undertaking until 1939 when she and seventy-four other men and women founded the

Historical Society of Carroll County. From 1953 until her retirement in 1962 she was the society's resident curator. At her retirement she spoke of her nine years as curator as "some of the happiest of my life."

During her tenure, the society built a fine collection of decorative arts, manuscripts, photographs, and newspapers. She also was curator of numerous exhibitions highlighting local history, developing educational programs that taught Carroll County history to adult and school-age visitors. Since her death in 1989 (less than a year shy of her 100th birthday), the Historical Society of Carroll County has sponsored an annual education awards program named in her honor for seventh-grade students.[1]

Contrary to Marie Webster's comment, Lillian did find the time to make a white wholecloth quilt[2] and actually saved time by machine-piecing the strips of white cotton sateen that make up both the front and back. The quilting designs, such as feather wreaths surrounded by a diamond-grid, are exquisitely worked twenty-four stitches to the inch. The border of the quilt is worked in running feathers with a clamshell filler.

141. Lillian Shipley (1890–1989) (Courtesy of Mr. and Mrs. Danial F. Shipley III)

She also stitched in her initials "L.S." and the date "1926." In 1960 Miss Shipley gave her quilt to her nephew, Daniel F. Shipley III, and his wife, who store it in a pillowcase, tucked neatly into a blanket chest.

1. The authors thank Mrs. Eleanor Shipley and Jay Graybeal, the director of the Historical Society of Carroll County, for allowing us to borrow from their biographies of Lillian Shipley.
2. Marie Webster, *Quilts: Their Story and How to Make Them,* revised edition (Santa Barbara, CA: Practical Patchwork, 1990), 86.

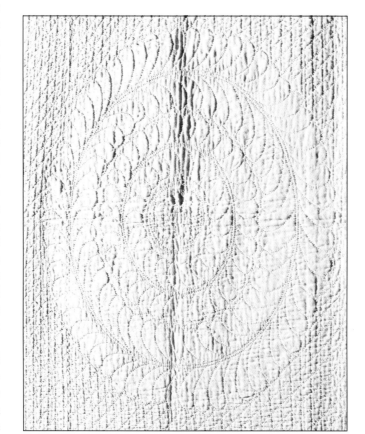

DETAIL OF WHITE QUILT, 1926

Made by Lillian Shipley (1890–1989)
Westminster, Carroll County
Cottons
82.5 x 79.75 inches
Owned by Mr. and Mrs. Daniel F. Shipley III

Wicomico County Quilts

PIECED BASKET QUILT, c. 1898

Made by Sallie Jane Hastings Nelson (1836–1909)
Hebron, Wicomico County
Cottons, embroidered inscription
80.5 x 80 inches
Owned by Letitia M. Bates

*L*ILLIAN NELSON WIMBROW acquired her love for quiltmaking from her mother, Sallie Jane Hastings Nelson. Even though Lillian was born late in her mother's life, she and Sallie made dozens of quilts together and alone. Although some were used and given away, Lillian's granddaughter still owns twenty-seven of their quilts.

Sallie Nelson and her second husband, Horatio (1818–85), spent most of their married life in Hebron, near Salisbury in Wicomico County. While Horatio farmed, Sallie kept house and brought up ten children.[1] After her husband's death in 1885, Sallie saw her village change from a sleepy crossroads to a town with a flourishing lumber industry, bank, church, stores, and a station on the Baltimore, Chesapeake, and Atlantic Railway. In the early twentieth century, a number of shirt and garment factories opened in Hebron, where taxes and power rates were low and female labor plentiful.[2] In 1890, after attending a Methodist revival, Sallie donated family land for a church, dedicated as the Nelson Memorial Methodist Church.

Sallie and Horatio's ninth child and fourth daughter, Lillian, was born in 1878. In 1898 she married Isaac Wimbrow (1876–1960), a farmer and dairyman who delivered milk to most of the residents of Hebron (142). After their marriage the Wimbrows moved in with the widowed Sallie Nelson. Once their new home was completed, Sallie joined the young couple at Wimbrow Farm (143). Like most farm fami-

142. Lillian and Isaac Wimbrow, in a photograph taken shortly after their 1898 marriage. The other photograph was taken about thirty years later. (Photographs courtesy of Letitia M. Bates)

PIECED COG WHEEL QUILT, 1900–25

Made by Lillian Nelson Wimbrow (1878–1938)
Hebron, Wicomico County
Cottons
95 x 71.5 inches
Owned by Letitia M. Bates

PIECED CROSS AND CROWN QUILT, c. 1898

Made by Lillian Nelson Wimbrow (1878–1938)
Hebron, Wicomico County
Cottons, embroidered inscription
79.5 x 79 inches
Owned by Letitia M. Bates

lies in the area, the Wimbrows raised cows and poultry and grew corn, melons, tomatoes, and strawberries. The period from March to November kept the whole family busy, but during the winter months the women made time for their needlework.

Lillian and Sallie quilted together and shared fabrics and patterns for more than twenty years. Of all the Nelson-Wimbrow family quilts, only three have embroidered initials to indicate which woman was the maker. A basket quilt is marked "SJN" and probably dates from the late 1890s, in the same period as the two quilts Lillian made just before ("LRN") and just after ("LRW") her 1898 marriage. Similar double pink and other printed fabrics were used in all three quilts.

The rest of the Nelson-Wimbrow quilts are more difficult to date and to assign ownership with certainty. The Double T (pp. 195–96), Schoolhouse, and Cog Wheel quilts, all containing similar red and green fabrics, probably were made by Lillian between 1900 and 1925. The Double T and Cog Wheel quilts also contain many striped cotton fabrics used by one or more of Hebron's shirt factories. Lillian's brother owned the M. N. Nelson factory; another shirt factory was located near the Wimbrow farm. For her backing on the Double T quilt, Lillian used white flour sacks marked "LL." Lillian's later quilts, made between 1930 and her death in 1938, demonstrate the popular use of printed feed sacks. They are pieced from a wide variety of small-figured colorful prints readily available in local stores.

Lillian initially made quilts with her mother. After Sallie's

death in 1909, Lillian may have joined in quilting with other women in the Hebron area. A chronicler of local history described the early social customs of Wicomico County in a 1932 publication.

Quilting parties were nearly as popular as bridge today. It was at these the debutante and matron alike gathered. As needles were drawn back and forth, conversation—and gossip—flowed freely. Of all the earlier customs, probably none survived so long as this institution.[3]

143. Nelson/Wimbrow family photographs shown against a block of Lillian Nelson Wimbrow's quilt. The Wimbrow home in Hebron, about 1920. The house the Wimbrows lived in earlier with Sallie Nelson is directly behind this house. Lillian Nelson, in center, with two of her older sisters, about 1895. (Photographs courtesy of Letitia M. Bates)

The patterns for most of Sallie's and Lillian's pieced and appliquéd designs have not been located, but examples of other twentieth-century quilts documented in Wicomico County indicate the wide popularity of several styles. Popular local patterns included the Double T, Basket, Schoolhouse, Fans, and Maple Leaf. Lillian or her mother made one or more quilts in all of these patterns. Newspapers, farming magazines, and mail-order services were probably the local method of pattern distribution. One of Lillian's quilts has a readily identifiable pattern—an appliquéd Morning Glory motif. This design was issued by Needlecraft Service, a mail-order company begun in 1933.[4]

Lillian and Isaac Wimbrow had two daughters, Ruth and Helen, born in 1900 and 1912. Lillian made many of her later quilts in pairs so that each daughter would have one. As late as 1932 and 1933 she made each a dated and initialed crazy throw. The Wimbrow daughters did not acquire their mother's and grandmother's love for quiltmaking, although Helen did embroider, crochet, and knit. All of Sallie's and Lillian's quilts now belong to Helen's daughter and Lillian's only grandchild, who continues to use and enjoy them in her home.

1. Interview with Letitia M. Bates, granddaughter and great-granddaughter of the quiltmakers.
2. Rural women, eager to earn extra money and less essential as farm laborers after the introduction of mechanized farming, moved into factory work. They were paid by the piece for cutting, sewing, and pressing shirts, at rates lower than those normally paid to men or to urban factory workers.
3. Charles J. Truitt, *Historic Salisbury Maryland: Including Historical Sketches of the Eastern Shore* (Garden City, NY: Country Life Press, 1932), 68.
4. Barbara Brackman, *Encyclopedia of Appliqué* (McLean, VA: EPM Publications, 1993), Pattern no. 37.42.

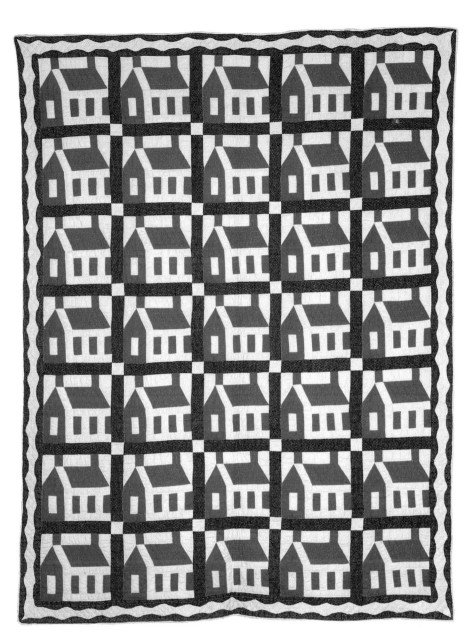

PIECED SCHOOLHOUSE QUILT, 1900–25

Made by Lillian Nelson Wimbrow (1878–1938)
Hebron, Wicomico County
Cottons
95 x 71.5 inches
Owned by Letitia M. Bates

Poffenberger Family Quilts

AFTER MONTHS AT SEA, George Poffenberger (Plaffenberger), his wife, and children finally reached land. The Poffenberger family had left their German homeland in 1733 in search of a better life in America. Sailing out of Dublin on the *Pink Mary*, they disembarked at Philadelphia. Stopping briefly at Tulpehocken in southeastern Pennsylvania, they then set out to join other German families in the sparsely settled lands of western Maryland. Over the next 200 years the Poffenbergers would become well established in Frederick and Washington counties.[1] By 1910 George F. Poffenberger, great-great-great-great-grandson of the immigrant, would be described in a local history as "one

of the most prosperous farmers of the Hauvers District . . . [who] attributes his financial success to honest toil and careful management."[2]

Reading a fragile volume of a county history is now the only way to learn something of this George Poffenberger. More tangible reminders, however, of his wife and daughters exist—their quilts. Several dozen quilts made by Elizabeth Poffenberger (1872–1965), wife of George, and two of their daughters, Nellie (b. 1897) and Mary (1898–1978), are still owned by family members, who have retained a lively oral history of the quiltmaking process.[3]

George F. Poffenberger married Elizabeth Routzahn, daughter of Frederick County residents Ludwig and Mary Marker Routzahn, in 1896 (144). They went to housekeeping in a brick house in the village of Ellerton, where George joined his father in the blacksmith business. Around 1906, with income from the forge not sufficient to support their growing family, the Poffenbergers moved to Sabillasville near the Maryland/Pennsylvania border. George farmed a 173-acre tract of land and was successful enough to receive a laudatory write-up in a Frederick County history published only a few years later. In 1912 the

144. Elizabeth Poffenberger with her granddaughter, Linda, about 1950. (Photograph courtesy of Paul and Gladys Poffenberger)

family packed all its household goods into wagons and crossed South Mountain to a 178-acre farm near Beaver Creek in Washington County (147). There the Poffenbergers ran a dairy herd and grew corn, wheat, and barley for market. It was at the Beaver Creek farm that Elizabeth Poffenberger and her daughters made most of their quilts.

Initially Elizabeth made quilts on her own. As the girls grew older, they worked with their mother (146). Most quiltmaking activities took place during the winter months when the farm's demands on their time were lower. Once the appliquéd or pieced top was completed, it was taken to Aunt Lottie (Charlotte Routzahn Hauver), who lived across South Mountain in Ellerton, to be marked for quilting. Drawing freehand with a pencil or using cardboard templates and a straight edge, Charlotte "laid off" the quilting pattern. She favored the popular motifs of her Germanic heritage, frequently drawing tulips and hearts in conjunction with classical wreaths, scrolling

Pieced and appliquéd Cherry Basket quilt, 79.5 x 79.5 inches, on the walnut quilting frame made by George F. Poffenberger for his wife and daughters.

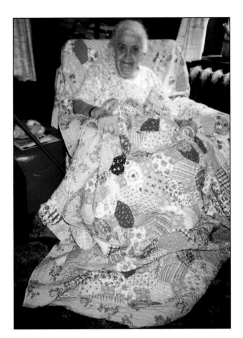

145. *Nellie Poffenberger in 1988 with quilt she finished in 1984. (Photograph courtesy of Paul and Gladys Poffenberger)*

their usual positions at the frame. Elizabeth always worked in the middle; Nellie being left-handed took the left side, and Mary quilted on the right side.[4]

Elizabeth, who probably planned most of the earlier quilts, got her patterns from family members, friends, and newspapers. Mary continued her mother's interest in collecting patterns; the family has retained many of her templates and mail-order patterns. During the 1930s, 1940s, and 1950s she obtained patterns from McKim Studios, *Rural New Yorker, Pennsylvania Farmer, Virginia Snow Patchwork Designs*, and *Aunt Martha's Favorite Quilts*. Mary also took inspiration from the patterns illustrated on Mountain Mist batting wrappers.[5]

The Poffenberger women used a variety of textiles in their quilts: some were scrap fabrics left over from the dresses, aprons, and other clothing they made continually; other scrap pieces they got from friends and neighbors. Some fabrics were ordered by mail, and

others were purchased locally. Butter-yellow cotton, a particular favorite, was used as a backing for quilts again and again in the 1930s and 1940s.

Three of the earlier quilts made by the Poffenberger women illustrate their proficiency, but determining which woman contributed to each step in construction is not always possible. Piecing and appliquéing on the three illustrated here are attributed to Elizabeth or Nellie, the quilting designs to Charlotte, and the actual quilting to Elizabeth, Nellie, and Mary.

The blue and white Feathered Star quilt is thought to have been made in the 1920s by Nellie, who usually took on the complex piecing projects. The small-figured indigo pattern recalls prints popular at the end of the nineteenth century. The quilting designs include Charlotte's usual elaborate combination of Germanic and classical motifs.

Elizabeth appliquéd the open Cherry Wreath quilt for her son Paul some years

feathers, and guilloches (148). For her services she charged her sister and nieces five dollars a quilt. A widow, probably living on a reduced income, Charlotte may have marked quilts for other local quilters.

During winter evenings the walnut quilting frame, made by George Poffenberger from trees on the Sabillasville farm, was set up in the living room next to the potbellied stove. When supper was over and the boys were sent to the kitchen to do the dishes, Elizabeth and her daughters set to work quilting by the light of an Aladdin lamp. Mary married Wesley Scott and moved off the family farm to live in a nearby community. Elizabeth and Nellie, who never married, continued to quilt together in the evenings. Mary walked to her mother's house in the mornings to lend a hand. When all three women quilted together, they took

PIECED FEATHERED STAR QUILT, c. 1925

Made by Nellie Poffenberger (b. 1897), quilted by Elizabeth, Nellie, and Mary Poffenberger
Near Beaver Creek, Washington County
Cottons
75.25 x 78 inches
Owned by Gail Poffenberger Yeiser

146. *Mary and Nellie Poffenberger in their twenties.* (Photograph courtesy of Paul and Gladys Poffenberger)

Grandmother's Flower Garden, Dresden Plate, and Boston Commons. They also made log cabin quilts, crazy throws, and quilts pieced from feed sacks, rayon crepes, ginghams, and plaid flannels, along with a wide variety of prints and solids. They usually made two or three nearly identical quilts so that each woman would have one when they finished. Mary took over the drawing of quilting patterns after Charlotte's death, and Nellie continued to make quilts after the deaths of her mother and sister. Today Nellie is no longer quilting, but she continued to work well into her eighties, finishing her last quilt in 1984 at age eighty-seven (145). The Poffenberger quilts, which span nearly a century, provide a lasting reminder of the quilt-making traditions of one western Maryland family.

147. *The Poffenbergers' Beaver Creek farmhouse during the late 1930s.* (Photograph courtesy of Paul and Gladys Poffenberger)

after his birth in 1913. The celebration of the bicentennial of George Washington's birth in 1932 could have provided the inspiration.[6] The cherry wreath revives a motif found on numerous Maryland album quilts of the mid-nineteenth century (p. 115).[7] This quilt also has Charlotte's characteristic quilted tulip patterns.

The pieced Cherry Basket pattern was popular with quiltmakers across the United States for many years.[8] Probably Elizabeth hand-pieced the baskets and machine-appliquéd the handles, using her sewing machine to assemble the blocks. Mary's collection of quilt patterns included another version of this design published by McKim Studios in the 1930s. The small-figured red and green calicoes recall red and green prints popular in Maryland from about 1835 to 1870.[9] Elizabeth pieced a Triple Irish Chain quilt, another revival of a traditional Maryland pattern, from the same fabrics.

The Poffenberger women continued to make quilts in a number of different popular patterns in the later decades, including the Lone Star,

148. *Detail of Cherry Wreath quilt showing tulip quilting patterns drawn by Charlotte Routzahn Hauver.*

1. Washington County was originally the upper section of Frederick County. It separated in 1776.
2. T. J. C. William, *History of Frederick County Maryland*, vol. 2 (Hagerstown, MD: L. R. Titsworth, 1910), 759–60.
3. Paul and Gladys Poffenberger were very generous in sharing their family history with us.
4. It is difficult to distinguish the different hands, although the quilt owners can spot Nellie's work on some of the quilts.
5. Most of the quilts based on these patterns were made after the 1934 cutoff date of the Maryland state documentation project.

6. We are grateful to Barbara Brackman for this observation. She pointed out, in a personal communication dated January 5, 1994, that she recorded an identical quilt. Both quilts are similar but not identical to a pattern published by Nancy Cabot in the *Chicago Tribune* in 1933. This pattern is indexed as no. 43.54 in Barbara Brackman, *Encyclopedia of Appliqué* (McLean, VA: EPM Publications, 1993), 124. A third quilt with a simplified version of this appliqué pattern has been brought to our attention by Sarah Shaffer, curatorial committee chair, Virginia Quilt Museum. The quilt, owned by the Virginia Quilt Museum, was made in the Piedmont area of Virginia. People living in the mountainous areas of Maryland and Virginia shared many of the same cultural traditions.
7. Also see Jennifer Faulds Goldsborough, *Lavish Legacies: Baltimore Album and Related Quilts in the Collection of the Maryland Historical Society* (Baltimore: Maryland Historical Society, 1994), Catalogue 31. This album quilt was made by a group of women in Harford County in 1862; it contains two closed cherry wreaths.
8. Barbara Brackman found in the Kansas quilt documentation project numerous examples of baskets with machine-appliquéd handles, beginning in the 1880s. Personal communication, January 5, 1994.
9. Barbara Brackman also has seen a number of these nostalgic calicoes on quilts made in southeastern Pennsylvania between 1880 and 1940.

APPLIQUÉD CHERRY WREATH QUILT, c. 1932

*Made by Elizabeth Routzahn Poffenberger
(1879–1965), quilted by Elizabeth, Nellie, and Mary
Poffenberger*
Cottons
79 x 89 inches
Owned by Paul and Gladys Poffenberger

Twentieth-Century Basket Quilt

THIS PIECED AND APPLIQUÉD quilt was one of many bedcovers made by Annabelle Watts during her lifetime. She and her sister Minnie Harrison regularly met with a group of local women to quilt. The sisters obtained their patterns from newspapers, magazines, and friends. Local dry-goods stores, scraps from friends, feed and grain sacks, and recycled household and dress goods were their preferred sources for the fabrics that they used in their quilts.

Minnie has stated that she and her sisters made quilts because it was something they liked to do, but they preferred certain patterns.[1] Minnie, for instance, made a pair of quilts in a tulip pattern, and to relieve the boredom of piecing the same pattern twice, she varied the color scheme.

The pattern for Annabelle's quilt (shown here) is unidentified. The central basket is similar to several patterns available in the early 1930s. Perhaps she adapted it from an Anne Orr or Nancy Cabot pattern from the local newspapers or one of the fashionable women's magazines such as *Good Housekeeping* or *Needlecraft*. The basket of flowers tied with a bowknot was a popular motif with quiltmakers during the colonial revival period. The classical symbolism of this design was attractive and echoed an earlier age. For Maryland quiltmakers in the twentieth century, designs had come full circle.

The bright pink-and-cream checkerboard pattern of the basket and field on Annabelle's quilt may have been inspired by the mosaic-like or needlework-inspired designs popular in the 1920s. Anne Orr, a needlework and quilt pattern designer from Nashville, Tennessee, was a trendsetter who promoted this particular style through her monthly column in *Good Housekeeping*, from 1919 to 1940.[2] Quilt historian Cuesta Benberry states, "The squared off look was not unusual in the first part of the twentieth century as that kind of design, using graph paper, was taught in art classes in schools nationwide, even at the elementary level."[3] The MAFCE documentation project recorded only two quilts worked in this unique style (p. 209).

Annabelle Cooper married Charles Watts, a storekeeper and waterman, in 1901. They had nine children, three of whom died before their first birthdays. The Watts family lived in the small community of Neavitt, located on the eastern side of the Chesapeake Bay. Charles Watts ran a store in Neavitt but supplemented his income by crabbing in the summer and oystering in the winter. The present owner acquired the quilt from Annabelle, her grandmother.

1. Conversation with Minnie Harrison, July 20, 1993.
2. Merikay Waldvogel, *Soft Covers for Hard Times: Quiltmaking & The Great Depression* (Nashville, TN: Rutledge Hill Press, 1990), 24–37. See also, Merikay Waldvogel, "The Marketing of Anne Orr's Quilts," *Uncoverings* 1990, vol. 11, 1991, 7–28.
3. Waldvogel, *Soft Covers*, 30.

PIECED AND APPLIQUÉD BASKET QUILT, c. 1930

Made by Annabelle Cooper Watts (1884–1949)
Neavitt, Talbot County
Cottons
93 x 77.25 inches
Owned by Alice D. Engle

The Dresden Quilt

149. Katherine McNemar Chance (1877–1968) on the Fourth of July at her home in Annapolis. (Photograph courtesy of Andrea Hinson)

150. Katie's sewing box with her tools and unfinished projects. (Courtesy of Andrea Hinson)

A PRINTED COTTON LABEL sewn to the back of this quilt identifies its maker as Katie McNemar Chance (1877–1968), a lifelong resident of Annapolis (149). The quilt was given to the present owner by the executor of the estate of Katie's daughter and sole heir, Marion Greer. At the time of Marion's death in 1986, little was known of her mother. Motivated by a curious nature and with unflagging persistence, the present owner searched through many boxes of household goods for some piece of evidence that might shed light on the life of Katie McNemar Chance. Luckily, she found a cardboard box filled with dusty family papers and old faded photographs of Katie Chance as a young widow with her daughter and son; photographs of a happy, fun-loving, middle-aged woman surrounded by the laughing young friends of her daughter, Marion (151).

The Dresden Quilt is the name of the pattern of Katie's quilt, a pattern designed by Anne Champe Orr (1875–1946) for *Good Housekeeping* magazine and first presented to their readers in the January 1932 issue (152). The same year Orr published a booklet, *Quilts and Quilting—Set 100*, in which the Dresden Quilt is included. Anne Orr, a needlework and quilt-pattern designer for *Good Housekeeping* for twenty years, was well known for her cross-stitch-style quilt designs. Historian Merikay Waldvogel states in her article

on Orr in *Uncoverings 1990* that "the years 1930 through 1935 were the peak in Anne Orr's quiltmaking offers." She also writes that Orr's popular booklet, *Quilts and Quilting—Set 100* "included cutting patterns and directions

151. Photographs of Katie Chance, her daughter Marion, and friends from the Naval Academy on the Fourth of July placed on another of Katie's quilts. (Courtesy of Andrea Hinson)

for eleven pieced quilts, hot-iron transfer patterns for two appliquéd quilts, and fourteen different quilting patterns. She also used a color insignia chart and working diagram to make the construction of her cross-stitch type quilts less tedious."[1]

Anne Orr offered full-color photographs in her booklet so that quilters could easily match colors. Katie Chance chose to follow Orr's pattern closely: the only variation from Orr's pattern published in *Set 100* is in the placement of the dark pink square in the border.

Katie Chance had a reason for choosing an Anne Orr pattern instead of a more traditional one, such as the pieced Nancy Cabot pattern found in her sewing box. Waldvogel analyzed Orr's marketing techniques, concluding that: she sold her patterns to women with time on their hands and to those who may not have made quilts before. Orr also made major changes in the function and design of quilts so they appealed to the modern woman who wanted a bedspread instead of a warm cover. Waldvogel found that Orr made her

PIECED QUILT, c. 1932

Made by Katherine McNemar Chance (1877–1968)
Annapolis, Anne Arundel County
Cottons
79 x 87.5 inches
Owned by Andrea L. Hinson

152. A detail of Anne Orr's Dresden Quilt (Photograph courtesy of Merikay Waldvogel)

patterns more accessible to more people by selling them through mail order and including a variety of price levels.[2] Katie Chance was one of only two Maryland quiltmakers MAFCE documented to use an Ann Orr pattern for a quilt (153).

When Katie died at the age of ninety-one in 1968, her death certificate listed her as a housewife. She seems to represent a successful marketing campaign by Anne Orr. She certainly had the time on her hands to make a quilt, and perhaps the pastel colors and the unusual cross-stitch-like designs appealed to her twentieth-century taste.

1. For more information on Anne Orr, see Merikay Waldvogel, "The Marketing of Anne Orr's Quilts," in Laurel Horton, ed., *Uncoverings* 1990 (San Francisco, CA: American Quilt Study Group, 1989), 7–28. The authors thank Merikay Waldvogel for identifying this quilt as an Anne Orr pattern.
2. Ibid., 16–21.

153. GARLAND AND BASKET QUILT, c. 1935, made by Estella Smith Stubbs (1865–c. 1955), Kensington, Montgomery County, Cottons, 96 x 105 inches, owned by Mr. and Mrs. John S. Stubbs Jr. This quilt is the only other made from an Anne Orr pattern that was documented by MAFCE. The pattern was first published in January 1934 in Good Housekeeping magazine.

Ruby's Quilts

I N THE EARLY 1930S WHEN Ruby Purnell was working with her mother for a family summering at the beach resort of Ocean City, Maryland, she was intrigued by a quilt she saw in a store window on the boardwalk.[1] She memorized the Rose of Sharon pattern, purchased the necessary pink, green, and yellow fabrics, and made her first quilt. Because she was an African-American and prohibited from attending most of the amusements in Ocean City, she spent hours after work in her room sewing with her mother. Ruby had learned to do appliqué work and other simple sewing in home economics classes in school. Not owning a quilting frame, she took her finished top to a friend, Eliza Collick, who did quilting as a business. Eliza charged Ruby $4 for quilting her top.[2]

About two years later, Ruby made her second and last quilt. She does not recall whether she saw the Hollyhock Wreath appliqué pattern in a magazine or an advertising pamphlet that came in the mail. She may have seen a pattern published around 1930 by McKim Studios and issued in their fourth series (154).[3] The red, green, and pastel fabrics for this quilt, as well as those for her earlier one, Ruby purchased locally in Snow Hill at William Goodman & Son's dry-goods store. This quilt top she also turned over to another woman for quilting, Mrs. Gillispie, who charged her $3.50 to do the work.

Ruby Purnell Waters, daughter of Georgeanna Harmon and George Purnell, has lived all her life in Snow Hill, Worcester County. She received her teachers' training from Bowie State Teachers' College and Morgan State College, and for many years

she taught lower grades in schools in Snow Hill and Berlin. Ruby recalls that in those days when schools were segregated, black children made do with secondhand books and furniture discarded by the white schools.[4] Ruby also ran the high school cafeteria and taught institutional cooking in the Newark vocational school in Worcester County. In 1939 she married Elwood Levin Waters, a farmer from Snow Hill (155).

When asked why she did not continue to appliqué quilts, Ruby Waters replied that marriage, raising a son, teaching, driving the school bus, and helping out on the farm left her little time for quiltmaking. In 1991 Ruby Purnell Waters was honored when her Rose of Sharon quilt was exhibited in the Maryland State House at Annapolis.

APPLIQUÉD ROSE OF SHARON QUILT, c. 1932

Made by Ruby Purnell (b. 1911)
Snow Hill, Worcester County
Cottons
80.5 x 66 inches
Owned by Ruby Purnell Waters

APPLIQUÉD HOLLYHOCK WREATH QUILT, c. 1934

Made by Ruby Purnell (b. 1911)
Snow Hill, Worcester County
Cottons
66 x 85 inches
Owned by Ruby Purnell Waters

HOLLYHOCK
WREATH

Along with all the Patchwork in our series, comes this applique design. Applique is really patch upon patch too, and this is a charmingly patterned block using 3 colors on a 16-inch white or unbleached background square 16 squares, either all applique or half of them just plain quilted, makes a 64-inch square, which with plain borders is ample for a quilt. There must be a wider border at the bottom both for use and better design.

Cardboard cutting patterns are made exact sizes of the 5 patterns here given. These do not allow for seams, so mark the goods around each pattern, but cut a seam larger and crease back to the pencil line. Baste very carefully, press and whip or blindstitch the units in place. Other plain colors or prints may be used, as lavender, blue or yellow with orange centers, pink with deeper rose or wine red with buff.

This is good size for an odd pillow, using scraps of silk on pongee or black sateen.

QUILT MATERIALS
AND CUTTING

Quilts are usually made of wash cotton materials, although silks are sometimes used in such patterns as Log Cabin, or the Friendship Ring, where one's friends are called upon to help furnish beautiful bits to make the patterns as variegated as possible. Woolens, even good parts of worn garments are excellent for the heavy type of coverlet, and such designs as Steps to the Altar, or Grandmother's Cross are suitable. Woolens are so apt to be dull, "practical" colors that it is imperative to have some certain unit of red, bright green, orange or such in each block.

Cotton broadcloth, percales, or fine gingham, the calico prints and such are used with muslin for wash quilts, or fine, high luster sateen of light weight and true coloring really makes the most gorgeous quilt of all. When the time comes to quilt you will know why we stress soft materials with no starchy dressing and not too close or heavy in texture, because the quilting is done through a pieced top, cotton filling and lining. Medium weight sheeting is excellent, now manufactured in standard 36-inch width and may be secured in a variety of colorings, so harmonious to the patchwork feeling. You may find these locally or write to the McKim Studios at Independence, Missouri, for samples or yardage at 30c per yard, postpaid.

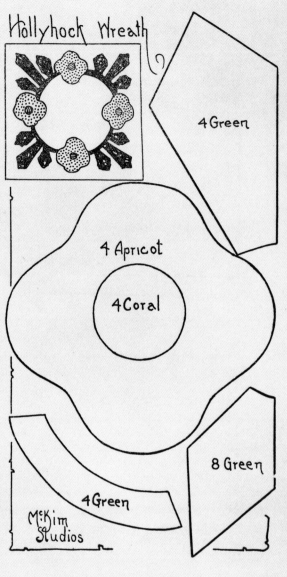

154. McKim Studios, Patchwork Patterns, *series no. four.*

1. By the end of the nineteenth century, Ocean City was Maryland's largest resort town and accessible to residents in Baltimore and the rest of the Western Shore by Chesapeake Bay steamship and train. Trains ran directly from bay to beach. Now the trip is not so pleasant, as weekend commuters fight bumper-to-bumper traffic driving over the Chesapeake Bay Bridge.
2. Interview with Ruby Purnell Waters, June 8, 1993.
3. Barbara Brackman, *Encyclopedia of Appliqué* (McLean, VA: EPM Publications, 1993), pattern no. 2.53. The McKim pattern is very similar to rose wreath blocks on Baltimore album quilts of the late 1840s and early 1850s. See Jennifer Faulds Goldsborough, *Lavish Legacies: Baltimore Album and Related Quilts in the Collection of the Maryland Historical Society* (Baltimore: Maryland Historical Society, 1994), Catalogue 12, 28.
4. Educational opportunities came slowly for rural African-Americans. There were no Negro high schools outside of Baltimore until 1916 and none on the Eastern Shore until 1919. Morgan State College and Bowie State College were founded in the late nineteenth century as small, private normal schools to train African-American teachers for Baltimore schools. Richard Walsh and William Lloyd Fox, *Maryland: A History, 1632–1974* (Baltimore: Maryland Historical Society, 1974), 515, 527–29.

155. Ruby and Elwood Waters, about 1945. (Photograph courtesy of Ruby Waters)

The Mudd Family Quilts

A YEAR OR TWO BEFORE her 1936 marriage, Emily Mudd of Charles County distributed hexagonal-shaped pieces of bleached muslin to female friends and family members and requested that each one embroider her name and place of residence (157). After receiving the embroidered patches, Emily pieced them together with cuttings from a variety of printed dress fabrics purchased at Kerr's Department Store in Waldorf. Mrs. A. J. Jones of Hughesville quilted Emily's Texas Star top.

Emily's quilt is a vivid and tangible reminder of friends and family. When she married William E. Rogerson in 1936, Emily gave up her job teaching in Hughesville, left

156. A postcard view of the Dr. Samuel A. Mudd House, also known as St. Catherine's. (Courtesy of Doris Brooks)

157. Emily Mudd in a photograph taken about the time she assembled the names for her friendship quilt. (Photograph courtesy of Doris Brooks)

her extended Maryland family, and moved to Richmond, Virginia. Her quilt, which accompanied her, contained not only the names of the women she taught school with but also the names of three generations of the Mudd family (158).

The name Mudd is well known in Maryland history. At approximately 4 A.M. on April 15, 1865, Dr. Samuel A. Mudd, a country doctor and tobacco farmer, opened the door of his farmhouse to two men—John Wilkes Booth, disguised by false whiskers, and David Herold. Earlier that evening Booth had fractured his leg leaping from the presidential box at Ford's Theater after firing shots that would mortally wound Abraham Lincoln. Dr. Mudd set Booth's leg and provided a room for him and his companion to rest for the better part of the day. After getting directions from Mudd, Booth headed south to Virginia. On April 26, he was sighted by soldiers, shot, and killed.

Dr. Mudd subsequently was arrested for failing to report to local military authorities the presence of odd strangers in his house on the night following the assassination of Lincoln and for denying meeting Booth on two prior occasions. A military court convicted Mudd and three others of aiding and assisting in the conspiracy to assassinate Lincoln, but their lives were spared. Four others, convicted of conspiracy, were executed. Historians have debated over the years whether Mudd recognized Booth and whether he played any predetermined role in Booth's escape route. Mudd was sen-

tenced to life at hard labor in the military prison, Fort Jefferson, located in the remote Dry Tortugas islands. In 1867 a yellow fever epidemic threatened the lives of most of the 300 prison inhabitants on the island. Mudd took charge of the care and cure of the sick. Two years later President Andrew Johnson issued Mudd a pardon, citing his work during the yellow fever epidemic and his "generous and faithful service to humanity."[1]

Two of Dr. Samuel A. Mudd's four daughters and his daughter-in-law signed Emily's quilt. In addition seven granddaughters and nine great-granddaughters were signers. Emily, the daughter of Claudine Louise

158. Detail with Emily's signature block.

PIECED AND EMBROIDERED FRIENDSHIP
QUILT, 1933–36

Pieced by Emily Mudd (b. 1906)
St. Catherine's, near Waldorf, Charles County
Cottons, embroidered inscriptions
82 x 56 inches
Owned by Doris Clements Brooks

T h e   M u d d   F a m i l y   Q u i l t s   215

APPLIQUÉD AND EMBROIDERED COLONIAL
BELLE QUILT, 1934–36

Made by Sister M. Samuela (Cecelia Dyer Mudd)
(b. 1914) for her sister, Emily Mudd
Marshall, Texas
Cottons, cotton embroidery
87 x 63.5 inches
Owned by Marie Frere Martin

Burch and Samuel A. Mudd Jr., grew up at the Mudd farm, then known as St. Catherine's (156). Emily, her mother, and sisters did a great deal of sewing and made most of their own clothes.

Emily's younger sister, Cecelia—or Sister M. Samuela as she was known in the Sisters of the Holy Cross Convent in Marshall, Texas—contributed an embroidered signature to Emily's friendship quilt (159). In addition to the small hexagon-shaped piece of muslin to embroider, Emily sent her sister a quilt kit in the Colonial Belle pattern. Sister Samuela, an expert embroiderer, had promised to make Emily a quilt for her intended marriage. Emily purchased the twelve-block appliqué and embroidery kit from the Rainbow Block Company of Cleveland; she probably acquired locally the

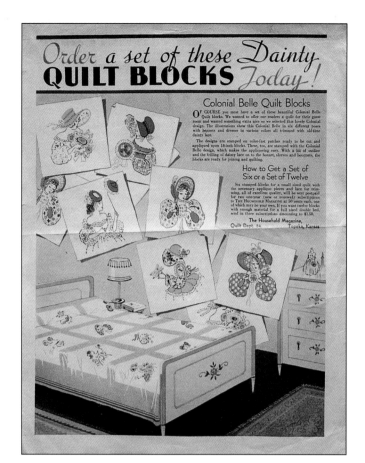

160. Advertisement for the "Colonial Belle" quilt blocks kit from the Household Magazine, Topeka, Kansas. (Photograph courtesy of Merikay Waldvogel)

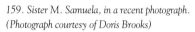

159. Sister M. Samuela, in a recent photograph. (Photograph courtesy of Doris Brooks)

bright lavender cotton used for the border[2] and may have ordered the quilt kit through one of the popular women's magazines circulating in Maryland in the 1930s or from one of the local newspapers.[3]

An advertisement for the kit in *The Household Magazine* stated, "The illustrations show this Colonial Belle in six different poses with bonnets and dresses in various colors all trimmed with old-time dainty lace. The designs are stamped on color-fast patches ready to be cut and appliquéd upon 18-inch blocks"[4] (160).

The Colonial Belle kit, with its impressive amount of embroidery, was an appropriate quilt for Sister Samuela to make; embroidery is still her favorite form of needlework. She recalled recently that the Colonial Belle kit was not particularly hard to make, but the embroidered hair became somewhat tedious

to work after many hours with the needle. Sister Samuela still does a little embroidery along with her other duties at the convent, which include teaching sixth- and seventh-grade math to students with special needs. She also enjoys lecturing to local audiences on the topic of her grandfather, Dr. Mudd.[5]

Today the gift shop at the Dr. Samuel A. Mudd House, now a historic house museum, occasionally has for sale needlework by Emily, Sister Samuela, and other Mudd descendants.

1. The story of Dr. Samuel A. Mudd's connection with the Lincoln assassination conspiracy is well known to Maryland residents. Many of the details cited here, including the quotation, were recalled in an article by Dixie Hoffland, which appeared in the Spring 1988 issue of the *Maryland Magazine*, 49–52.
2. The Rainbow Block Company was owned and operated by William Pinch of Cleveland, Ohio, from the 1920s until his death, when it was taken over by his daughter. The company sometimes went by the name "William Pinch, Quilt Block Specialist."
3. According to Cuesta Benberry, the Rainbow Block Company never sold paper patterns, only quilt kits. Quiltmakers traced the patterns from the kits and circulated them through "round robins," or groups of people who exchanged by mail ideas, objects, and information about quilts and quiltmaking. Correspondence between Cuesta Benberry and Merikay Waldvogel, April 4, 1993.
4. *The Household Magazine*, Topeka, Kansas, the Mildred Dickerson Collection, owned by Merikay Waldvogel. We are grateful to Merikay Waldvogel for sharing research from the Mildred Dickerson Collection with us.
5. Telephone conversation with Sister Samuela, September 6, 1994.

Tercentenary Quilt

161. Cover from the souvenir booklet published by the Maryland Tercentenary Commission. (Photograph courtesy of the Maryland Historical Society)

On MARCH 25, 1934, A group of patriotic Marylanders commemorated the landing of the *Ark* and *Dove* at St. Clements Island with the dedication of a large stone cross. In mid-June of that year a water pageant featuring replicas of the two ships culminated in a re-enactment of the landing of Leonard Calvert. Maryland dignitaries, some descended from the first settlers, played the roles of Calvert, other passengers, and native Americans. A local ship captain assumed the role of Richard Loe, master of the *Ark* and owner of Maryland's earliest documented quilt (p. 23). The following day, the governor dedicated the reconstructed state house of 1676 in nearby St. Mary's City. The festivities in southern Maryland, along with the "historico dramatic pageantry in Baltimore City," marked the three-hundredth anniversary of the founding of the colony of Maryland.[1]

Marylanders celebrated this historic event in individual ways. One Maryland woman, possibly a resident of Frederick County, made a bedquilt with forty-eight hand-pieced blocks based on the repeated design of the state flag.[2]

The Maryland flag, adopted in 1904, bears the arms of the Lords Baltimore. The red and white cross of the family of Alice Crossland (Argent and gules a cross bottony counterchanged) is quartered with the black and yellow arms of Leonard Calvert (Paly of six or and sable a bend counterchanged).[3] Their son George Calvert was named first Lord Baltimore and granted the proprietorship of Maryland. His son Cecil, or Cecelius, the second Lord Baltimore, received the Maryland charter from Charles I in 1632. On November 22, 1633, Cecil's two younger brothers, Leonard and George, set sail from Cowes, England, to claim their brother's land.

This quilt, made in 1934 to celebrate Maryland's tercentenary, brings the story of Maryland's quiltmaking traditions full circle. With its brightly dyed cotton textiles and sociotechnic function, it is far removed in time, style, technology, and use from the flock quilt carried ashore by Richard Loe on that eventful day in March 1634.

1. *Maryland Tercentenary 1634–1934* (Baltimore: Maryland Tercentenary Commission, 1934), 15.
2. The quilt was purchased by dealer John Newcomer from an estate in Frederick, Maryland. He gave the quilt to the Maryland Historical Society in 1991.
3. Thomas M. Coakley, "George Calvert, First Lord Baltimore: Family, Status, Arms," *Maryland Historical Magazine*, vol. 79 no. 3 (Fall 1984), 255–69. There is some dispute regarding the family of George Calvert and the unusual arms adopted by the Lords Baltimore. According to fairly strong tradition George Calvert's mother was Alice or Alicia Crossland, but no contemporary evidence confirms this. There is also no clear proof that the quartered arms adopted by George Calvert follows rules of English heraldry. Evidence suggests that the Calverts employed the Paly of six, or black and yellow motif, for personal use and the quartered arms in their capacity as lords-proprietors of their provinces.

PIECED MARYLAND FLAG QUILT, c. 1934

Made by unknown quiltmaker for Maryland's Tercentenary
Possibly Frederick County
Cottons
83 x 64 inches
Owned by the Maryland Historical Society

MAFCE Acknowledgments

*I*T WOULD NOT BE AN EXAGGERATION to say that 6,000 persons were involved in the Maryland Association for Family and Community Education (MAFCE) quilt documentation project that encompassed documentation days, quilt conservation workshops, and exhibitions that eventually led to this publication. Every person involved contributed time, talent, and resources. For these contributions, the organization says, "We thank you!" Although "thank you" seems inadequate, there is the knowledge that each person involved shared in the recording of a piece of Maryland history that is a special gift to future generations who acquire and read this book.

> We conserve what we love
> We Love what we Understand
> We Understand what we are Taught
> —*Author unknown*

Thanks to the MAFCE Quilt Publication Committee: Elaine Crow, Chair; Kenner Ashby, Rita Bastek, Josie Bruzdzinski, Gene Crabtree, Belinda Crews, Christine Fanning, Jean Frost, Louella Marlin, Barbara Perry, Ellen Pusey, Alice Skarda, Helen Totura, Virginia Voit, and Evelyn Ziegler.

Our project could not have been accomplished without help from numerous people and sources, including the following:

Statewide use of libraries, churches, schools, museums, and other building sites were donated for this project. For these numerous donations of space as documentation sites, we are especially grateful.

The Maryland 4-H Center, University of Maryland, College Park Campus, and the Maryland State Fair and Agricultural Society, Inc., served as quilt show facilities and sites.

Especially valuable and extremely appreciated was the donation of vault storage space for the quilt show in September 1990 by the Annapolis Banking and Trust Company. In tandem with storage was the generous contribution of the use of St. Anne's Episcopal Church meeting rooms for four days. The talent, energy, and hard work of Lucinda Dukes Edinberg made the show a reality, along with the show cosponsor, the Annapolis Quilt Guild. Also, thanks to Russell J. Balge, Ph.D., for designing the entrance to the September 1990 quilt show.

Of course, we could not have pursued this goal without money. Major funding sources were the Annapolis Quilt Guild, the Baltimore Heritage Quilt Guild, and the Maryland State Arts Council. A special thanks goes to the numerous volunteers who sold raffle tickets, quilt pins, and other items as fundraisers.

For documentation data entry, we thank Kathleen Shatt; for photography, Richard and Ann Rohlfing of R.A.R.E. Photographic; for legal guidance, attorney H. Douglas Schenker; for data storage, office facilities, and support staff, we thank the Anne Arundel County Cooperative Extension Service, University of Maryland, advisors, Madeleine Greene, Dr. Margaret Ordonez, and Ella F. Smart; and special thanks to the owners of the 2,400 quilts who shared their treasures!

The project could not have become a reality without the MAFCE Quilt Documentation Committee: Alice Skarda, Chair, 1988; and Belinda Crews, Chair, 1989 to present.

Volunteer members from the following member associations are the reason this project was so extensive and so successful. MAFCE is particularly appreciative of the work of local cultural arts and documentation chairmen and their committees:

Alleghany County Association for Family and Community Education

Anne Arundel County Association for Family and Community Education

Baltimore City Association for Family and Community Education

Baltimore County Homemakers, Inc./Association for Family and Community Education

Calvert County Association for Family and Community Education

Caroline County Association for Family and Community Education

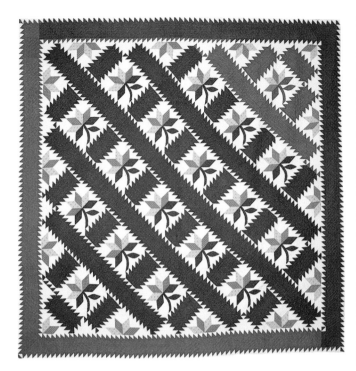

Pieced Peony quilt, 1835–45. Made by Ann Amanda Floyd Dunbar (1819–1903), Dameron, St. Mary's County. Cottons, 98 x 97.5 inches. Owned by Lucie Dunbar Abell.

Carroll County Association for Family and Community Education

Cecil County Association for Family and Community Education

Charles County Association for Family and Community Education

Dorchester County Association for Family and Community Education

Frederick County Extension Homemakers, Inc., in association with MAFCE

Garrett County Association for Family and Community Education

Harford County Association for Family and Community Education

Howard County Association for Family and Community Education

Kent County Association for Family and Community Education

Montgomery County Association for Family and Community Education

Prince George's County Association for Family and Community Education

Queen Anne's County Association for Family and Community Education

Somerset/Wicomico/Worcester County members, in association with MAFCE

St. Mary's County Association for Family and Community Education

Washington County Association for Family and Community Education

Wicomico County Association for Family and Community Education

Worcester County Association for Family and Community Education

To the extension agents in the twenty-three counties and Baltimore City who advised and assisted with the project, a sincere thank you.

Also, to the members of various quilt guilds around the state who assisted with documentation days.

In addition, we thank the experts who enriched the programs of quilt show days with their lectures:

Quilt appraisals, Mary Louise Day; Restoration and conservation, Margart Ordonez, Ph.D.; Dated crazy quilts, Kathy Jung; White on white quilts, Anne Oliver; Woodbourne Quilt, Peg Lucas; Political quilts, Sue Hannan; Slave-made quilts from the antebellum South, Gladys Frye, Ph.D.; Maryland quilts, Gloria Seaman Allen; Historic significant colors in quilts, Susan McKelvey; National Museum of American History Collection of Quilts, Joan Stephens; Appraising quilts, Patricia Steiner; Crazy quilts, Rosemary Gately; Textile conservation, Fonda Thomsen; African-American quilts, Steven Newsome; and History of Maryland quilts, Nancy Gibson Tuckhorn.

Maryland Association for Family and Community Education